ETHICS AND ORGANIZATIONS

Issues in Business Ethics

VOLUME 15

Ethics and Organizations

Understanding Business Ethics as a Learning Process

by

JOSEP M. LOZANO
ESADE, Barcelona, Spain

KLUWER ACADEMIC PUBLISHERS
DORDRECHT / BOSTON / LONDON

A C.I.P. Catalogue record for this book is available from the Library of Congress.

ISBN 0-7923-6463-5

Published by Kluwer Academic Publishers,
P.O. Box 17, 3300 AA Dordrecht, The Netherlands.

Sold and distributed in North, Central and South America
by Kluwer Academic Publishers,
101 Philip Drive, Norwell, MA 02061, U.S.A.

JK

In all other countries, sold and distributed
by Kluwer Academic Publishers,
P.O. Box 322, 3300 AH Dordrecht, The Netherlands.

English translation of
Jozep M. Lozano, *Ètica i Empresa*, Proa, Barcelona, Spain, 1997.
Translators: Daniel Arenas and Patricia Mathews

Printed on acid-free paper

Printed in the Netherlands.

To my sons Oriol and Xavier

CONTENTS

INTRODUCTION: LIKE OIL AND WATER?

Is business ethics possible? If we take into consideration declarations, polls, and opinion articles, it is desirable and necessary. But those who call for it usually overlook another question: Is it possible? Or, if you prefer: Is it feasible? Because although many people call for business ethics, deep down most of them believe that the relationship between ethics and business is more or less like trying to mix oil and water.

What we need is not a further call for business ethics. We don't need to deliver more sermons or make any more statements. What we need is to make ethical proposals that are feasible within the framework of organizations and can be made an ntegral part of business practice. We need to propose a form of ethics that can speak the language of business, even if sometimes a critical tone of voice is required.

The increasing talk about business ethics might be nothing more than another example of the changes ethics has undergone in recent years. It has become a true rhetoric of slander. Talking about ethics is all too often an elegant way of speaking ill of others. Nonetheless, this sometimes seems to be justified inasmuch as a great deal of the progress made in business ethics has been the result of reactions against actions that triggered personal and social rejection.

It is such reactions that explain the fact that business ethics is often expected to help eradicate anything that is considered objectionable. This is a negative view of business ethics and one which is much more concerned with what should not happen in the business world than with what is desirable. It is much more concerned with setting limits than with broadening horizons. In short, people often call for more ethics, but what they want is more control. Now, however, they realize that this control is no longer gained simply through penalties and outside pressures. Instead, control is now expected to come from within, on the assumption that taking a generous dose of ethical vitamins will give one the necessary strength to resist the undesirable.

From this follows, for example, the interest in business codes and corporate culture, the formulation of which provokes a beatific smugness or, simply, alibis and justifications for anything that might happen. Without denying their usefulness as a tool in the development of organizational learning processes, business codes are often nothing more than an updated version of a desire for control. And, more often than not, corporate cultures are just an expression of a desire to merge personal values with corporate goals. In short, with this approach one can succumb again to the temptation to reduce ethics to just one more management tool, subordinate to corporate aims and functional to corporate objectives.

Fashions with a hidden agenda aside, I think that concern with business ethics is the expression of a problem that has yet to be fully resolved. And, at the same time, it is a symptom of some social and cultural changes which far surpass the manifest demand for business ethics. The rapid changes that have taken place in recent years have overwhelmed what was formerly a comfortable supply of conceptual and institutional resources. If some discussion is now under way - on the advent of the information society, the future of the welfare state, or the possibility and legitimacy of governing world interdependence - this is not only because the answers are changing, but because the questions are changing too. And, in this new game of questions and answers, questions about ethics in organizations take on a new dimension.

This new situation forces us to ask whether it is sufficient to automatically extrapolate to businesses and organizations those ethical approaches constructed on the assumption that the subjects of actions and human decisions are isolated, ethically self-sufficient individuals. Obviously, it is not a question of individuals being absorbed by the organization, or being subordinate to it. But neither can we be satisfied with an ethical discourse that leaves individuals defenseless before the organization, so overloaded with demands they are unable to fulfill them. This would ultimately lead only to frustration, cynicism, or indifference.

When we raise the question of whether ethics should accept the fact that we are living in a society of organizations rather than a mere society of individuals, we are expressing our concern about demands for responsibility and the inherent need for self-regulation. This demand is not simply a matter of good intentions but a recognition of the power of business firms and organizations in an interdependent world. In this context, it is impossible to understand, orient, and justify human action with a unidirectional discourse that limits itself to going from ethics to business, not vice versa. The task then is start with concrete experiences and projects, and from there construct an ethical proposal capable of understanding the reality of our organizations and becoming an integral part of their development.

Beyond fashions, beyond public relations maneuvering, beyond nostalgia for pre-modern forms of cohesion, what we are addressing here is the challenge posed to ethics by the fact that we live in a society of organizations, and what this implies: that human action has a specifically organizational dimension; that it goes beyond individual wills because it is neither absorbed by nor identified with them. It is in this context that it makes sense to ask whether it is possible to develop a body of ethical thought capable of adequately understanding organizational practices and decisions. Obviously, this problem cannot be solved if we implicitly believe that the relation between ethics and business is the same as the relation between oil and water.

In this context I propose to engage in an analysis of Business Ethics. I will attempt to not merely repeat what others have already said, but instead take into account the fundamental contributions this discipline has made. Through this analysis I aim to show how a business ethic is possible and viable. My goal then is to make a critical reading of the main contributions of business ethics in order to integrate the concept in organizational learning processes.

The first chapter is an introduction to the framework of ethical reference that has guided both my analysis and the presentation of its results. In the second chapter I review the history of Business Ethics and how it came to be the identity of an academic discipline. Chapter three shows how some of Business Ethics' problems of identity are intimately linked to its difficulties in trying to achieve a truly interdisciplinary perspective as well as to the merely instrumental and acritical use of ethical theories that sometimes appears in Business Ethics proposals. In this chapter I also point out that some of these difficulties could be better addressed within a framework of civic ethics. In the fourth chapter I discuss an issue that has proved valuable (in terms of both its contributions and its limitations) in shaping Business Ethics thought and its constitution as an academic discipline; namely, the issue of corporate social responsibility and, in this context, the issue of whether a business firm is a moral person.

Immediately thereafter I analyze the core aspects of Business Ethics that make it possible to construct a form of ethical thought that deals specifically with organizations. Taking this analysis as my basis, I attempt to shape a model that reconstructs Business Ethics in terms of a learning process. I will begin this analysis in chapter five by presenting the stakeholders' understanding of the business firm (underscoring how this perspective relates to consequential ethics and responsibility ethics). The analysis continues in chapter six with a study of the contributions made by organizations' codes of ethics and "missions" (underscoring their relation to deontological ethics and constructivist ethical approaches). Chapter seven continues along the same line as the two previous chapters, examining the make-up and development of organizational cultures (underscoring their relation to virtue ethics).

Once these references have been made and justified, I propose ways to integrate them in organizational development processes. Chapter eight therefore emphasizes the actual decision-making processes and the processes that constitute the strategies and purposes of organizations. I do this on the assumption that integrating the various dimensions of business ethics is simultaneously a practical problem and a problem of theoretical coherence. Precisely for this reason, it is in integration that the credibility of business ethics is at stake.

Lastly, in chapters nine and ten I conclude by attempting to situate my proposed approach within the framework of the processes of organizational and social change taking place in a society whose viability is increasingly contingent on information and knowledge technologies. Thus my study culminates in a proposal to situate Business Ethics in the setting of organizational learning processes (presenting the learning process as a particular way of understanding the make-up of organizations, a way that is well-suited to the new social and technological situation). My progress towards this final proposal is guided by a strong conviction: I believe that the challenge involves making the ethical perspective, in all its dimensions, a key factor of organizational learning, ensuring that this perspective is always an integral part of the entire learning process. I do not propose this view of Business Ethics as a process of organizational learning as an alternative model, or as a norm or prescription. Rather, I consider it an approach or a framework of reference that can help us order and integrate the diverse elements that should make up the daily practice of ethics in business life.

I would not want to conclude this introduction without thanking Patricia Mathews and Daniel Arenas for the painstaking care with which they traslated my original text from Catalan to English. I would also like to thank the Fundació Catalana per a la recerca for its contribution towards funding this translation.

CHAPTER 1

BUSINESS ETHICS AS APPLIED ETHICS

In recent years there has been a growing tendency to link the words "ethics" and "business". No doubt this might be just another of the many fashions that periodically hit business schools and the mass media. But, fashion aside, I believe that this tendency reflects concern about a problem that is as yet unresolved, a problem that is one more symptom of social and cultural changes that probably exceed the manifest demand for corporate ethics. The growth and ambiguity of this demand is evident simply in the increase of publications, courses, and seminars that have appeared in recent years. But this quantitative boom also poses a specific new challenge that simultaneously affects corporate management and applied ethics: the challenge of explaining an ethical proposal that is adequate to the contemporary reality of corporations and organizations and can be framed in both conceptual and operational terms.

Underlying this need and challenge we find a critical social reaction to a number of actions that have lately taken place in all kinds of organizations, both public and private. But we can also find many other things, such as uncertainty about the future of the welfare state and the prospects of governability, given the mid- and long-term consequences of certain business actions. Furthermore, after a period in which the company was viewed with suspicion and strongly criticized, an attempt is now being made to revalue it culturally and socially. Now, however, companies seek their legitimacy not simply in their own activities and criteria of action but in rethinking them from the standpoint of ethics.

In a different order of things, this challenge also plays a role in the reaction provoked by the crisis of ideologies. Substantive discourses and the institutions that voiced them have fallen into a certain disrepute that has liberated the corporation: it is no longer less valued than political parties, trade unions, churches, or the media. Quite the contrary in fact. But then the corporation becomes subject to excess expectation: in this case an appeal to ethics would make some demands on the corporation that go beyond its economic possibilities.

At another level, the appeal to ethics in corporations could also express a certain change in individual values. Overwhelmed by the complexity of contemporary problems and unable to tackle them, individuals seek the meaning and motivations of life in their immediate surroundings. And since work occupies a fair share of their time, an appeal for ethics would channel and express a personal need for foundations, motivation, and meaning.

Inasmuch as there is considerable controversy over the subject, we need to ask how to address this demand which is formulated in terms of corporate ethics and ethics in the corporation. And we must do this by placing ourselves above the diverse motivations, interests, and situations that this issue can call forth. Ultimately, the challenge consists in elaborating a sufficiently rigorous answer in terms of applied ethics. I think that, just as bioethics has been the response to some questions and challenges that were literally unthinkable some years ago, the dialogue between ethics and corporations is a sign of an awareness of a new reality. In today's world human action is irrevocably an organizationally mediated action. It appears, therefore, that to think about human action in ethical terms also entails thinking about it in specifically organizational surroundings inasmuch as this action takes place through corporations and organizations. Indeed, the demand for corporate responsibility and the need for self-regulation evinced is not a mere desire, but the consequence of acknowledging the power of organizations in an interdependent world. In this context, it would appear impossible to understand and guide human action with a one-way discourse that moves from ethics to the corporation or vice-versa. What we need is an integration that allows us to understand the reality of corporations and organizations, and understand them within a frame of reference that is ethically sustainable.

Consequently, my point of departure is the recognition that in today's society action cannot be understood only as action by individuals or a set of individuals. Human actions are increasingly performed by corporations and organizations of all kinds. And life styles, values, types of society, etc. are also shaped by decisions made and implemented by organizations. I feel that this cannot be viewed only in individual or personal terms. There is a collective dimension (specifically organizational) that goes beyond individual wills and neither culminates in nor is identified with them. I therefore think that it is necessary to strive to develop a form of ethical thought capable of properly understanding organizational practices and decisions.

We should then ask to what extent, in what sense, and with what limitations can one propose an ethics appropriate for executive functions and the demands of corporate and organizational practices. I think that the best way to do this is through a study of the basic contributions of what is usually called Business Ethics.[1] Here we must recall that U.S. academic and corporate circles have a long tradition of proposing ways to construct an ethical approach to corporate actions. Although a great deal of work in this field has also been done in Europe - not least with the deliberate intention of breaking with the dependence on American production and creating a new approach that would take European ethical and corporate traditions into account, American BE boasts much more material, experiences, and approaches which make it an unavoidable reference.

This does not mean that we should passively accept the contributions of American BE. On the contrary. But indeed a systematic analysis is inevitable if we want to contribute anything from the European cultural context. This more systematic approach seems to me worthwhile because corporate ethics is sometimes confused with a collection of recipes aimed to satisfy the consumer's taste. My aim is to construct a framework for understanding corporate ethics (from the standpoint of management) that will make it possible to channel experiences and processes in such a way as to make this understanding viable as corporate ethics.

In fact, everyone acknowledges that there is a great deal of available information and contributions to the various fields of BE. Yet we lack a sufficiently developed frame of reference that would provide a systematic basis in which to situate all possible studies. For instance, in 1990, after thirty-two interviews with some of the most important BE scholars and theoreticians, Kahn acknowledged that the absence of any

---

[1] Henceforth I will use BE to refer to Business Ethics. I personally think that it is more appropriate to speak of organizational ethics. Pruzan and Thyssen (1990) also think so. However, since the predominant denomination is obviously business ethics and this is the subject of my research, I will refer to it as BE.

type of frame of reference is one of the most important sources of frustration for BE researchers.

Obviously, I do not aim to make up for this lack. But I do want to make clear that an analysis of the themes that I consider central in BE has led my research towards the objective of constructing a model that would allow us to situate the themes at issue within a minimally coherent global perspective and, at the same time, propose a broader hypothesis for understanding BE which would, in turn, point towards a direction in the field of applied research and in the fields of education and consulting. For, lest we forget, what is at issue here is to work on applied ethics and, therefore, make ethics applicable (and the latter is not always taken sufficiently into account by those who have made ethical discourse their private property).

1.1. BE: a case of applied ethics?

In recent years ethical reflection has addressed questions that are much more immediately related to issues that are close to people's everyday lives. There is no denying that issues open to public discussion, such as abortion, genetic engineering, the thousand and one varieties of corruption, the growing role of professional people in the ordering of social life, the ecological crisis, the arms race, the persistent habit of resolving conflicts by military actions, social and economic inequality, and so many other challenges that face our societies pose all kinds of answer questions, even moral ones.

The attempt to answer these questions has favored the appearance and development of what is usually called "applied ethics". Applied ethics has been gaining ground not only as a result of changes in the philosophers' profession but, above all, as a result of increasing perplexity about what we should do. New questions have been posed not only because of the technical progress, new forms of power, and the planet-wide interdependence and complexity which are shaping human life. The ideological crisis and the cultural pluralism that characterizes our societies today have also played an important role. All this has resulted in ethics becoming a "hot" property, often due to the pressure of a demand which expects ethics to resolve the problems that overwhelm our lives and that other disciplines or approaches have failed to solve.

On this point, however, I think that we are still suffering from a lack of mediation and the dualism between ethics and economy in the modern age (KOSLOWSKI, 1987). This lack becomes onerous when experts' research on the foundation of ethics or metaethical issues ends up in a divorce between ethics and moral life. The possibility of an ethics that is also inherent (and not merely incidental) to the diversity of life spheres has been ignored on all too many occasions.

In dealing with this issue, I think that the division between "moral" and "ethics" continues to be enlightening. It attributes "moral" with everything that concerns the immediate expression of some kind of proposed life meaning or action. Thus, in contrast, I will consider ethics as a philosophical and critical reflection on morals, a reflection that, because it aims to give a reason for and understanding of "moral", orients action, albeit not directly. Ethics could therefore be properly said to be moral philosophy. Both ethics and morals are plural, but whereas "moral" is used as an adjective for various life meanings and proposals, "ethics" is given adjectives according to the philosophical approach involved. Nonetheless, I do not think that these divisions should exclude one another. Instead they are two extremes on a continuum of possible positions.

According to conventional classifications, we should consider BE as a particular form of applied ethics. The problem, then, becomes how to conceive what is referred to as "applied ethics" and how to work with it. To begin with, when we accept the division mentioned above, talk of ethics does not refer to solving particular cases but to the frames of reference from which they can be addressed and within which we act, as well as to the justification and foundation of these frames. Consequently, BE should not be reduced to a particular moral proposal - or, more literally, to a normative proposal - for managing organizations.

But the very label "applied" linked to ethics raises doubts and causes reticence. Isn't qualifying ethics as applied (or as practical, as is also done), either a self-contradiction or a redundancy? Though necessary,[2] it seems insufficient to say that ethics only aims to guide action indirectly, but not immediately because its elaboration is theoretical. Probably the origin of the label "applied" is also related to the fact that ethics has centered on questions that often seemed disproportionately removed from the biographical and historical problems of moral life. However, the successive turns that philosophy has taken throughout this century have directed it towards themes more closely linked to human life, which might make it appear more practical or applied when compared with the philosophy of the past.

This is a fairly recent development as is its translation to the academic world: the neologism "bioethics" first appeared in 1970 and BE was consolidated as such during the 1980s. Likewise, the 1970s saw the appearance of institutions and journals devoted to several "practical" problems. As ethics took this practical or applied turn, the status of this approach became an issue. The problems addressed were not protected by a solid theoretical tradition and posed new questions for which philosophers did not always have suitable concepts at their disposal and which, above all, were questions that should not be treated as being - or even susceptible to being - philosophers' exclusive property.

Such problems stem from the diversity of professional and political practices, where casuistry (and even deontology) fail due to their lack of a single code of reference. In fact the various situations that have led to the high point of applied ethics usually have at least one common element : the experiencing of a conflict of values. What is basically at issue here is whether values - even the most fundamental ones - can be completely clarified without any reference to situations in which they are liable to become conflictive. It is the attention to situations that makes it more and more evident that it is not possible to talk about values by talking only about values.

And it is here where the ambiguity of the term applied ethics becomes apparent. I think that this ambiguity lies, above all, in the fact that it can suggest an approach very similar to proposals that presuppose a single code. It can even be instrumental in orchestrating a return to the traditional model not only of moral authority but also the authority of morals. The idea of "application" has a deductive connotation, as though it were enough to simply clarify or justify one's principles when tackling situations, and

---

[2] In a pluralist context, I believe that the identification between ethics and morality is really only possible when one embraces the claim (or the nostalgia) of the single moral code.

then only the minor "practical" problem of applying these principles would remain. This would be a secondary problem that depends only on one's will or the circumstances, but does not affect the principles or the norms clearly established independently of them. Therefore "applied ethics," can suggest and presuppose a top-down approach where the weight of ethics naturally falls on the top.

Brown (1987) has clearly expressed the implicit assumptions involved in accepting the existence of an "applied ethics". This can be summarized in four points: (a) applied ethics is an application of ethical theory; (b) there exists a complete body of ethical theory and of well-founded moral contents waiting to be applied to practical problems; (c) there is a division of labor which consists of non-philosophers posing the problems and philosophers providing and applying the theory; (d) professional ethics is the result of applying general ethics (which does not contain any specific element from each practical field) to the profession or the occupation at hand. There is no need to add that the contemporary cultural context and the philosophical scene make any applied ethics identified with these claims absolutely unfeasible. However, when it comes to taking action, this does not prevent many people and groups from behaving as though applied ethics consisted precisely of this. In my opinion what renders inviable the model of applied ethics understood as a top-down process that leads from theory to practice is not only social reality but also an ethical reflection that is sensitive and attentive to the diversity of dimensions of moral life.

However, the fact that applied ethics cannot be understood as a deductive process does not mean that the approach should be reversed and would consist of some sort of inductive process which does not aim at constructing principles (due to the diversity of approaches necessary to do so), but at contributing practical orientations commonly accepted at the moment of resolving conflicts. Hence, the issue is not to shape a "bottom-up" practical ethics. Once we have accepted that moral problems emerge in the context of a social situation that must be taken into account, it is not necessary to continuously invoke this context, although it is necessary to keep it always in the back of your mind. All normative proposals demand some type of specifically ethical justification and do not emerge directly and acritically from social and professional practices without any "reflective moment" being involved.[3]

Hence, although we cannot acritically accept either a deductive or inductive model of application, we cannot fail to acknowledge the theoretical and practical problem posed by the articulation and interpenetration of the diverse contributions that must be taken into account when we deal with any problem of practical ethics. I therefore think that the status of applied ethics will be established in parallel with (and not prior to) the development of the various ethical positions which are characteristic of specific areas.

This will entail fine-tuning and complementing the various ethical approaches, promoting dialogue among them, reformulating them in the context of the situations in which one wants to integrate and develop them with the contributions of other disciplines (and viceversa as well). Because one of the intrinsic requirements of any

---

[3] Something that, incidentally, is not always easy to propose or accept because the new practical problems and the difficulty of constructing a common frame of reference are often experienced as an obstacle and a complication when decisions must be made and time is a scarce resource. Analysts and thinkers are considerably more tolerant of doubt and uncertainty than people who will ultimately be responsible for the decisions they make.

practical ethics is knowing the reality you want to deal with, we cannot claim any legitimacy for the development of practical ethics if we ignore what are sometimes called - somewhat presumptuously - the mere fields of application. In other words, applied ethics requires a change in everyone involved, including philosophers, and consequently cannot be left only in the hands of philosophers. Shared approaches will therefore be necessary and I suspect that, given the complexity of the problems that must be faced. an interdisciplinary approach will be an indispensable condition for the survival of the hermeneutical circle that embraces ethical theory and situational contexts.

I find the approach that opts between considering applied ethics as either a province or as a process (EDEL, 1986) very enlightening- not least because it is so expressive. In my opinion, a "province" would refer to a more or less fixed and self-sufficient academic discipline with its particular experts, while a "process" would refer to a reflective and theoretical process that accompanies the development of professional (individual or collective), organizational, institutional, or social projects, and is imbued with them, without being identified with or limited to these projects.

I aim to deal with BE as a process. This will consequently involve a close look at the contributions of various moral philosophies and how we should understand the viability of ethical principles within the particularities of various fields of action. But in the medium term I think that another consequence will be that the questions raised by the field of applied ethics will bounce back towards the various moral philosophies and force them to rethink some of their assumptions.

Nonetheless, the circular nature of applied ethics requires a specific ethical dimension. The coordinates of its elaboration must be clearly drawn. And I will do so here, starting from the observation that "discussion in practical philosophy has always nourished itself from three sources: Aristotelian ethics, utilitarianism, and the Kantian theory of morality."[4] This is not the time to discuss when this "always" starts, or whether these three sources are the only ones. Still, it is true that they are the dominant ones today and, above all, they are the ones used almost exclusively in BE.

The problems and perspectives of applied ethics mean that the confrontation among the various moral philosophies and the claims made by each one become a question of whether the various spheres of life can be properly understood from the standpoint of only one of the existing ethical models. In other words, "in questions like the ones that have been occupying us, there is possibly no theory that could not be attacked or considered blameless. What is reasonable is rather to examine what is useful in each ethical theory."[5] Obviously, setting criteria that permit us to consider some approach as useful is already, in a direct way, an activity directly typical of moral philosophy, just as is, to use an expression I find more suitable, underscoring the "truth" contained in each ethical theory. Such truth is very often found in what each one of these theories proposes and also sheds light on the blind points and shadows detected in the others.

---

[4] Habermas, 1991, p. 317.
[5] Ferrater, 1981, p. 35.

1.2. BE as "applied" ethics: a preliminary proposal for integration

In the case of BE, I do not think that business should be considered an already constructed reality in which ethics would only be a value added feature. Nor should ethics be considered a self-sufficient discourse which is just waiting to come down to earth and be adapted to business without being affected by it. But the truth is that, because of the need to give an answer to practical demands (and sometimes the tendency to give functional answers to corporate needs), BE has not managed to sufficiently integrate the disciplines that converge in it. As a result, more than interdisciplinary dialogue we often find a conglomerate of disciplines or the predominance of one of them. This is confirmed, for example, when we observe the predominant use of various ethics: frequently their use is only instrumental as though the various ethical traditions were preexisting conceptual tools ready to be used for dealing with corporate practices or theories which would ultimately be what would determine the conditions for using the various ethical approaches.[6] I think that what is needed to develop BE is not only an interdisciplinary dialogue, but also an integrated consideration of various ethical approaches. Thus my point of departure is the conviction that a closed model should not be used when addressing BE, but that we should use some coordinates[7] that constitute a framework in which the ethical problems posed by organizational management can be situated and understood in the light of their specificity.

Indeed, the different ethical proposals usually do not merely affirm themselves, but they also do so by disputing the proposals to which they are opposed; and often they stake a certain claim to exclusivity or preeminence. This is very significant in the field of ethical thought as such. Nonetheless, my hypothesis (at least in relation to BE) is that a good way to understand ethical theories from the standpoint of "applied" ethics is to adopt an approach similar to the one Ferrater adopts when he proposes "integrationism": "Given two positions in conflict [. . .] each position can be considered as a position-limit, labeled by one or more concepts-limit; the insufficiencies of one position can be corrected by shifting to the opposite position, which then functions as complementary [. . .] From this point of view, the position I defend can be called integrationism. Integrationism is, nonetheless, only a method, it is not a conception of reality."[8] It is true that approaches such as this one might be viewed as some sort of eclecticism or even opportunism. But it is a risk we could run provided that we do not cease to justify the various proposals that are continually being made.

In fact, to give a current example, in the controversy between liberalism and communitarism, scholars have already pointed out the importance of searching for what Thiebaut (1992a) calls the "truth" of each of these approaches. I think this attitude can be broadened to the point where moral doctrines are not treated as different and rival classes of morality among which one should choose, but as complementary aspects of the same moral life. I think that if it really focuses on the problems and challenges

---

[6] Ethical approaches that are, moreover, most often used in a relatively simplified way in many versions of BE.

[7] For reasons of space I cannot go into a detailed discussion and justification of these coordinates, but will only give a synthesis of them here.

[8] Ferrater, 1979, pp. 84-85.

generated by human situations, "applied" ethics will gradually move in this direction. In short, we should not ignore the fact that "our action, when it is ethically relevant, is the result of a struggle and a tension between irreducible poles. And it is not a question of one being imposed over the other [. . .]. Rather, the tension should always be maintained."[9] I feel that the tension is maintained in at least two ways: on the one hand, by addressing each theory's specific dimension of morality; on the other, by addressing aspects of morality that each ethical theory points out when it criticizes other theories for not taking them into consideration. I further think that when there is insurmountable opposition between two ethical theories the best way to change this sterile opposition into a fertile tension is by introducing a third ethical view.

However, an ethical approach which aims at a minimum of integration does not aim to reach it only in discourse, as if we were once again obsessed with searching for an all-embracing synthesis. Integration does not look for a completed synthesis, but aims at keeping tension alive. In this sense, and returning now to BE, my whole approach is based on a concept of this tension as referring to organizational processes, and not as enriching a definition of what an organization is. For this reason I consider it important, at least symbolically, to use the verb "to organize" rather than the noun "organization" (RITCHIE, 1988), since it then becomes much more apparent that BE's references are not concepts, but organizational processes. Incidentally, I believe that this is the only way we can overcome the separatist paradigm that is a legacy of the duality between ethics and economy .

Thus, as a frame of reference for BE I propose what I call a hermeneutics of responsibility, in contrast to what in practice ends up being nothing more than submission to the heteronomy of results (economic or corporate). This hermeneutics of responsibility stems from an integrated and integrating understanding of the utilitarian, deontological, and virtue ethics traditions within the framework of BE and in dialogue with it.

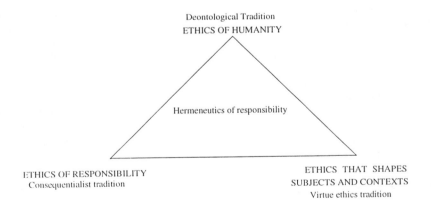

[9] Camps, 1988, p. 13.

In my opinion BE should adopt the utilitarian tradition's consequentialist structure. Thus, it should also embrace the demand to consider knowing reality as ethically relevant in order to avoid the dissociation between moral discourse and what takes place in reality.[10] However, I prefer to talk more about responsibility than about consequentialism since responsibility involves taking into consideration the power of the actor. Taking into account the power of organizations and addressing the consequences of their actions and decisions is what identifies BE as an ethics of responsibility in a world where the increase of scientific and technical power is inseparable from its organizational structure. Still, we should realize that in order to operate with responsibility from an ethical standpoint, it is not enough to state that responsibility is important. The consequences are not ethically relevant unless there is a criterion that makes them relevant, and this is something that is usually forgotten. Nor can we forget that acts also shape the moral identity of the actors. Therefore, for BE the acknowledgement that consequences are important does not mean that everything depends exclusively on these consequences. The preferences expressed in them and the quality of the subjects who provoke them are also ethically relevant. Thus, as an ethics of responsibility, BE should address the consequences of actions for the affected parties. But this attention cannot be separated from the capacity to understand and interpret the criteria and purposes that govern them and the constitution of the agents who bring them about. Hence, as an ethics of responsibility, BE cannot separate attention to the consequences of organizational actions from a critical treatment of organizational preferences, priorities and decision-making criteria.

From the tradition of virtue ethics, BE borrows its recognition that the subject of moral life is a person and that any ethical proposal must therefore refer to the many dimensions that constitute a moral subject. BE should not think only in terms of ends and results, as if the fulfillment of certain personal, professional, and organizational values will take place at the end of a long road. BE also refers to the very process of constituting organizations as such (and the people who are part of them). To the extent that BE involves some organizationally contextualized practices, it demonstrates that it is not indifferent to an organization's shared traditions (in terms of values and styles of action), just as it is not indifferent to their consequences. And what is more, BE recognizes that organizations shape their ethical identity as they develop a way of acting that also acknowledges the internal goods they aspire to reach in terms of organizational purposes. Accordingly, one of BE's contributions is precisely to favor a shared construction of meanings within the corporation in relation to the goods that are brought into play in organizational life. Thus, BE is not reduced to calculating the consequences in decision-making; it also includes a dimension of discernment that includes the shared creation of organizational purposes, assuming that in fact each organization promotes certain virtues and certain vices in its way of doing things and in its everyday practices and legitimizes a view of human excellence that can be reached through its professional and organizational practice.

In short, BE starts with the assumption that organizations are groups that shape the character and values of the individuals who form part of them. Because of this, we can

---

[10] I think that this also includes the acceptance of effectiveness and efficiency as values that should not be considered merely instrumental.

consider organizations as ethical spaces. It is from this perspective that BE also considers the organization as a field that is - or can be - a catalyst of human quality, whose ethical analysis cannot be reduced to the social consequences of individuals' actions.

Radical acceptance of the deontological tradition allows BE to avoid being reduced to a simple professional deontology. BE cannot be reduced to a simple declaration of abstract duties but must always combine any reference to universal values and principles with an affirmation of the humanity of individuals and acknowledgement of their moral autonomy. BE should therefore be an ethics able to overcome in practice a merely preconventional approach, but it must also be able to sidestep the danger of confining itself to being simply the affirmation of a conventional morality. In other words, BE has to make it possible to accept the organizational contexts of a postconventional approach that is typical of the deontological tradition. But it must do so recognizing that this approach cannot be institutionalized or materialized separately from corporate practices.

Within the framework of BE, the postconventional perspective should be thought of as an internal moment in the organizational processes, which BE can frame and regulate, but not substitute in their specificity. Thus, BE cannot be operative if it simply affirms universal principles and values. But, should it forget them, BE could vanish as an ethical reflection, given that the concept of BE as an ethics of humanity allows it to set the limits of what is humanly intolerable and to indicate the horizon (limits) of what cannot be renounced.

But the fact that BE is an ethics of humanity should not make us forget that BE is also an ethics of responsibility (and increasingly of co-responsibility) because BE cannot be a direct discourse on the principle of humanity. The principle of humanity is an ethical perspective which is a dimension that is – or could be – at stake because it critically addresses everything that concerns the viability of organizations (as, for example, the quality of the subject they foster, the moral climate they favor, the criteria defining their purposes or decision-making processes). The principle of humanity, however, cannot be conceived as a final goal; it is an internal moment of organizational life, which refers both to the moral autonomy of the individual and to the recognition of the other as a valid interlocutor. And, therefore, I do not consider it a corrective or descending principle, but a continuous ethical backdrop that needs some degree of institutionalization. The ethics of humanity is not a direct object of BE, but it is the frame of reference that makes responsibility, values, and shared values intelligible.

This frame of reference is what allows me to propose and maintain an integrated conception of BE (as ethics of responsibility, ethics that shapes subjects and contexts, and ethics that refers to, and is founded on, the principle of humanity). And I propose to provisionally call this concept the hermeneutics of responsibility, in contrast to what I call the heteronomy of results.

In my opinion, it is very important to present this proposal of a hermeneutics of responsibility as an integrated approach because it is not a question simply of affirming or adding together various ethical traditions. Moreover, I think that the ethical quality of the above three dimensions which should be integrated in BE is devaluated when each is taken separately as an absolute value or when attempts are made to reduce BE to any one of them.

Whenever one ethical dimension becomes an absolute reference responsibility is reduced to a simple consequentialism which ignores the criteria and finalities that make it intelligible as well as the principles that frame it and the attention to the actor. Conventional values are then reduced to a cultural identity closed in itself, impermeable to criticism, incapable of both self-criticism and dialogue, and without any consideration of their responsibilities. And humanity is reduced to the affirmation of abstract principles, insensitive to context, indifferent to consequences, and ignorant of concrete human subjects.

Consequently, BE should show how all the following considerations are viable and significant : the consideration of the consequences of actions for the affected parties ; the consideration of the principle of humanity which includes the acknowledgment of others as valid interlocutors ; and the consideration of the need to shape a certain conventional morality which enables individuals to identify with the practices and goods that are at stake in each organizational project. Should one want to visualize this triple consideration, I think it would be best to depict it circularly rather than linearly because each of these dimensions becomes fully intelligible only when it is interpreted together with the other two in a process of organizational development.

In other words: in a society of organizations, BE has to be viable and has to become an ethics of responsibility, an ethics that generates conventional morality and as an ethics that affirms the principle of humanity.

BE should become an ethics of responsibility because it should be able to take into consideration the power of organizations in our society; a power that must be understood in both its technical and specifically organizational aspects. Only if we explicitly accept the challenges posed by the power of organizations can we sustain our efforts to take into consideration the consequences for those who are affected by this exercise of power. This means that the preferences and priorities reflected in organizations cannot be taken as a kind of datum which admits no further thinking. On the contrary, responsible acknowledgement of organizational preferences and priorities entails a critical analysis of the interests and objectives that govern organizational life, because this acknowledgment must start with and refer to them, but it should also filter them by considering everything that is at stake in decision-making processes.

BE should become an ethics that generates conventional morality because it cannot overlook the fact that organizational life educates, shapes, and channels human desire through the goods and practices inherent to it and only in relation to them. It proposes a certain understanding of human excellence; it promotes certain habits and styles of action that are not the result of adding together those of the individuals who constitute the organization; it legitimizes values and generates meaning and motivations; and it promotes a social construction of reality that gives identity to those who take part in the organization and can be understood in moral terms. From this perspective, an organization is also - or can be - a catalyst of human quality, although it does not aim at this directly but in relation to its raison d'etre. Therefore, the organization can only attempt to be a catalyst within this frame of reference.

Lastly, BE has to become an ethics of humanity. It is not simply a matter of what not to do but also a matter of where we are going. Nonetheless, BE does not directly address these issues. Instead they are addressed through organizational practices. This is BE's particularity as well as its ambiguity, since BE cannot consist of a discourse about the universal values of the principle of humanity.[11] But no organizational process can ignore these values if it wants to ethically construct its raison d'être, its values, its social responsibility, and the organizational project itself. For this reason I also suggest that it is not necessary to conceive the principle of humanity as a final goal, but that it should be conceived as an internal moment of (or background to) organizational life, which continually affirms human dignity and which ultimately recognizes that individuals have dignity and not a price. This approach takes us beyond conventionalism, but it does not prevent us from criticizing abstract humanity, especially when this is proposed as if it were possible to ignore the reality of concrete human beings and social systems. "For it is clear that the subject of ethics is not an omniscient and powerful god, but we ourselves, the same subjects who are involved in political, economic, professional or, simply, ordinary life. Ethics is nothing but the response that aims at giving meaning to and directing the various dimensions of existence. As a response, ethics must, then, proceed in the wake of the problems that are continually appearing and will inevitably be polluted with the uncertainties and miseries that they involve."[12] In line with Cortina's approach (1993), I think that the principle of humanity is fundamentally some sort of coordinating conceptual frame or like a common melodic background to all spheres of corporate life.

Having reached this point, the task is to determine, in reference to these coordinates and in relation to the particularities of organizational life and institutionalization processes, what constitutes an ethics that adequately refers to corporations and organizations. This is what I shall try to do in the following chapters.

---

[11] The principle of humanity comes into play when we have to critically reflect on questions that directly affect organizational life, as for example the quality of the subject that organizational life promotes, the quality of the world of life that it protects internally and promotes externally, the quality of its decision-making processes, the criteria that operate in setting its purposes and objectives, its willingness to alter preferences and priorities, and its capacity to also adopt a social perspective.

[12] Camps, 1988, p. 9.

CHAPTER 2

BUSINESS ETHICS: AN ON-GOING PROCESS

2.1. Introduction: A Progressive Self-awareness

The difficulties in methodically systematizing an understanding of BE stem from at least one fact: the discipline is still very young. Thus it is still in a phase in which increased production has neither resulted in a general consensus about its scope nor in a shared formulation of its presuppositions. Although agreements can be detected in many areas and experiences progressively reveal fundamental coincidences, I feel that the panorama still responds to a situich shared framework of referenceation in wh. Among other reasons, it would not be easy to establish the diversity of initiatives, proposals, and approaches has not materialized in a what would sanction such a framework as valid. In contrast, what cannot be denied is the increasing growth of work that refers in one way or another to this reference: Business Ethics.

As my goal is to understand - and not only describe - BE, any attempt to be exhaustive would be condemned to failure from the very outset. What is indispensable first of all is an approach that aims to shape a certain perception of the whole, starting from the diversity of the fragments (which indeed vary greatly in both quantity and quality), given that it is not yet possible to compare and critically contrast already constituted global approaches. I feel, however, that in coming years BE will culminate the process of its self-awareness as well as the configuration of its identity. It has been noted (Vidal, 1990) that we are still searching for a reasonable paradigm for BE. But it is necessary to add that this search has already given us enough elements to enable us to shape a more complete picture of the discipline.

In this chapter I attempt to explore the process of progressive self-awareness in BE. This process of self-awareness has been a bottom-up process developed basically in the U.S., although in the 1990s it has experienced a boom in Europe as well. I think one can broadly state that BE's leap forward was triggered by two fundamental expansions: one internal and the other external.

As far as internal expansion is concerned, BE has progressively ceased being a purely academic question or purely business issue and has gradually become a theme that is considered incomplete if it is approached only from the world of academia or only from the business world. Thus, the enrichment of BE has been paralleled by the emergence of a tendency to increasingly transform it into an object of careful consideration in both the academic and business worlds.

The external expansion is geographical in nature: in recent years concern with BE has ceased being fundamentally American and become European as well. This means that BE now has a larger and more complex social and economic reality as its reference. Although it is undeniable that the bulk of the written production has been, until recently, predominantly American, European approaches increasingly attempt to make an original contribution.

To summarize my view, I think that the key is not only to be found in the different social and economic traditions, but also in a crucial difference in the frame of mind used to approach these problems. While the American tradition is based on the premise that the economic system is good (and tends to view ethical values in relation to how businesses and organizations function), the European tradition tends to critically question the ethical values of the economic system itself (often with the implicit assumption that, once this point is clarified, only a secondary practical problem will remain: how to apply them). In any case, as this dichotomy is overcome and as BE's interdisciplinary and international character develops, this discipline, together with bioethics, will become the most important point of reference for the development of applied ethics. In addition, it will be the new source of questions addressing ethical theories.

Before looking ahead, however, we should first look back for a moment. Thus I will devote this chapter to reconstructing the emergence of BE. I will do this by discussing both its historical evolution and a number of elements that have contributed to shaping it up to the present day. In short, to use Kohlberg's terminology, I will attempt to show that up to now BE has primarily focused on constituting, supporting, or legitimating what we could call a conventional morality that is adequate to the functioning of businesses and organizations. I think that this is due to reasons of both social context and philosophical tradition. Socially, the issue of BE very often arises as a consequence of the recognition of business practices of a pre-conventional nature. Philosophically, the issue of BE very often stems from the different crises of legitimization in a social and economic system that is neither questioned nor wants to be questioned For this reason I believe that ultimately the most radical question one can ask of BE is that it clarify whether it is an ethics capable of incorporating a post-conventional dimension. I consider this question essential to understanding BE's constitution as a process that ranges - or can range - from a simple reaction to a reality shaped by a pre-conventional morality to the construction of a perspective capable of incorporating a post-conventional dimension. I contend that unless we understand this, we will be unable to understand the development of BE's perspectives and possibilities.

2.2.   A first historical approach to BE

Whatever the period of reference, there tends to be agreement on one point: the origin of concern with BE. It stems from the "social demand and internal pressure"[1] to reprehend business practices that are considered immoral and even scandalous. This origin has weighed heavily on BE, which has often focused primarily on avoiding repetition of such practices rather than directly promoting an alternative understanding of organizational practice.

In fact, only in a very broad sense (which I think should be abandoned) can one talk about BE before the first half of this century. Granted, concern about issues that have later been addressed within the framework of BE dates back to far earlier. But I think that one can safely say that, up until recently, these questions were posed mainly in terms of ethics and economics, or in terms of economic ethics, but not in terms of BE.

---

[1] Fernández, 1992, p. 29

In addition, when this more generic perspective is adopted BE becomes confused with economic ethics and one ends up finding BE in all the authors and traditions that throughout history have voiced concern about the ethics of the economy and economic systems as well as the ethics of individual actions in economic transactions. It is obvious that there must be some link between BE and economic ethics (in other words, there is always some kind of economic ethics behind BE), but it would be advisable to ask whether there is a more specific feature that could enable us to set some reasonable bounds when we talk about BE.

In my opinion, although the connection cannot always be made sufficiently explicit, the appearance of BE is a consequence of the appearance of what Chandler (1977) called the visible hand of management. If we ignore the view that confuses BE with some kind of economic ethics, we will see that in fact attempts to understand BE historically (and specifically) situate its origins in a moment when the process described by Chandler had already taken place: the appearance of big firms as opposed to small traditional businesses; the formal - and hierarchical- organization of these new firms; the emergence of managerial career paths defined in professional terms; the separation of management and ownership. This was already significant in the first half of our century and a growing concern about the ethics of action in big companies and thoughts about corporate management stem from this time. But this early concern had three particular features. First, it was formulated in terms of disenchantment or criticism of the social results of the generalization of a market economy; which were in sharp contrast to some ideals of the liberal tradition. Secondly, the approach that treated the issue in terms of one-on-one relationships continued to prevail (although this began changing to an approach that questioned what management as a profession involves). Thirdly, the discussion took place mainly within the framework of religious traditions that did not actually treat BE as such, but tried to "apply" particular moral perspectives to the business world.[2]

During the sixties - as both cliché and history remind us - there was a growing mobilization against what "identified" the American way of life: some fundamental symbols of this criticism were counterculture and demonstrations protesting the Vietnam War. This was also a time when the social consequences of corporate actions were called into question: first, the ecological impact of industrial development and secondly the consequences of promoting consumerism as a life style. Concern for the social consequences of business actions caused a new question to be raised - a question that was ultimately formulated as corporate social responsibility. This meant that, when analyzing business, viewpoints (and interests) other than those of owners and managers had to be taken into account. The most important point of this new perspective is that problems focus on organizations rather than individuals.

This change was based on the assumption that "there is one kind of social contract implicit between society and companies: companies have obligations to society, which must control their actions. Consequently, companies must design their policies in the knowledge that they will be accountable to society".[3] Thus, companies know that, on the

---

[2] Still, however, it must be acknowledged (Mahoney, 1990) that religious traditions made a decisive contribution to developing a social ethics, one of whose repercussions took the form of BE.
[3] Kerhuel, 1990, p. 17.

one hand, they have to consider their obligations to different social groups and, on the other, they are forced to anticipate some social demands that cannot be considered in, or rather reduced to, mere economic terms. The sixties were a boom period for authors writing about BE, and this meant that the academic world began to be concerned about education in this field.

Nevertheless, "the development of the field of business ethics began in the 1970s. Theologians and religious thinkers had developed the area of ethics in business and continued to develop it. Professors of management continued writing and teaching on corporate social responsibility. The new ingredient added to this setting was the entry – for a variety of reasons – into the area of a significant number of philosophers." [4] As an example, let us review three milestones on this path of development. On the one hand, there was the famous article by Friedman (1970), who summed up his controversial thesis in the title of this article, "The Social Responsibility of Business is to Increase its Profits"; On the other hand, there was Rawls' Theory of Justice (1971), which, among many other things, signified the legitimization of philosophical concern about economic issues, and lastly, biomedical ethics began developing at this time.

The advent of philosophers was, in fact, linked to a concern about clarifying the moral status of business firms. Obviously, this did not imply abandoning concern for individual questions, but it was decisive because it marked the beginning of thinking that was specifically directed at the ethics of organizations as such . Still, it must be stressed that very often ethical thoughts couched in business terms continue to take management's view of the company as their point of reference.

Nonetheless, by the end of the seventies there were new perspectives and concerns. It has therefore been stated that the first half of the eighties was the beginning of the consolidation of BE and that it was not defined or consolidated as a separate discipline until around 1985 (De George, 1987). In short, during the eighties a true explosion of initiatives took place and revealed the existence of widespread dedication to the study of what was explicitly labelled as BE. [5]

It should not come as a surprise, then, that academic production started to grow and be formally systematized. Thus, as far as journals are concerned, the Business and Professional Ethics Journal was the first to appear. It was followed by the Journal of Business Ethics; Economics and Philosophy, and Business Ethics Quarterly. At the same time bibliographic compilations begin to appear. And finally, in 1987, De George recognized the existence of seventeen centers devoted to promoting BE-related initiatives in one way or another. If we look at these dates (and recall the dates of the first attempts to pinpoint the history of BE - all dated after 1985) I feel it is plausible to situate the constitution of BE as a fully autonomous - and academic - discipline during the first half of the eighties.

---

[4] De George, 1987, p. 202.
[5] Two studies by the Center for Business Ethics (one of the most prominent organizations in the field) confirm this. One of them referred to the teaching of BE (Hoffman & Moore, 1982): almost a third of the most important 1200 schools and universities offered courses in this subject, two-thirds of which bore the title BE (up 500% from 1973). The other study (Center for Business Ethics, 1986) reported that of the 1000 important companies in the U.S, one-fifth had taken some steps to institutionalize ethics, even though the great majority referred solely to drafting some ethical code.

2.3.   The recent development of BE in Europe

It could perhaps be said that European interest in BE lagged behind that of the U.S. It is necessary, however, to qualify this statement because Europe has a long tradition of addressing issues inherent to BE, even if this particular name (which is also an approach) was not adopted until the second half of the eighties. Before that, these subjects came under headings such as "Economy and Society," "Social Ethics," "Economic Ethics," etc. It is fair to say that, although the US is the acknowledged leader in the field, there has always been a strong awareness of the need to formulate a different approach: an approach that would be more consonant with the European socio-economic, managerial, and academic reality, going beyond mere imitation of what has been called the US "ethicsmania".[6]

I believe that two facts of a social and economic nature contribute particularly to an awareness of the difference between Europe and the U.S., an awareness that is especially strong in Europe. On the one hand, political and social traditions have given rise to various forms of capitalism. [7] On the other, in Europe discussion has often been excessively ideological, regarding the business world with a certain disdain. Perhaps for this reason the crisis of ideologies has triggered a boom in values in the business world, which sometimes seem to simply fill the void created by those ideologies rather than actually replacing them. To these two global considerations it would be necessary to add other differentiating factors: Europeans are less prone to taking legal measures to settle conflicts; they are more eager to connect BE with philosophical or sociological approaches to problems; European companies are somewhat less inclined to draw up codes of ethics; Europe is more sensitive to the danger of making BE a way to legitimize companies and is therefore more aware of the danger of instrumentalization. Europeans have less confidence in self-regulation, which is linked to the anthropology of liberal individualism, and they place greater weight on the social values inherent to dominant political traditions.

In my opinion, a key event in bringing BE awareness to Europe was the creation of the European Business Ethics Network (EBEN) in 1987. This organization aims to foster relations between the academic and business worlds and thereby become a network that supports BE development in Europe through courses, publications, congresses, contacts between institutions and research centers, etc. Apart from its annual congresses, which have been held since 1989, the association has promoted the creation of individual networks in a number of countries, among them Germany, The Netherlands, the United Kingdom and Spain. Another milestone was the appearance of three journals: Etica degli affari, Business Ethics. A European Review, and Entreprise Éthique. Moreover, as of the mid-eighties several European centers turned their attention - fully or partially - to BE, among them: The Business Ethics Research Center and the Institute of Business Ethics in London; the Centre d'éthique de l'entreprise in Paris; the Chaire Hoover d'ethique économique et sociale in Louvain; the Institute of Business Ethics in Saint Gallen, the Business Ethics Center of Budapest, the Center for Ethics and Economics in Stockholm, the Seminario Permanente Empresa y Humanismo

---

[6] Lipovetsky, 1992, p. 263.
[7] See how Albert (1991) and Thurow (1992) have placed the alternative between diverse forms of capitalism at the center of a debate about the process of globalization of the economy.

in Pamplona, and the Fundación ETNOR in Valencia. They are not the only centers and institutions working with BE (as one can see from the attendance at EBEN meetings), but I feel that they are the most significant ones dealing directly with BE.

In sum, my opinion is that the future of BE in Europe lies in contributing something different to both the most concrete aspects of BE and to its status. Europe's economic and social history, its philosophical traditions, and its academic developments can all help shape some distinguishing traits.

2.4.   What issues should BE address?

As we have seen, diverse factors have converged to shape BE. Its development is due not only to an accepted internal logic, but also to outside pressure and demands regarding what companies and organizations do and what is expected from business schools. We can take Brooks (1989) as the paradigmatic attempt to synthesize the variegated elements at the root of the demand for BE: a) society's distrust of corporate activities (and, therefore, a need to reconstruct their legitimacy); b) the demand for a better quality of life, which increases internal and external expectations of companies; c) the demand that managers do not limit their actions to merely seeking profits for owners; d) the acknowledgment of corporate power and the ensuing need to regulate and publicly link together the diverse interest groups in our society; e) increased public concern with these issues and the increased publicity given them; f) the greater complexity of corporate objectives, which can no longer be limited to seeking short-term benefits. I consider it necessary to add to all these elements one that is both a cause and a consequence of the demand for BE: business schools' reflections about their raison d'être, about the kind of training they should provide and about the type of education they should propose.

Nonetheless, if what we want is to understand the process of constitution of BE and to situate it in context in order to propose our own reading, our next step should be to identify the object of BE.

2.5.   BE: a first attempt at a systematic ordering

The slightest attempt to systematize the development of BE has always encountered an obstacle, which is that "the traditional approach to ethics is an individualistic one. Our notions of morality, moral worth, and moral praise and blame have derived primarily from consideration of the human person as a moral agent".[8] Obviously, it does not intend to question basic ethical references, such as autonomy or freedom. However, it does intend to express a certain caution with respect to the dangerous desire to explain human action ethically through terms, concepts, and paradigms that refer exclusively to the individual as a human agent because these actions cannot be reduced to actions understandable in individual terms, whether they be isolated or aggregated. It has therefore been observed (Preston, 1975) that one of the dangers that always threatens BE is that it might appeal to approaches that cannot take into account - either explicitly or implicitly - the specific particularities of companies and modern organizations.

---

[8] De George, 1990, p. iv.

Thus, from both an analytical and methodological standpoint, it seems to me important to acknowledge a distinction that I feel has already been accepted within the framework of BE and which, to give a European example, can be summed up in the subtitle of Sacconi's book (1991a): Individui, imprese, e mercati. In other words, BE can be understood as a three-tier ethical reflection: ethics in relation to the economic system, in relation to companies and organizations, and as applied to the actions of individuals in their professional roles and their institutional functions. Although in general terms there is a basic consensus on this division, I still think that we need to more precisely situate some of its elements.

The "macro" perspective of BE refers to the ethical analysis of economic systems and, more concretely, to the ethical justification of the market. But it is at this point that one of the levels of ambiguity - and, in my opinion, insufficiency - can already be glimpsed. We could imagine this ambiguity as a tension between two extremes. At one extreme, the issue is to understand "macro" thinking as a search for the moral justification and legitimization of the system in which companies act. Such thinking would solely aim to emphasize and justify the internal moral values of the market economy as if they were both self-justified and self-sufficient. And, at the opposite extreme the issue would be to understand "macro" thinking in the context of construction of an economic ethics that cannot be limited exclusively to business ethics. As Conill puts it, "There has been a split between the ethical and the technical aspects of the economy and this split constitutes a social problem to which we have as yet been unable to give an answer either in theory or in practice".[9] In other words: I think that, within the framework of BE, we need to specifically reflect on a differentiated "macro" level (and not limit ourselves merely to an introductory reflection on BE issues) about economic ethics or, more simply, about the ethics of capitalism (which is too often taken for granted or assumed).

The "meso" approach to BE involves analyzing the ethics of corporate actions by companies operating within the capitalist system, Up until now this was the predominant subject of study, although we should not forget other organizations and institutions that have also been directly involved: trade unions, consumers' associations, etc. Nevertheless, here too there has been a mixture of two different approaches. On the one hand, there is the need to understand companies and organizations as such ethically, and this includes on-going discussions about their moral status. On the other hand, there is the need to understand various concrete organizational practices, also from an ethical point of view. This distinction -often not theorized - is embodied in the tables of contents of almost all BE textbooks. After a brief introduction to some ethical reflections there is usually a description of what a company is and what its social responsibility should be, and immediately afterwards various chapters about practices, specific fields and functional areas, which usually account for the bulk of the book. In any case, it is necessary to recognize that the "meso" approach is inseparable from the corporate concept adopted in each case. This means that sooner or later BE will have to ask itself the following question. Is it limited to choosing from among the different concepts of the company the one considered most adequate to its aims? Or, rather, does

---

[9] Conill, 1993b, p. 201.

it aim to constitute itself as another element that should be taken into account when we want to explore the concept of what a company is and how it operates?

When Sacconi (1991a) suggests that the question of property and the question of management and authority are basic issues at the "meso" (or intermediate) level, he points out that there is a third level; namely, the "micro" level. This refers to the ethical analysis of individual relations and actions insofar as they respond to a professional role or to an organizational function.[10] Nevertheless, it is usually not entirely clear to what this "micro" level refers, whether to the link between personal moral values, ethical principles and professional values; the extent to which individuals' accept the deontology and conventional values of a particular profession, or individuals' appropriation- passive or critical - of corporate values. I think that the "micro" level should include all three aspects and I would say that they are, in fact, already included if we take into account the entire BE production. But they have not been jointly systematized. Indeed, when one considers the individual, there seems to be no criteria for deciding which of these three aspects should be emphasized other than from each author's personal, and often incompletely explained, personal preference.

In short, it seems amply accepted that in present-day BE three distinct levels of ethical questions should be analysed and addressed: the system, the organization, and the individual. The problem, however, is how these three levels can be linked. Obviously, it is not enough to address them successively or to distinguish them analytically. And acknowledging these three distinct levels without integrating them is a constant danger in BE, particularly in view of the fact that most authors do not seem aware that this danger exists. My answer to this question is that the object of BE thought should be the organization and it is from the organizational perspective that we need to seek the articulation of the three levels: organization, system, and individual. By taking this approach the organization does not become merely a specific object of reflection; it also acts as a go-between between system and individual.

Stating that the organization is at the center of things obviously does not deny that moral life is the expression of human development, the realization of a personal and social life-project. And we must acknowledge that BE runs the risk of overflowing its space between individuals and society: "in this case, the individual is threatened with being absorbed in the company and the company runs the risk of absorbing the social dimension".[11] Obviously we must be alert to this risk. But it is also risky not to take the organization sufficiently into account, at least from the standpoint of ethics. I therefore believe that BE should deliberately proclaim its perspective from the field of organizations (rather than limiting itself to simply acknowledging the distinction between the three levels). After all, "the corporation is a social invention designed to accomplish the moral task of serving the social needs of human beings."[12] Surely it is not necessary that its proclaimed intention and this characterization of its task be deliberate and explicitly discussed. Nonetheless, they are the result of a thought process that comprehends the typical organizations of modern societies within the context of the

---

[10] For this reason it is important "to acknowledge that individual and organizational ethical reflection are not mutually exclusive but are iterative parts of a process which inevitably shape and interpenetrate each other." (Epstein, 1987, p. 371)

[11] Kerhuel, 1990, p. 19

[12] Fasching, 1981, p. 64.

development of these societies. And for this reason, "just as individuals must reflect on the moral significance of their actions – including their business actions – so too, corporations through their boards of directors, top management, and other business persons involved in collective decisionmaking, must consider the moral implications of collective action."[13]

Our "society of organizations" (Drucker, 1992, Perrow, 1987) has ultimately turned human life into a corporate ecosystem in which "the company is no longer an organizational system but an arrangement of various levels of operation. Therefore, the company is not a sociological concept but a social reality which must be deconstructed by analysis."[14] Thus BE does not have to devote itself to debating the definitions of the company, but to understanding -together with other approaches- its reality. The three-level distinction acknowledged by BE (system, organization, and individual) should, in my view, be understood as a result of the acknowledgment of the specificity of the organizational level (or, to put it another way, as a result of the conviction that BE is not possible unless we take an ethical approach to the organizational levely).

Consequently, BE should first of all not be confused with a mere practical application of economic ethics to business firms, nor should it be reduced to this. Neither should it seek legitimacy in economic ethics alone. BE development needs the specific and autonomous development of economic ethics. BE should be open to a dialogue with economic ethics because it needs to consider the perspective of the system. But this does not mean that it can be self-sufficient when it comes to constructing an economic ethics that would provide its framework and basis. Indeed, one might be surprised by the speed with which BE texts usually confront (or avoid) this question. However, I consider far more symptomatic the resistance to BE that occurred as soon as some people perceived it as a possible criticism of the market economy. It is as if from certain perspectives BE could only be valid in the framework of a market immune, as such, to any ethical critique. Before proceeding any further, I think it would be a good idea to briefly discuss this resistance.

Secondly, BE should not be confused with a practical application of individual moral values to the company, and neither should it be reduced to this. Clearly, it should not shrink from the acknowledgment that what is ultimately at stake is individual development and moral quality. But BE addresses human action to the extent to which it is mediated by and contextualized in the organization. Hence it does not reduce professional ethical problems to a question of individual morality and it does not simplify individual moral life into some kind of adaptation to professional ethics. Accordingly, I believe that BE cannot be reduced to, or dissolved in, the treatment of ethical questions characteristic of professional practices and reflections on the values of work. Rather, it should do this only to the extent to which these questions arise within an organizational setting.

In my opinion, the two types of resistance (one which emphasizes the system and one which emphasizes the person) have a fairly symptomatic common denominator: avoiding that corporative and organizational actions are questioned in terms of ethics. As a result, they accept BE only to the extent to which it is a kind of conventional

---

[13] Epstein, 1987, p. 371.
[14] Touraine, 1969, p. 150.

moral, reducing it to a derived (or "applied") consequence of the values of the system or of personal values.

2.6. The acceptance or rejection of BE as a possible (il)legitimization of predominant practices and values

There is a long tradition of rejecting BE or the social responsibility of companies precisely on the grounds of defending values inherent to business practices. There is also an equally long tradition that views BE as an appropriate approach to the values inherent in business practices (but only to the extent to which it coincides with these values). In both cases, the following question arises: to what extent does BE consider itself as justified only when it has proven that it does not intend to be or to become an illegitimization of the values inherent in economic practices (which would thus become implicitly unquestionable)?

What often happens is that BE is justified in terms of the parameters of reference provided by the values of the economic system, which therefore makes it contingent on these values. In this approach, the BE discourse is often identified with - and justified by - the acceptance of a way of life that is considered to have its roots in society. And thus no attempt is made to ground it in a specifically ethical discourse. I think this interpretation is decisive to understanding BE because it has one consequence that is rarely taken into consideration. To put it briefly: BE tends to use ethical theories and refers to them, but it sometimes tends to justify itself primarily within the framework of what we could call "the predominant social project", and not so much within the framework of ethical thought.

We can state that understanding BE in the framework of its identification with the American system of values is a recurrent theme. This is true to the extent that when attempts are made to justify or criticize BE, it often seems that it is not really BE which is under discussion, but these values.

We should take into account the fact that the three-level analysis of BE (system, organization, and individual) is not always synonymous with a properly ethical analysis that deals with all three levels. Instead, what occurs in practice is that ethical theories are used to analyze company ethics, although on the assumption that these companies operate within the framework of an economic system that provides values (also of a moral type) and whose ethics are not directly subject to justification (not to speak of questioning). The American mark on BE not only involves accepting the market economy system (which could, to a certain extent, be understandable). It also tends to an axiological identification with the practical form that this system has taken in the U.S. and with the understanding of certain values as typically American (that is, as unquestionably normative).[15] In my view, this could explain BE's failure to develop its connection with an economic ethics that, in turn, has a global perspective that exceeds its geographical references. Despite the many contributions BE has made to the specific understanding of corporate and organizational ethics, this failure at the root of BE should not be overlooked. It must be noted not only as an academic detail, but because it also has practical consequences: the poorer BE's connections with economic ethics,

---

[15] For a detailed analysis of this, see Lodge, 1997; De George, 1982 or Cavanagh, 1984.

the more likely it is to be perceived - whether accepted or rejected - as an ethics that is a mere function of an economic and social system, and as corrective or motivating ethics (or simultaneously corrective and motivating) within a particular economic and social system. In contrast, the more closely BE fits into a framework of economic ethics (without being absorbed by it), the more necessary it will be to develop a specific body of ethical thought about the fact of organizational reality.

Thus I think De George (1993) is right when he says that the future of BE must necessarily involve creating a network of world relations that will foster dialogue among the approaches taken in different countries. Only true internationalization can allow the key transition: in this internationalization discussion on typical aspects of the organizational and individual levels can provoke the need to specifically think about the link between BE and the field of economic ethics.

Thus BE's credibility is at stake as it attempts to ensure that reflections on companies and organizations deal with their specificity, and do not reduce them to a scenario which acritically mirrors predominant social and economic values.

2.7.   The impossible dissolution of BE in individual ethics

Another way to question the very possibility of BE would consist of reducing the whole problem to the issue of the moral character of individuals as such, i.e., the issue of personal moral values. Nonetheless, I think that this type of approach essentially errs in not paying enough attention to the fact that the subject of BE is not only the individual. What is at issue here is whether companies can also be the object of ethical thought, and whether such thought has consequences for the individual as well as for the organization itself. In other words, the individual-only approach simply "frees" the company from any ethical consideration. Not surprisingly, De George (1982) connects this reduction of ethics to the individual dimension with the myth of business as something amoral: thus, morality would be a personal matter, alien to the logic of business, which would then be inherently amoral.

Furthermore, if we observe the diversity of studies about managers' beliefs and viewpoints on these issues, we will see that it is impossible to reduce BE to a question of personal ethics. Despite differences in views on other matters managers' are agreed that one needs an organizational view. This view does not suppress the individual dimension, but shapes it in a decisive way, at least in the sense that within the company individuals' acts always take into account some internalized perception of what the "company" as such wants and expects. In other words, it is not a matter of denying that ethics always has an individual dimension, but of affirming that BE cannot stress only individuals without understanding the organizational dimension as a structural and structuring ingredient.

2.8.   The ethics of organizations as the core of BE

In short, everything leads us to conclude that BE should be an ethics of companies and organizations that understands them from an ethical standpoint as such. In my opinion this reference to the organizational dimension should be the element that defines the specificity of BE. Thus I start from the assumption that BE involves reflecting on three levels of analysis: system, organization, and individuals. All three are necessary, have their own entities, and - at the same time - are nonviable except in relation to the other two. But the core of BE should be the organization because thinking about the ethics of organizations necessarily includes the other two levels, because as it is not possible to think about the organization without showing its connections with ethical questions involving the economic and social system, on the one hand, and personal and professional aspects, on the other. In other words, where BE's legitimacy is at stake is in its capacity to become an ethics of companies and organizations.

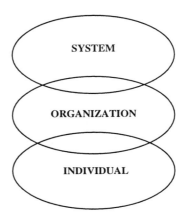

Thus BE cannot be dissolved in either professional ethics (since today this type of ethics requires an organizational perspective which, in the case of managers, is indispensable) or in personal ethics (which, in reality, always ends up incorporating an understanding of the organizational context).

But neither should BE be reduced to being an application deduced from economic ethics (even though economic ethics are needed as a frame of reference to keep BE from being a simple conventional morality); nor is it the simple embodiment of the characteristic values of the economic sphere. I believe that an ethical understanding of the particularities of organizations is what prevents BE from being a simple application deduced from economic ethics or a simple embodiment of the values of the economic sphere.

Certainly, BE is explicitly open to questions of personal and professional ethics, which it considers as intrinsic; and it is also explicitly open to questions of economic ethics and values, which it also considers as its own. Therefore, it does not exclude either of them. But as BE it includes them to the extent to which these questions are now articulated and integrated as an ethics of organizations and companies. Thus my proposal to structure BE on the "intermediate" level (the organization) does not pretend to reduce all of BE to the organizational level, but only aims to affirm that its specificity lies on this level. This approach can be BE's contribution (and perhaps also its limitation) as applied ethics.

CHAPTER 3

BE'S SELF-AWARENESS: UNRESOLVED TENSION AND A CALL FOR INTEGRATION

3.1.   BE: one discipline or two?

We know then that "the ethics of corporations, in the final analysis, is not simply a matter of having ethical workers and managers, or of having ethical procedures, policies, and structures, but also of operating in a society that requires corporations to act ethically. A corporation is a central and key element between the individual and the system. It should be seen as such and the three levels of business ethics analysis-the individual, the corporation, and the system of American free-enterprise as a whole-should not be artificially separated and treated in isolation. The ethics of corporations is inextricably tied with the ethics of the other two levels."[1] But this assumption leaves one problem unresolved: once its object is minimally clarified, how does BE deal with its comprehension? It is at this point that one can corroborate what was said in the previous chapter: BE is still immersed in its own period of constitution, as can be seen from discussions about its theoretical framework and the perspective from which BE thought should be developed.

What is essentially at stake in the field of BE is solving a problem inherent to all applied ethics: finding the interdisciplinary approach needed to address the types of issues that arise in applied ethics. Here, BE is constantly threatened by a fundamental danger that has been clearly formulated by Trevino & Weaver (1994): Is it one or two disciplines? Trevino and Weaver identify two types of academic approaches to BE: one is a more normative and prescriptive approaches; the other is more empirical, and therefore more explanatory, descriptive, and predictive. Obviously, the problem is not merely one of approach. What is actually at stake is the very concept of the discipline: each approach - when taken to its extreme - can be understood as a certain paradigm.[2] In any case, for Trevino and Weaver the tension is clear: the BE umbrella shelters two disciplines: Business ETHICS and BUSINESS Ethics.

Using five variables (the academic background of the people who cultivate these disciplines, the language they primarily use, their implicit assumptions about human moral actions, their theoretical purpose and its application, and their evaluation of their fundamental theory, Trevino and Weaver propose the following distinctions: [3]

---

[1] De George, 1990a, p. 180.
[2] Kuhn, 1962.
[3] Trevino & Weaver, 1994, p. 115.

Normative and Empirical Approaches to Studying Business Ethics

Categories	Normative Approach	Empirical Approach
1) Academic Home	Philosophy, Theology Liberal Arts	Management Social Sciences

2) Language
   Definition of ethical
   Behavior/action
	Evaluative
	Action that is right, just, fair
		Descriptive
		Ethical choices, decisions (right
		or wrong)

3) Underlying Assumptions Human Moral Agency	Autonomy, Responsibility	More deterministic Reciprocal causation
4) Theory Purpose, Scope, and Application	Prescription & Proscription Abstract Analysis & Critique	Explanation/Prediction Concrete & Measurable Influence actual behaviors
5) Theory Grounds, Evaluation	Reflection on business practice Rational critique of moral judgements	Empirical study of business practice Ability to explain, predict, solve business problems

Obviously, I do not consider it necessary to identify these distinctions empirically, as if they were clearly and separately detectable in the different ways of addressing BE issues. But they do reflect the problem of fitting together the diversity of approaches used to address BE problems. Moreover, attempting to do this is not merely the result of an obsession with classifying everything theoretically or conceptually. It also has pedagogical consequences: "in general theologians seem most interested in motivating students to act morally; philosophers are interested in moral reasoning and theoretical problems in the area; professors of business concentrate on case studies and concrete applications."[4]

Lurking behind these distinctions, we find not only the typical problem of integration required by any "applied" ethics, but also an additional problem: "the absence of ethical reasoning in the development of management from the early twentieth century has been a major factor in allowing technique to displace, rather than supplement, ethical reasoning in management."[5] We should thus take into consideration the fact that, if integration of the diversity of perspectives does take place, it will somehow lead to a redefinition of some of the presuppositions of management theory.

Not surprisingly, therefore, a repeated BE issue is clarification of its intellectual and academic status. This refers especially to two things: on the one hand, establishing BE's theoretical frame of reference as applied ethics (i.e., its possibility of being an applied

---

[4] De George, 1987, p. 206.
[5] Donaldson, 1989, p. 206.

ethics,), and, on the other, BE's practical relevance as applied ethics (i.e., the "place" it occupies or can occupy in corporate and organizational development).

As regards BE's possibilities of being an applied ethics there is increasing agreement that the key questions are of a methodological nature.[6] And thus, although the concrete questions are of great importance and immediately trigger demands and discussion, one always returns to the need to specify the ethical framework and corporate model adopted. In fact, BE's greatest temptation is to avoid going beyond the descriptive stage, which is the fundamental problem with the discussion about its academic and theoretical status.[7]

In my opinion, this explains why more global approaches to BE have always emphasized the study of its strictly ethical and critical dimensions and its conceptualization as the crucial tasks that will enable its scope to be defined.

In contrast to the above, concern about the practical relevance of BE focuses much more closely on its intermingling with business practices. In principle, this does not seem to be more than a demand made on BE as applied ethics. But when BE aims to stick close to the reality of corporate and organizational life, there is always one imminent danger: BE might ultimately end up being subordinated to prevailing market values, making a normative reading of them. In other words, BE might become synonymous with conventional moral thought. It is one thing to take into account how companies see themselves and their environment and another very different thing to accept these views as normative. It is thus important to realize that, "the negative response of business is in part a result of business's view of itself. The American business corporation developed in a certain way. As it developed it was studied and described by sociologists and organizational theorists. In an attempt to be value-free in their approach, they described the business corporation as they found it. Their descriptions have in turn become the model taught to business students and rising young managers. These managers have believed what they were taught and have come to hold that the descriptions correspond to what the corporations should be. This is a mistake. It is a mistake that can and should be corrected. And it is a mistake that, if corrected, can have significant results in freeing the corporation for organizational change."[8] That is to say, the problem of constituting an ethical frame of reference for BE is inextricably linked to organization theories' frequent tendency to convert organizational practices into norms.

In short, the question of whether BE is one discipline or two is clear, pertinent, and thought provoking. But it is also ambiguous. In what sense is it acceptable? It is acceptable because it discloses that BE has not yet reached an articulated integration between what originates with ethics and what originates with business, nor has it been clarified how this integration can be achieved. Such integration has not been achieved

---

[6] Donaldson, 1989, p. 61.

[7] As regards its academic status, De George considers that the development of BE must make some progress on the following seven points: 1) maintaining instruction at undergraduate level, 2) developing courses for MBA programs, 3) taking research as a key to academic development, 4) shifting from the treatment of ethically negative aspects of corporate life to the development of BE as a positive proposal, 5) improving integration -still scarce - among philosophers, theologians, and business school faculty, 6) shaping a closer relation between scholars and business people, 7) paying more attention to the developments in Europe. I believe that these seven points continue to be valid today. (De George, 1987).

[8] De George, 1983, p. 161.

even in terms of teachers'preparation, the education that should come as a result, establishing a sufficiently recognized and accepted body of knowledge, the existence of a shared frame of reference within which to approach the questions at hand, or in shaping an explanation about what its "application" to business reality consists of (above all, if the issue is to clarify whether BE comes after the definition of this reality or actually participates in its definition).

The still open debate on all these points converges towards the issue of the integration of ethics and business and indeed to the very definition of BE. But, in my opinion, the answer to the question of whether BE is one discipline or two (more business or more ethics), should be NO right from the start. It is not two disciplines if this means that the difference between them consists only of a lesser or greater distance from the reality of the business world. We have already seen that BE exists only insofar as it refers to this world and stems from it. It is not two disciplines if what this means is that one can take either a fundamentally ethical approach or one confined to accepting and proposing a conventional morality. We have already seen that BE exists only insofar as it is constituted as applied ethics. Therefore, I consider it more pertinent here to stress that, more important than discussing whether BE is two disciplines, is the fact that in BE there is still an unresolved tension between "ethics" and "business." I will devote the following section to discussing this unresolved tension. As I will emphasize, the fact that the tension is not resolved is due to the prevalent reality in the world of corporations and organizations and, to some extent, reflects it as if thought were its photographic negative.

3.2. Managers' moral reasoning as a metaphor for and expression of the problem

According to De George (1991) BE is faced with four threats: the threat of not being sufficiently competent, the threat of unfulfilled expectations, the threat from co-operation, and the threat that critical ethics will be replaced by descriptive ethics. Even though the first and third threats seem characteristic of the academic world and the second and fourth to BE's echo in society, I think that a careful reading of De George's arguments leads to the conclusion that all these threats ultimately boil down to one: the danger of reducing BE to an acritically presented conventional morality. As De George points out, there would be an opposition between Business Ethics and Ethics in Business.

Indeed, according to De George, "what is gaining such success and popular attention is not business ethics in the academic sense, but ethics in business [....] Businesses, on the whole, are not interested in the academic field of business ethics. Many of them are interested, however, in inculating conventional morality in their employees. [....] Instruction in business ethics as an academic subject aims to produce critical ethical thinkers. But this is not what many who call for business ethics courses want."[9] In my own words, I would say that BE is sometimes confused with an affirmation of conventional morality, a confusion that De George identifies by making a distinction between the ethical evaluation of corporations and the ethical practices in corporations.

---

[9] De George, 1991, pp. 43, 54, 49.

Harking back to Goodpaster's (1983) distinction, De George points to the danger of overlooking the justifying, critical, and foundational aspects of BE and restricting it to promoting certain practices that are described as desirable. He acknowledges that many activities presented as BE (in business schools as well as in corporations) fundamentally aim to inculcate certain values that can help subjects better adapt to corporate objectives and economic practices. Indeed, the very use of ethical theories and teaching materials is aimed more at fostering integration than critical analysis, often with the argument that this is closer to corporate reality and avoids abstraction or pure theory. De George makes it very clear that he has nothing against conventional morality, but he is opposed to identifying BE with the advance of a conventional morality in corporations and organizations because this would be tantamount to relinquishing the ethical perspective.

In this context, Kohlberg's conceptual framework could to be helpful [10] in clarifying the dilemmas of BE.[11] Among other things, it allows us to see that a demand for conventional morals prevails in the world of organizations because that is what corresponds to the extent of moral development actually reached. An analysis of how managers act in their day-to-day practices and how they cope with decision-making reveals that the problem is not that there are two disciplines; but that ethical discourse moves on a different plane than the discourses that usually emerge in the exercise of managerial functions. Seen from this angle, approaches like Trevino's (1986) enable us to grasp some aspect of conventional morality through an analysis of organizational culture, understood as "the common set of assumptions, values, and beliefs shared by organizational members. Organizational culture influences thoughts and feelings, and guides behavior."[12] Thus we can state that most managers make their decisions at a conventional level (around stage 3). Consequently, from the standpoint of moral judgment the organization's working and cultural environment determines their moral conduct within the organization.

Thus, addressing organizational reality (and the organization as the generator of conventional morality) is not only a question of acknowledging the significance of the context, but also involves assuming that "organizations wishing to promote moral behavior that is consistent with moral reasoning may need to find managerial structures

---

[10] I think there are least five reasons why this is so: a) it emphasizes the construction process of values and objectives; b) it emphasizes the moral discourse to the extent that it functions within a situation (and this allows it to be sensitive to both *ethics* and *business*); c) it emphasizes the decision-making process and enables value conflicts present in all moral decisions to be addressed; d) it focuses attention on the process of individual evolution and hence approaches moral development in the light of the individual's actual situation; e) it conceives rationality as inseparable from recognition of the other, which turns moral development into an open process in which everyone involved exchanges viewpoints and participates. But, above all, I feel that Kohlberg's conceptual framework (which identifies three levels in the evolution of individuals' moral judgments: (preconventional, conventional and postconventional) allows us to take a more operative approach to the tension between ethical discourses (which, to a greater or lesser extent, belong to the postconventional level) and the moral discourse of most people, which usually does not go beyond the conventional level. I believe that by operating with the distinction – and the links – between Kohlberg's three levels, the problem of disassociation between ethical discourse and corporate reality can be made more intelligible rather than being experienced as an unsolvable problem. I have presented this idea in Lozano, (1995).

[11] For a presentation of Kohlberg's approaches to studies about managers' moral reasoning, see Bird et al., 1989; Carroll, 1987; Conry & Nelson, 1989; Fritzsche & Becker, 1983; Gellerman, 1986; Hunt & Chonko, 1984; McMurray, 1973; Trevino, 1986; Weber & Green, 1991; Wood et al., 1988.

[12] Trevino, 1985, p. 611

and systems that encourage individual managers to take personal responsibility for their decisions and actions."[13] Research suggests that managers interested in fastering ethical conduct in the organization should encourage change processes, assuming that "powerful organizational norms, reward systems, and structures may serve to constrain or even retard moral reasoning."[14] This might explain why managers in their day-to-day practices do not take normative moral theories into consideration when they make decisions, while, in contrast, they do take into consideration the weight of conventional moral views. "The individual comes to the organization with a particular level of cognitive moral development and other individual characteristics. But, moral action takes place in a social context and can be influenced heavily by situational variables. Therefore, ethical/unethical behavior in practical situations is not simply a product of fixed individual characteristics, but results from an interaction between the individual and the situation. [....] Organizational culture also can play an important role in the moral development of organizational members."[15] An organization culture that, let it be said in passing, always takes on the guise of the models on the same and higher levels.

Therefore, personal moral reasoning can even be a dependent variable: "the perceived ethical climate was reasoned to be a potentially powerful force in directing the ethical decision-making behavior of managers in the firm."[16] Research reveals that, when making decisions, managers do not tend to act in accordance with a moral judgment that they have reached individually, but in accordance with a moral judgment created by the organizational context. Thus the question is actually not whether BE is more business or more ethics. The idea is to elaborate a proposal that enables us to rethink business reality in a way that takes into account the demands of business and the demands of ethics from the very outset, without trying to join them as if they were two separately constituted approaches.

Otherwise, it is clear that one of the most important dangers threatening BE is that it may end up diluting morality in an organizational culture, in identifying the former with the latter if it is understood as a way of managing organizational values. While it is true that every organization implies a system of values not all values are moral, neither are all values equally justifiable, nor does the mere fact of incorporating an awareness of values in the decision-making process mean that an ethical perspective has been adopted. These values can be reduced to no more than a pragmatic expression of one's own interests or to the acritical acceptance of the values assigned to the organization and its managers or transmitted by its most immediate surroundings.

This is the reason why I think that if we acknowledge the reality of managers' moral reasoning we will be able to understand why BE's demands and ethical proposals are fundamentally expressed in conventional terms: because in the world of corporations this conventional level has not yet been reached, or because it is the level on which one tends to act. Or is it because the need to avoid actions deserving of rejection still outweighs the need to propose what is considered desirable? If this is the case, we must conclude that the capacity to generate a conventional morality is a necessity and a success factor as well as a threat for BE. Nonetheless, this conclusion also allows us to

---

[13] Trevino, 1992, p. 453.
[14] Trevino, 1992, p. 456.
[15] Trevino, 1986, pp. 610-611.
[16] Elm & Nichols, 1993, p. 818.

think that there is no radical and insurmountable contradiction between a more conventional and a more critical approach to organizational ethics. Rather, they can be understood as two dimensions to be stressed in the process of personal and organizational development. As will be seen in the following chapters, I believe that the problem should not be posed in terms of academic disciplines (one?, two?), but in terms of an organizational process.

If we do not keep in mind the need to integrate the two approaches, we be forced to confirm, on the one hand, the contraposition between Business ETHICS and BUSINESS Ethics, and on the other hand, between BE and ethics in business, which is precisely what must be overcome. Nonetheless, in my opinion, it is very important to acknowledge that there is always a greater danger of clinging to a conventional outlook than of moving ahead.

We should not forget that BE today is an issue in our society, which is marked by segmentation in the many different groups to which individuals belong, fragmentation of narratives, the heterogeneity of value paradigms, and the absence of a socially binding meaning. In short, we are faced with an ideological pluralism (of ideas and beliefs). This pluralism embraces various life styles, criteria and norms of conduct because it is inseparable from the attachment of each individual to different groups (professional, family, community, friends...), with their corresponding practices and ideals. It is a pluralism that can end up being interiorized as a kind of aggregate of values and life histories associated to different roles. Thus the need for a conventional morality and the contemporary pluralism of the different groups to which we belong raise the question about the extent to which corporations and organizations are expected to fulfill some social, and not strictly economic, functions. This is, in sum, what in my opinion is expressed by the tension detected within BE; it is a tension that can scarcely be resolved if BE only looks to itself for resources. As soon as the company is considered as a social institution, BE needs to be placed within a minimal framework of ethics that then makes it possible to wholeheartedly accept the pluralism of values and sustain different ethical options and commitments.

Ultimately, the issue here is nothing other than the challenge of discovering how to approach the integration of conventional and postconventional approaches with organizational ethics. This is the challenge that BE must confront today because ethics in business can undeniably end up being a simple legitimization of conventional morality, just as Business ETHICS can end up being not only critical, but also abstract and dissociated from reality. However, we can ask ourselves to what extent Ethics in business and BE, or Business ETHICS and ETHICS in Business, are in reality two antagonistic approaches or whether they are complementary, susceptible to being fittogether and integrated while preserving their differences in emphasis, perspective, and content. The issue is therefore, to attempt to articulate this complementarity.

3.3.   Integration in the framework of BE: a demand- at least- acknowledged

BE has increasingly questioned its own status as applied ethics by integrating contributions from philosophy, from organization and management theory, and from organizational and business practices. It must be acknowledged, however, that this self-examination has mainly taken place in those texts that reflect on the reality of BE, rather than those that merely present it. Nonetheless, I think it is a good thing to be aware of the different ways of handling the integration of the various experiences and disciplines converging in BE because these differences illustrate the extent to which such integration is still an unresolved question. It is a question that arises whenever attempts are made to justify BE's raison d'être or its frame of reference, and which apparently disappears when BE deals with concrete problems in the business world.

Seen from this angle, and going beyond a possible analysis of BE's readings of ethical theories, the main question that remains to be answered concerns the place of ethics in BE and the degree to which ethics is used as a mere toolbox[17] available to whoever possibly intends to act according to moral criteria. That is to say, the issue concerns the extent to which BE, rather than making an innovative proposal about organizational practices, has consisted of submitting some ethical approaches to the demands of the business world.

3.4.   Beyond ethics as a toolbox

Referring to BE as a "toolbox" is not a kind of irreverence on my part. It is a symptom of BE's very self-awareness that this expression is used by BE researchers. In my opinion, it reflects an attitude that is very closely connected to the understanding of applied ethics as an approach that confronts a particular aspect of human reality with certain standards and criteria, which are assumed to already exist. Thus ethics is perceived as an external contribution, foreign to the reality to which it is applied. In this view, ethics would have an entity in itself and the application of ethics would come later, once its legitimacy has been established.

I do not consider the image of the "toolbox" to be neutral by any means. It reflects an approach that views ethical theories as a set of tools available to whoever decides to use it, applying it to a reality that is perfect and unequivocally understandable even before these tools are used. The "tool" metaphor is generally used to explain the objectives of the ethical component in a curriculum: a course on ethics, it is said, will give students the tools they need to analyze ethical issues and resolve ethical dilemmas.

This understanding of ethics as a toolbox manifests itself in the way ethics is usually presented, even if one does not use this image. As we can verify if we analyze the most cited books on BE, this presentation of ethics confines itself to offering the reader some ethical theories without going into how they can be used as an argument and without proposing criteria or references for the moments when tensions between priorities or perspectives in the various approaches arise. All this usually remains vague.

To put it another way, the use of ethics as a toolbox can serve in practice as an alibi for a lack of responsibility. Ethical discourse appears as an unquestionable and stable producer of prescriptions (one must then recognize its basic traits in order to use it correctly). The relation an individual ultimately establishes with these prescriptions is, in a first phase, almost one of submission and, in a second phase, one of arbitrariness: submission because it passively receives the rules that say what must be done, arbitrariness because, faced with a possible diversity of orientations, the apparent

---

[17] Padioleau, 1988, used this image to sum up his presentation of BE.

freedom of decision seems more like a situation of indefinition. Everybody will see what they think needs to be done since ethics stops giving assistance at this point.

Thus the acritical perception of ethics as a toolbox often found in BE reinforces the tendency to handle ethical concepts as though one could use them outside the systematic and cultural context that renders them meaningful. But, in addition, the ideal of ethics as a toolbox is perfectly in tune with two conspicuous features of customary BE approaches in the US. On the one hand, deontological ethics is reduced to Kant, with manifest ignorance of the contributions of thinkers like Apel and Habermas. On the other, the weight of the Aristotelian tradition is negligible (although it must be admitted that in this respect the scales have begun to balance out in recent years).

The absence of explicit references in the proposals of dialogical ethics has not been pointed out due to some academic urge to take into account all contemporary ethical perspectives. I point it out because it illustrates two important traits of BE. First, it is usually an ethics of monological character, linked to an individualist outlook which is more prone to making decisions-and in any case to justifying them as an internal question (personal or organizational)- rather than engaging in discussion with those who have different perspectives or interests. Secondly, BE usually has the sensitivity to point out as an ethical criterion the significance of taking into account those affected by it (although it talks more about consequences than about affected parties), but it scarcely acknowledges them as interlocutors, as we will see when we deal with stakeholder analysis.

The absence of references to the Aristotelian tradition shows, in my view, that conceiving ethics as a toolbox implies a sensitivity to what is done, but not so much to who does it, or should do it. It is no accident that a recurrent argument among BE teachers is whether BE should be limited to giving cognitive or intellectual information or whether it should somehow attempt to alter some aspects of the characters or some of the attitudes of those that receive this training. Furthermore, I feel that the absence of an Aristotelian perspective is closely linked to the understanding of decisions as moments or events - attained through analysis and calculation - and not as processes that some subjects develop in a context. Considering decisions as processes also requires an interpretation and a comprehension of the actual social structure in which they take place. But conventional presentations of BE hardly ever raise questions about decision as discernment (and therefore also as an interpretation of the situation) and understanding in terms of what practices are performed in organizational life (and therefore the question about what goods that are at stake in it).

In my view, this monological perspective, which is quite insensitive to the problem of configuration of subjects, together with the lack of a frame of reference, leads BE to understand itself as an applied ethics in a deductive sense. Ultimately, underlying this perspective, one finds what Mulligan (1987) has called the "two cultures" in business education. That is, after seeing a contraposition between the humanistic and the scientific approaches, he concludes that the latter has ejected the former and that, although they can both make some contribution to business education, it is very difficult for them to do so because they start from very different philosophical assumptions.

In what terms, then, can one attempt an integration of different perspectives within BE? I think that it can be attempted above all as a demand, which lately has been more and more emphatically stated, to overcome the view of BE as a producer of conventional morality as well as the view of BE as a toolbox. But the question of integration can only be adressed if it is accepted from the start that the economic point of view is insufficient (although indispensable) to understanding and orienting organizational life. The trouble with adopting only an economic viewpoint is that it cannot serve as a complete guide for decision making. Companies are not simply the abstract firms of economic theory but large-scale organizations which coordinate the activities of flesh and blood human beings. The task of productively organizing the work of people who interact with other people requires that some attention to be paid to ethics. The ethical climate in the work place has a significant impact on corporate economic performance because companies operate in a complex environment with many stakeholders to whom they must continually justify their activities.

Thus this integrative approach does not merely underline from the practical point of view the need to integrate economic, legal, and moral perspectives when managing an organization. It also emphasizes that management always requires a diversity of perspectives: indeed, integrating different points of view is nothing new. Managers must juggle finance, production, marketing, personnel and many other factors in order to achieve a good economic performance. Inevitably there is tension among these different viewpoints. The outcome should be a decision that is ethically defendable so that it simultaneously satisfies the legitimate demands for economic gains and the company's legal obligations. In other words: it is not necessary to understand the tension between the different perspectives as a disturbance, but as a resource and an opportunity for management. And, above all, it is not necessary to understand business management as a unequivocal practice, which would be disturbed only after the eventual integration of ethics.

Now, this integrative perspective implies adopting an approach that BE does not usually take into account (and less so when it emphasizes the conventional accent): constructivism. In other words, awareness that the integrative perspective is not the passive result of putting together already defined elements and creating some kind of ethical puzzle, but the active result of forming an understanding of organizations. Thus I think that the integration within BE is something more than complementing [with ethics] the analytical techniques derived from accounting, economics, finance, management and marketing. Certainly, integration requires some level of organizational institutionalization. But, above all, it also needs to stress procedure and construction. This emphasis assumes that ethical questions do not manifest themselves as a dichotomy between two perfectly known alternatives, but in the form of options that set in motion a confluence of values. We never decide between clear and distinct options or between pure values, but between limited possibilities that set different values in motion, often in conflict with each other.

Thus the claim of integration seems to even more persistently demand a frame of reference from which it can be addressed. The objective of integration clearly amounts to emphasizing BE as professional and organizational self-regulation. But it is also true that, if one avoids the debate about how the frame of reference for BE and its concretions is built, BE can end up being reduced to just another symptom of a certain postmodern disposition inasmuch as it would ultimately legitimize any organizational proposal. Hence, once the need for integration is affirmed, it is important to ask BE just what this integration involves.

Responses on this point are just beginning to emerge. Awareness of the need for integration has not yet created a consensus about its traits. Indeed there is no agreement about the "place" where this integration should take place or where it can be catalyzed, whether in universities or in business firms. Nevertheless, I think that going beyond this dichotomy is part of solving the problem. The problem should be situated in the context of creating a new mutual relationship between university and corporation, a relationship linked to a new understanding of learning processes. Thus a new path in BE has begun to unfold: a concern for its presence in the context of organizational constitution and development processes. In other words, one cannot talk about integration in merely conceptual terms, but only to the extent to which integration as such can take place in organizational management processes.

I am convinced that the development of BE lies beyond confining itself to its own improvement as a hypothetical toolbox for supposedly ethical management. Rather, it will entail constructing a model that allows us to simultaneously address organizational complexity, take into account the multiplicity of dimensions that shape moral life, and act on the assumption that "there is no action or inaction, decision, structure, state, process, relationship, institution, procedure, rule or attitude that cannot have an ethical dimension." [18] What is at issue here is not only whether BE is able to enrich or complement certain views or theories about corporations and organizations but also whether it can propose a specific global understanding of them, a consequence of which will be to give a direction to their own development.

3.5. A note about civic ethics as a possible framework for BE

It has become clear that a minimally articulated integration between Business and Ethics requires some kind of frame of reference to make it possible. Yet BE has not developed an ethical perspective that would rovide a context for and serve as a bridge between moral philosophy and BE as applied ethics. For example, it has not realized that "economic and business ethics have an important task as an embodiment of civic ethics and, therefore a tremendous social importance in the civic education of individuals in an open society".[19] One might add, however, that this setting of BE in civic ethics takes place fundamentally in European contexts.

The question about civic ethics is raised in a social and cultural context of axiological pluralism, and recognizes it as such. This recognition means that it attempts to understand its context in terms of ethics and not only sociologically or culturally. What is at issue then is not only recognizing the absence of a unified system of shared social values. We must also acknowledge some common minimal values that would allow us to sustain life together while admitting that there are still irreducible differences in some basic assumptions. The transcending of moral monism should not necessarily result in a void or in indifference linked to the belief that "anything goes" or the belief that what "goes" is strictly private (in the sense of non-communicable or incommensurable). Even if it includes the recognition of dissent, civic ethics does not assimilate it to some kind of social or moral disintegration. Rather, it becomes a cause and effect of both tolerance and solidarity, offering the possibility of mediation between

---

[18] Donaldson, 1989, p. 83.
[19] Conill, 1993b, p. 199

a diversity of moral standpoints. In this sense, one can talk about civic ethics as a moral minimum that is shared by the diverse moral options (thus, strictly speaking, it does not clash with any of them). Civic ethics then becomes a concrete horizon of reference for all of social life: civic ethics is the common moral minimum accepted by a particular society within the legitimate moral pluralism. But this acceptance does not originate with a simple consensus of superficial opinions or through self-seeking social pacts.

In fact, "civil morality fits into the context of moralities of minimum values i.e. moralities that solely propose the axiological and normative minimums shared by the conscience of a pluralistic society. Individuals must have full freedom to propose their own maximum values on the grounds of which the members of this society can then make shared moral decisions in questions of applied ethics."[20] As we can see, in this approach civic ethics connects both with pluralism and with applied ethics.

Civic ethics presupposes then "that moral norms lose the absolute and definitive character which seems to have accompanied them down the ages and which - in my opinion - retain as the central points of morality the procedural principles, the values that necessarily accompany these principles (autonomy, equality, solidarity, impartiality), the rights of the participants in the dialogue, and their attitudes, which can be governed either by the 'moral' interest of satisfying universalizable interests or by the selfish interest of exclusively benefiting oneself or one's own group Thus good will that involves deciding according to universalizable interests continues to be essential."[21] Civic ethics therefore connects also with that minimal anthropology whose reference and horizon are a conception of the individual as a valid interlocutor, able to universalize, reaching autonomy through mutual recognition symbolically mediated. Hence the significance of encouraging dispositions, attitudes, and virtues that shape the social and cultural ecosystem of civic ethics and its presuppositions.

Seen from this angle, the other dimension that provides the setting for civic ethics becomes decisive. We referred to the differentiated recognition of minimum common moral values and the plurality of proposals about moral life. Now we must also refer to their function in sustaining different types of applied ethics. Thus we should take into account the fact that civic ethics is not directly present in the various fields, institutions and projects that accept it as a structuralizing reference, but is present in a mediated way. In a complex society one should talk about spheres of morality where personal and organizational projects are generated in relation to the goods at stake in each of these spheres. Hence we can affirm that civic ethics is built also with elements drawn from the various fields of applied ethics. In this approach, the flow goes in two directions: civic ethics sustains applied ethics, but is socially materialized through them. And thus we can affirm that "an improvement in the quality of institutions, an ethics of institutions or of organizations, which is urgent today in order to imbue social life with moral content, does not depend on the application of majority rules, but rather on reflection about which are its proper ends and what kind of specific rights for individuals, what kind of common responsibilities, attitudes, and procedures must necessarily be accepted in order to attain them"[22] Thus, the frame of reference in which

---

[20] Cortina, 1993, p. 204
[21] Cortina, 1993, p. 219.
[22] Cortina, 1993, p. 66.

BE must be situated is one of an ethics of institutions in the context of civic ethics. And it should not be reduced to being a way to resolve conflicts of action from a moral point of view, a way to regulate organizations' internal and external relations, or a way to give guidance to corporate management.

In this sense, civic ethics can become a mediating factor between moral philosophies and BE (without which the relation between business and ethics can easily take the form of wanting to unite two essentially separate approaches). Moreover, it can encourage greater BE attention to the anthropological presuppositions with which it operates. Consequently, it can strengthen BE's need to be sensitive to the social context, and therefore strengthen an understanding of corporations and organizations that would include the question of their contribution to society. Finally, the perspective of civic ethics can promote greater BE attention to its own sphere of morality. This would lead BE to raise the question of how to foster through corporations and organizations a greater attention to the goods and practices that are at stake in their activity. In addition, it would lead to the need to foster in business life the ethos and values that correspond with those of civic ethics. It is in this sense that I consider it legitimate to talk about corporations and organizations as a space of moralization.

CHAPTER 4

AN ILLUSTRATIVE DEBATE: CORPORATE SOCIAL RESPONSIBILITY

4.1. Introduction

We have seen that the progressive configuration of BE becomes inseparable from the need to more closely integrate the perspectives and elements converging in it. From the methodological standpoint, the distinction between system, organization and individual has played a crucial role in this process of configuration. Above all, the key factor was the progressive concentration of BE in the organizational sphere. But seen with some perspective, we can also affirm that the debate about the corporation as a moral subject and -most of all- the debate about corporate social responsibility were essential in this movement towards the organization.

In fact, the question concerning what kind of ethical reflection about the company one should engage in was first raised in an indirect fashion through two other questions. One inquired whether the corporation could be given the same treatment as individuals in terms of ethics. The other asked whether one might have expectations of the corporation other than those attributed to it by the economic system.

It is possible, I think, to give an interpretation about why BE, in the initial moments of its constitution process, focussed on these two issues. Briefly: the emphasis on the corporation as a moral subject and on corporate social responsibility reveals that, unless an ethical understanding of the organization is worked out, BE has no choice but to operate with resources deriving from ethical thought about individuals or about the system. As my analysis aims to show, it is because there had been little or no thought given to the organization that it became an issue whether the corporation can be treated as a moral subject (as the basis for justifying and developing BE) and whether the company has purposes and justifications other than those attributed by a view which only considers the dynamics of the economic system.

Both debate about the corporation as a moral subject and debate about its social responsibility are a paradigmatic manifestation of BE's constituting process inasmuch as they express the desire to construct a specific body of thought about corporate and organizational ethics. Yet, at the same time, these debates reveal their dependence on the individual and the system as the fundamental references for an ethical reflection about the corporation. Thus, not surprisingly, as BE has developed as such, the problem of corporate social responsibility and the problem of the corporation as a moral subject have tended to disappear as problems or, at least, have ceased to be the main BE issues. Whereas the latter problem has almost entirely vanished, the former has only partially disappeared. Lately, concern about corporate social responsibility and corporate citizenship is reemerging, but in a different context: reflections about the corporation in a context of globalization.

4.2.   A preliminary question: Is the corporation a moral subject?

"The thesis that corporations are moral persons has brought considerable discussion, but inconclusive results."[1] Nevertheless, one must add that this thesis has also contributed with a series of proposals, analyses, and arguments that, once liberated from their context, have been an important thematic reference in the world of BE. To analyze these contributions, it would be indispensable to trace them in the context of each author's particular approach, but I cannot go into such detail here. The authors who have made the most decisive contributions to this debate (and the ones who have become points of reference) are P. French (1979, 1984), K.E. Goodpaster (1982, 1987), J. Ladd (1970, 1986), M.G. Velasquez (1983, 1988), T. Donaldson (1982, 1987), P. Werhane (1985), and R. De George (1981, 1986, 1990a). French and Goodpaster represent the most belligerent positions in favor of understanding the corporation as a moral subject; Ladd and Velasquez, the most openly opposed to it; and Donaldson, Werhane, and De George - each with his particular traits -represent more intermediate positions.

In short, debate about the corporation as a moral subject has led to a progressive awareness that the entire discussion was so implicitly ambiguous as to be endless. This ambiguity stemmed from the tendency to talk about the organization in the - metaphorical - framework of an idea of the "person." Despite this and despite the fact that the discussion has not led to shared conclusions, I think it has generated a set of elements that have helped shape BE.

In my view, the fact that Morgan (1986), in his seminal book about organizational images, does not include it as a relevant image is an unmistakable sign that the person (moral or otherwise) has not been recognized as an adequate paradigm for understanding the organization. Instead, Morgan, like many others, underlines the dangers of trying to confine the understanding of organizations to one of the images that we have created for them, and the dangers of trying to cram into one image all the relevant things that can be said about organizations. Along similar lines, Berger (1967) had already warned that one must be very careful when formulating any kind of affirmation about the "logic" of institutions because such logic does not lie in institutions and their external functions, but in the way these are treated when one reflects upon them.

An analysis of the discussion about understanding the corporation as a moral person reveals the need to take such precautions. Paradoxically, this discussion has excluded all consideration about the metaphysical and historical presuppositions of the proposed analogy. Indeed, in the comparison, the discussion has been restricted to only one of the dimensions of the person: to everything that refers to decision making and to intentionality in actions, and therefore to the attribution of responsibility. Thus, from the standpoint of the "person" metaphor, the question about the corporation tends to refer to the issue of free decision, in contrast to the representative fiction that characterizes the legal tradition. Hence, paradoxically, the debate does not actually deal with subjects and their constitution or recognition. It only deals with their decision making and the acceptance of responsibilities insofar as they can be attributed to a subject, but not insofar as they can constitute a subject.

---

[1] Pfeiffer, 1990, p. 473

Thompson (1986) has noted that what is at stake here is the need for an adequate theory of the organization, since otherwise we use models of responsibility originating in the military or legal traditions, which prove insufficient to explain the problems posed by the actions of contemporary organizations. From the traditional point of view, the corporation is identified as a hierarchical structure that can only function on the basis of submission and control, while moral problems appear only as a circumstance that limits the actions of individuals within the organization.

Thus, oddly enough, the fundamental problem is that discussion about moral personality might end up masking discussion about the corporation, its theorization, its raison d'être, and its objectives. And it masks this discussion because it is based on a metaphorical shift from the person to the corporation, overlooking the specificity of each level. What is latent in the way discussion about the corporation as a moral person has developed is not actually the stated problem but the need to properly understand what it means to say that human action today is also an organizationally mediated action, and the consequent need to build a paradigm for understanding the organization in terms of ethics.

This has been clearly pointed out by Sacconi (1991a) when he emphasizes that what we may affirm about the organization in terms of ethics depends, to a great extent, on how we describe it. But much more is at stake here. One must also realize that this question places new demands on contemporary ethical thought. The need to find a framework that enables us to reflect (ethically) about the corporation is not simply a common denominator of the different positions in the debate. It is also an acknowledgement of the problems implied in analyzing the corporation, taking into account the different disciplinary approaches.

Now, assuming that "the fundamental problem of the corporation in modern society is a problem of rationality"[2] - precisely because ethics is also rationality- I think that the challenges BE faces are not met if we limit BE only to passively choosing the most adequate organizational paradigm for its development (as if BE had no choice other than to be a passive receiver of what organizational theory devises on its own). On the contrary, BE has to contribute actively to constructing an organizational paradigm. I think that the most problematic aspect of the claim to identifying the corporation as a moral person is that it ends up blocking the possibility of ethical creativity. For, in reality, this claim assumes that BE's problems can only be resolved by referring to what has already been established by some ethical tradition or some conventional morality.

Obviously, this does not mean that I underestimate the importance of this debate as a catalyst of thought and a way of putting certain themes forward. Above all, it has stressed the need to acknowledge that the corporation has its own entity, one which is not adequately treated from an ideological point of view. The issue then is to clarify the purposes of organizations and whether they are limited to those shaped by their legal status as well as to those shaped by their profit-earning function. It should not come as a surprise that one of the increasingly recurrent subjects of discussion has been whether the morality of the corporation can be dealt with by considering only the results of what corporations do. Here we find a change of perspective because the question that has been raised is whether it is also possible to evaluate internal organizational dynamics

---

[2] Marzal, 1983, p. 23.

(since corporate action is only intelligible when we take into account the fact that it is a human action performed by human beings), rather than merely the results of corporate action. Furthermore, the question is whether this evaluation of internal organizational dynamics also affects the corporation's purposes and the goods and goals that are specifically at stake in each organization.

In my opinion, what the debate about the corporation as a moral subject has accomplished is the recognition that ethical reflection about the organization is possible and that the organization must be distinguished from the individuals that constitute it. Nevertheless, I think one could have made the same points more clearly by distinguishing between ethics and morality. This would have allowed us to make a distinction between the affirmation that only individuals are endowed with life and moral personality, and the affirmation that it is possible to reflect ethically about human institutions, precisely because they are human creations and because it is through them that human beings act. I also think that addressing the problem by asking whether the corporation is a moral person amounts to taking a stance that ends up blocking the debate because, on the one hand, a monological model of person seems quite insufficient to give an ethical account of collective actions as well as organizationally mediated actions, and, on the other, it seems rather insensitive to the demands of an ethics that must meet the requirement of thinking about human action in the context of an organizational society and a scientific and technical age.

At any rate, discussion about the corporation as a moral subject also allowed BE to explicitly state some of its core themes. Among them I would emphasize the need not to forget that what should be taken as reference is what organizations do.[3] One should also note the attention paid to decision-making processes and the importance attributed to the way in which organizational policies and goals are formulated, as well as to their corresponding business structures. Lastly, one must emphasize that, in its final phases, the debate about the corporation as a moral subject gradually began to consider corporate character and culture (as a way of taking into account other elements of organizational life, as for example those that refer to shared habits and beliefs).

But what was probably most important for the field of BE was the distinction between talking in terms of the corporation's moral responsibility and talking in terms of the corporation's social responsibility (a distinction that has not always been perceived as such, so much so that at some point in the discussion the two adjectives were used as synonyms). It is advisable then to show their differences; differences that correspond to - in fact, stem from - adopting approaches whose understanding of the organization is based on very different frames of reference, even if at times they might seem complementary. Whereas talking about the moral responsibility of corporations usually refers to the paradigm of the moral person, talking about corporate social responsibility tends to refer to the paradigm of the system (social and economic) and to the function which that paradigm attributes to the corporation. From the point of view of ethical reflection, this does not imply only that it is necessary to think critically about the corporation as a social institution. One should also criticize the assumption that any moral evaluation of the corporation can only be made from the point of view of the

---

[3] Although the links between corporate responsibility and individual responsibility as a member of the corporation have not yet been made clear.

dominant social values and from what society, at a given moment, expects from the corporation. It is for this reason that the contributions made in the debate about corporate social responsibility have had such relevance in the context of BE.

4.3.   Corporate social responsibility

Corporate social responsibility was undoubtedly the most important theme in the field of BE up until the time it became fully constituted as an autonomous discipline. But it was also necessary to make a distinction between BE and corporate social responsibility in order to avoid confusing them, as has happened from time to time.

Although many contributions have been made to this debate, the underlying issue is relatively simple: justifying that corporate purposes are limited to such purposes as are a function of the economic system to which the company pertains. If so, this system would then become the only frame of reference for understanding these purposes. The question is to establish whether economic and legal responsibilities cover all that can be said about (and all the responsibilities of) the corporation and therefore whether the corporation has any other criteria for action apart from maximizing profits and observing the law.

Nevertheless, the discussion about corporate social responsibility has revealed other underlying problems. First is the obvious problem about how to understand such responsibility, since those who affirm and those who deny it do not understand it in the same way. But it should be noted that talking about corporate social responsibility always has at least two sides, which, though inseparable, should not be confused. One side is the discussion about what corporations should and should not do. The other is the most appropriate way of conceiving the corporation. These two sides share a common denominator: the problem of legitimizing the corporation, both inwardly and outwardly.

4.4.   Is the corporation in question?

"The concept of corporate social responsibility originated in the 1950s, as American corporations rapidly increased in size and power. And the concept continued to figure prominently in public debate during the sixties and seventies as the nation confronted pressing social problems such as poverty, unemployment, race relations, urban blight, and pollution. Corporate social responsibility became a rallying cry for diverse groups demanding change in American business."[4] Nevertheless, I don't consider it farfetched to date the use of the term "social responsibility" somewhat earlier than Frederick et al do (1988). Rather than to a definition, the term refers to the problem about the extent to which corporations are (or have been) concerned only with maximizing profits. But once this point is conceded, we risk, if we are not careful, going back to the very origins of capitalism and considering Smith's The Wealth of Nations and the social impact of Calvinism as the first point at which corporate social responsibility is addressed. If we do this, all the approaches that put forth some kind of active concern for society's most disadvantaged members will be considered as forerunners of corporate social responsibility. This would indeed be interesting, but it thwarts any attempt at precision.

---

[4] Boatright, 1993, p 385.

We find a more concrete precursor of the characteristic approaches to corporate social responsibility in the first steps leading towards what could be called business philanthropy. Dating back to the beginning of the twentieth century, this approach was obviously very closely intertwined with what is known as the "charity principle" (Frederick et al., 1988). The novelty was that philanthropy was no longer considered an individual act (as something coming from the manager or owner of the corporation) but as something characteristic of the corporation or business as such. This charity principle was complemented by the "stewardship principle," which opened the door to the belief that corporations -and, above all, managers- not only produce profits for the owners but also manage social resources. Thus they had to take into account the consequences of their decisions for all those affected by them. "These two principles, the charity principle and the stewardship principle, became the foundation of corporate social responsibility. The charity principle urged business firms to give voluntary aid to society's unfortunate or needy groups. The stewardship principle urged them to be trustees of the public interest, which meant that they should act in the interest of all members of society who are affected by the corporation's operations." [5]

It is in the fifties, however, that one finds the "first wave" (Frederick, 1986) of studies addressing the theme of corporate social responsibility. This first wave explored the problem of the interrelation between corporation and society, and questioned the corporation's lack of attention to the social implications of its activities. At this moment there were not too many operative or normative proposals. But there was an awareness that the prevailing forms of action in corporations needed to be changed since there is something about the rules governing corporate behaviour that does not work. Some of these norms were: focusing solely on maximizing profits, taking into account only shareholders and owners, taking the observance (or non-violation) of the law or the externalization of costs as sole references. At the same time as these and other similar common features of customary business practices were questioned, a critical social current was born and began questioning the predominant economic and social system. Both these elements were often embodied in the critique of the corporation. In addition, this criticism of the system to which corporations belong played a prominent part in protest actions and public opinion in the sixties. And, increasingly, those in charge of corporations also underwent a change in sensitivity and focus.

This marked the appearance of a basic coordinate which tends to frame discussion about corporate social responsibility: non-reduction of the corporation to its economic function, attention to all groups included in the business activity, and corporate involvement in solving social problems. "The period 1965-1975 was an important period for the corporate social responsibility concept. A consensus developed within academic and business circles, driven in no small measure by the social, political, and economic upheavals of the times, that business and their managers must indeed be "socially responsible." Still, no agreement as to what precisely the term meant emerged." [6] It was, however, in the early seventies that there began to be a clearer outline of the pertinent themes to be included (and therefore discussed) in the field of corporate social responsibility. It was then too that some minimal limits to this concept

---

[5] Frederick, et al., 1988, p. 30.
[6] Epstein, 1987c, p. 5.

were set and even a complementary concept (Corporate Social Responsiveness) proposed in order to express and distinguish between the different conceptual options for addressing the question or simply the dimensions included in it.

The idea of corporate social responsibility posed the problem not only of what corporations did, but also of how they slanted their actions, and therefore, how they could respond to, and even anticipate, new social demands. This meant that attention to social issues was understood as something that needed to be incorporated into strategic planning processes and, accordingly, one began to test mechanisms and techniques that would allow progress to be made along these lines.

The 1971 declaration of the Committee for Economic Development played a very important role in this process. The Committee considered corporate social responsibility not only as a management concept or a question affecting each corporation individually, but one "which emphasized the social role of business as an important instrument for social progress in a pluralistic society."[7] And for this reason it raised the question about what corporations should do in relation to ten specific social problems: economic growth and efficiency, education, occupation and formation, civil rights and equal opportunities, urban development, pollution, preservation and environmentalism, culture and the arts, medical attention, and government actions.

In short, this declaration was a public recognition that the social contract on which the actions of corporations were founded had changed because society expected much more from corporations than in the past. "There were three concepts around which CED's 1971 theory of social responsibility was constructed: social voluntarism, enlightened self-interest, and a government-business partnership."[8] Put more clearly, the question was not only the search for short-term benefits but also cooperating with the government to resolve social problems.

The declaration of the Committee on Economic Development shows the public significance of the discussion and, in turn, its dependence on the demands of the social context. Frederick (1981) has made this clear by comparing this declaration with another made by the same committee in 1979 in which it returned to a greater "orthodoxy" in its approach.

Although it recognized the legitimacy of certain social purposes, the 1979 declaration stated that this should not be seen as a justification for moving towards more tightly regulated markets or turning corporations away from what constitutes their competence in the economic arena. This contrast has raised the question about the extent to which the 1971 declaration - and, indirectly, everything referring to corporate social responsibility - is merely the business world's more or less ideological response to stormy and troubled times.

From the historical perspective of the formation of BE as a discipline, discussion about corporate social responsibility represents, above all, the consolidation of the transition from individual to corporation as the object of ethical reflection, even if this transition fundamentally involves thinking about the corporation's place in society, its

---

[7] Epstein, 1987c, p. 5.
[8] Frederick, 1981, p. 23. Enlightened egoism involved seeking social welfare because this is the company's greatest guarantee of short-term survival. Social voluntarism addressed the ten problems mentioned above and cooperation with the government was considered an option when there were not enough volunteers to achieve social progress.

contribution to society, and what legitimizes its existence. It is a reflection about the corporation with a strong ethical component (although, as we shall see, not only ethical), which is viewed, however, from the standpoint of the economic system and the society in which corporations act. To put it graphically, we could say that discussions about the corporation as a moral subject opened the door to the possibility of an ethical reflection about the corporation, whereas discussion about corporate social responsibility opened the door to the possibility of an ethical reflection about the corporation.

Like discussion about the corporation as a moral person, discussion about corporate social responsibility also raised various issues that were later accepted in the framework of BE. But this discussion about corporate social responsibility had an even greater impact because it facilitated a series of approaches to the corporation that, as I will demonstrate in the following chapter, are indispensable for an ethics of the organization. Before analyzing this, however, it is important to review in greater detail the outcome of discussion about corporate social responsibility.

4.5.   Friedman: the most controversial reference

When I discussed the history of the debate on corporate social responsibility, I deliberately omitted any references to the role played by the opinions of Milton Friedman, the most widely quoted author on the subject. Friedman's belligerent attitude leaves no room for doubt: corporate social responsibility is non other than increasing profits. Friedman's position became so commonly accepted that one can safely say that acceptance or rejection of Friedman's position influenced many authors' approaches to corporate social responsibility.

Friedman expressed his opinion about the issue in two particularly important works (1962, 1970), although only the second one is a point of reference, among other reasons because its title has become a sort of watchword. It is worthwhile, however, to analyze them separately here since Friedman's position is not exactly the same in both cases and I feel that this is important in terms of clarifying the problem.

First, it must be noted that even in his first book Friedman expresses two opinions with regards to corporate social responsibility. These two opinions are not exactly the same: one of them refers to the individual who acts in the market and the other to the corporation as such. In fact, what primarily interests Friedman is rejecting any justification for monopoly. In his opinion, monopoly essentially involves a disturbance of the functioning of the market, since it limits the possibilities of voluntary exchange by actually limiting the alternatives at each individual's disposal.

According to Friedman (1962), talking about social responsibility could only make sense in the case of a monopoly. It is difficult then to maintain that the company has any social responsibility beyond what is expected of any citizen: obeying the laws of the state and living in accordance with their norms. Friedman realizes that the idea that corporations and trade unions have a social responsibility beyond serving shareholders or members has gained currency. But he considers that this idea is due to a fundamental error in understanding the character and nature of a free economy. In a free economy the corporation has only one social responsibility: to utilize resources and carry out activities aimed at increasing profits, provided that it abides by the rules of the game, i.e. it acts in free and open competition without fraud or deceit. Similarly, the social responsibility of union leaders is to serve the interest of the members of their unions. It is up to the rest of the citizens to establish a legal framework within which these activities can be carried out. The corporation is not responsible for solving social problems.[9] The corporation is an instrument of the shareholder, who is its owner. Thus whoever wants to make donations will make them individually; otherwise all we are doing is promoting the separation between ownership and control.

Some years later, Friedman (1970) dealt directly with the question of corporate social responsibility, arguing in favor of the thesis enunciated in his title. In short, in a free system of corporations and private property, managers are employees of the corporation's owners. They have direct responsibilities towards their employers. Their responsibility consists of conducting business according to their employers' interests, which will generally be to make as much money as possible, although in accordance with the basic rules of society embodied in the law and ethical habits. Since the responsibilities of managers are simply those of an agent of the corporation's owners, they should not be confused with the responsibilities managers have as private individuals -which they can accept voluntarily. When managers talk of social responsibility this would mean nothing more than using money that is not theirs in a way that is not beneficial to their employers. This money can only be spent as employers wish to spend it. If managers don't do this, what they do in fact is charge a sort of tax, and this is the function of government.

This argument works also for shareholders who impose criteria other than maximizing profits. Only the individual owner is an exception, since he can obviously do whatever he wants with his money[10] and can engage in the "social" activities that benefit the corporation in the medium or long term. But Friedman believes that one should then say that this is done out of interest, rather than disguising it with a doctrine that does not correspond to reality, even if it is a convenient way to avoid the public discredit often suffered by corporations, businesses, and capitalism.

To sum up, Friedman feels that the doctrine of corporate social responsibility involves accepting the socialist viewpoint which holds that political rather than market mechanisms are the best way to allocate scarce resources to alternative uses. The difficulty of exercising social responsibility illustrates the great virtue of the private and competitive corporation, which forces individuals to be responsible for their actions and makes it difficult to exploit others for selfish or non-selfish purposes. One can do well, but only on one's own account. Hence Friedman always draws the same conclusion: the doctrine of corporate social responsibility is a fundamentally subversive doctrine and the corporation's only social responsibility is to increase profits in open competition, without deceit or fraud.

Friedman's position has been so important because, as Carson says "many people appeal to profit maximizing (or profit maximizing within certain rules) as a moral principle and use it as a basis for defending various business actions and policies on

---

[9] And since he thinks this affects his own personal interest Friedman explicitly states that corporations should not make donations to charity or to universities

[10] Although this implies levying a surcharge on his customers and then having to abide by the consequences of the market.

moral grounds."[11] One should perhaps add that, as a principle excluding all moral considerations, this is one of the central issues of the debate as posed by Friedman.

As Bowie (1991b) has pointed out, Friedman's approach and that of those he calls "Friedmanites"[12] totally depend on a neoclassical perspective applied to the issue of corporate social responsibility. Put in my own words: it depends on a view of the corporation that is consistent with an interpretation of the market that has been established as a norm. In any case, this view is only able to see the corporation in terms of maximizing profits.

The confrontation with Friedman and the Friedmanites takes place on three levels: concerning some basic elements in his analysis, concerning the understanding of corporate social responsibility, and concerning the absolute dominance of maximizing profits. I will not go into the details of the criticisms made about some of the elements of his approach (although as they are important) since they do not go to the heart of the matter.[13] In my opinion, the two fundamental questions are, first, the understanding of corporate social responsibility together with the concept of corporation that it presupposes, and second, the place of profits in business ethics. I will talk about the first issue in the following section, but it is also necessary to provide a setting for the second one in my analytical approach.

It has been pointed out that Friedman's economism is the expression of an inadequate social philosophy. This can be due not only to an approach characteristic of economic science, but also to particular presuppositions accepted in particular cultural contexts.[14] It has also been emphasized that "the appeal of Friedman's paper is achieved at the price of misrepresenting business itself. This is the first of his empirical errors. His characterization of business as an autonomous activity is simply false, empirically. Business does not operate in regal isolation, totally disconnected from other areas of life."[15]

Obsession with profits reflects the belief that the market is the only reference to be taken into account. But one thing is to acknowledge that nobody has demonstrated that profits should not be a business priority and quite a different one to reduce all understanding of the corporation to a matter of maximizing profits: "Rather than

---

[11] Carson, 1993, p. 22

[12] Sohn (1982) calls them fundamentalists.

[13] Many criticisms of the Friedmaniste approach emphasize its tendency to identify corporate social responsibility with corporate efforts to solve social problems, thus excluding from analysis the relations between ethics and law and between ethics and social responsibility. It is also surprising to think that, given that shareholders and owners can only protect their own interests, managers should and would not do likewise.

[14] "Our European model will go further than that because we consider that this is only one kind of human progress. It does not necessarily imply social progress, political progress, cultural progress, scientific progress, or spiritual progress.
More and more, we will have to give a proper answer to the questions: economic and technical progress: How? For whom? For what? These questions have to come out of a political process, a concerted action process: a distinctively European process. When I read some articles my colleague, Professor Friedman of Chicago, he says these are irrelevant questions for the business firm. The very concept of societal responsibility of business is a subversive concept in a free society. But when I hear his response, I feel that Europe is different." De Woot, 1992, p. 5.

[15] Grant, 1991, p. 907.

eliminate the goal of profits, a more reasonable approach seems to be to introduce other goals, i.e. moral goals, into the corporate decision-making structure.[16]

Thus, in the positions paradigmatically expressed by Friedman, two separate questions are mixed and assimilated: what is the best way of understanding the corporation and how relations between ethics and economics fit together are articulated in the corporation; there are questions that should be specifically dealt with. I think that to a large extent these issues are addressed in Friedman's approach, although they are not properly the issue of corporate social responsibility as such. In fact, from Friedman's perspective, everything that can be said ethically about the corporation (which, it must be acknowledged, is not much) should be dealt with by talking only about the system and the individual: a direct discourse about the corporation in terms of values is not possible.

I think, however, that one can embrace Friedman's analytical scheme, although in a direction totally opposed to his proposal. As I have emphasized thus far, I believe that the methodical distinction between system, organization, and individual should not lead us to claim that three self-sufficient and mutually isolated discourses can be constructed. On the contrary: there is always an area of intersection between these discourses. The ethics of organizations should necessarily be included in an ethics of the system or the social context in which these organizations act. It is thus not possible to have a corporate ethics that does not fit into the framework of economic ethics.

But reducing the corporation to an economic dimension that maximizes profits ultimately reduces the corporation to a market function. It identifies the corporation with its shareholders or owners and simplifies the understanding of its internal dynamics. It presupposes, moreover, a more than arguable anthropology, insofar as it totally and schizophrenically dissociates what is characteristic of managers as persons and citizens from what defines them as managers, which is reduced to the managerial functions they embody. Friedman seems to take this dissociation for granted and also accepted as a norm.

Because it is so radical, Friedman's position is usually the first to be presented when corporate social responsibility is addressed. But it is by no means the only one and the diverse proposals that take a positive view of corporate social responsibility should also be considered.

The first step beyond economic reductionism usually involves asking whether the law would be sufficient to provide corporations with a frame of reference to regulate and orientate their actions. It was Stone (1975) who, in an often quoted text, maintained that the issue of corporate social responsibility is raised precisely when one becomes aware of both the contributions and limitations of the law. In fact, acknowledging corporations' economic responsibilities tends to include accepting their legal responsibilities. However, these responsibilities are not only to the shareholders and owners, but also affect employees, customers, suppliers, and any others involved in the corporation. The law has progressively extended these responsibilities (and thus it has offered yet another argument for those who consider that adopting only the viewpoint of owners and shareholders is not enough). In reality, couldn't the increase in corporate legal responsibilities be considered as implying an obligation to respond to social

---

[16] Donaldson, 1982, p. 168.

expectations and that these responsibilities are in themselves a sufficient frame of reference for corporate actions? Furthermore, if we take this perspective into account, shouldn't we say that there has always been social responsibility?

There are various reasons for maintaining that the law is insufficient to attain what society expects from corporations. Legal penalties do not always achieve their aims. Even if the impact of penalties were adequate, the law is a reactive institution which does not anticipate new or unusual circumstances. The law usually emphasizes negative aspects and fundamentally tends to establish limits for action. The law tends to reflect the accepted practices in an economic sector without situating them in a broader social context. Moreover, the law usually acritically adopts the belief in maximization. The workings of legal institutions depend in part on the habits and attitudes of the lawyers and jurists who embody them, on the possible manipulation of public opinion by corporations, and on the legislators' very knowledge of the subjects they regulate.

Obviously, these reasons refer to different kinds of problems, in some cases quite heterogeneous ones. The issue here is not to engage in a debate about the limits and justification of the laws, but rather to recognize and accept what is proposed by this line of argument, namely, that neither the market nor - in this case - the law fully expresses what societies expect from corporations and, thus, they cannot be the only criteria and frame of reference for corporate action.

It is therefore necessary to say that corporate social responsibility presumes an understanding of the corporation in the social system in which it acts. But this means that understanding of the relations between corporation and society is not shaped only from the standpoint of the classical economic model or from the legal model. We must build a model able to account for organizational reality in a more complex way, and also able to account for society's expectations of organizations. The point is to realize that a corporation seen as a legal phenomenon is not the same as a corporation seen from a sociological viewpoint. From this perspective, I agree with Touraine that "the corporation is no longer an organizational or social system but an arrangement of various levels of operation. The company is therefore not a sociological concept but a social reality which should be broken down by analysis."[17]

Here is where it becomes necessary to think carefully about relations between corporation and society, and the social legitimization of the corporation. To a large extent, the issue of corporate social responsibility focuses precisely on this broader issue and therefore addresses the issue of what business activity means in terms of the quality of social life. For the same reason, some authors have insisted that at the end of the discussion on corporate social responsibility we will encounter the basic problem of legitimizing corporate behavior. This legitimization cannot come from the simple conversion into norm of what managers and corporations do or have done at a particular moment[18]

---

[17] Touraine, 1969, p. 150.

[18] "The American business corporation developed in a certain way. As it developed it was studied and described by sociologists and organizational theorists. In an attempt to be value free in their approach, they described the business corporation as they found it. Their descriptions have in turn become the model taught to business students and rising young managers. These managers have believed what they were taught and have come to hold that the descriptions correspond to what the corporations should be. This is a mistake. It is a mistake that can and should be corrected." (De George, 1983, p. 161).

Thus, "where the law ends," a process of corporate self-understanding begins. It is a process of interpreting what it does, of accepting this interpretation, and of contextualized creation of its identity. It is here that discussion gets underway on what corporate involvement is, should be, and can be in the communities where corporations act, which is essentially what is at stake in the discussion about corporate social responsibility. For this reason, I also believe that the concept of social responsibility can be related to corporate strategic planning in two basic ways. First, it can be helpful for a corporation to decide what type of company it wants to be. Secondly, the idea of corporate social responsibility - whether accepted by the company or not - helps Management decide how the corporation will try to attain its goals. It is important, then, to see how the idea of corporate social responsibility can be understood.

4.6. The diversity of arguments about corporate social responsibility

It is enlightening to read the mandate [19] given to the committee appointed by the Quebec Chamber of Commerce to work out a frame of reference for handling corporate social responsibility: " In winter 80-81, the Chamber of Commerce Board of Directors decided to form a committee whose mandate would be as follows: Propose to the Chamber's Board of Directors: (1) A definition of corporate "social responsibility" (2) A definition of the principles that constitute the corporation's social role (listed by order of priority and, if possible, with relative weight of importance). (3) A formula (the simplest possible) for measuring corporations' accomplishment of their role in society."[20]

There are numerous and varied texts that deal with corporate social responsibility without having received this mandate, although they don't always respond to these questions either accurately or in the order listed here. These questions seem to be quite obvious if one wants to address the issue. Thus I do not attempt to be entirely faithful to the Quebecois mandate. Instead, I will try to mirror both the plurality of the discussion and, above all, the implications it has for my analysis of BE.

It does not seem appropriate to start with a discussion about different ways of accepting corporate social responsibility. It is more pertinent to start by reviewing the pros and cons that have been presented. Admittedly, the most suitable procedure would be to examine the definitions first and then move on to the arguments. But, given the great diversity of definitions, I think that explaining different arguments will more clearly reveal the emphases placed on different aspects of corporate social responsibility and the areas one assumes should be included there. Presenting these different arguments will enable us to better and more systematically arrange the themes proposed for understanding corporate social responsibility.

To avoid making an excessively heterogeneous list, I have chosen to group the research conclusions analyzing various arguments for or against corporate social responsibility under five headings: economics, management, politics, socio-culture, and ethics-morals. Evidently, in each bloc there are some arguments that recur more than others (and very often reflect the degree of their acceptance). But the most important thing is to realize that the same argument is sometimes used to support the idea of corporate social responsibility and sometimes to oppose it. It is often difficult to

---

[19] Mandate that we take only as a paradigmatic example here.
[20] Quebec Chamber of Commerce, 1982, p. 3.

discover not so much the concept of corporate social responsibility reflected in these arguments, but the types of business practices they refer to.

As is to be expected, economics-related arguments[21] are very important. Arguments against corporate social responsibility are the following: (1) Using company resources to achieve social goals entails a decrease in efficiency since it diverts the company from its objective of producing goods and services at the most competitive prices, adds costs its competitors do not have and also diverts the company from its specific goals. (2) Since society ultimately pays all the costs, someone will have to bear the cost of corporate responsibility (fewer profits, the shareholders; lower salaries, the employees; higher prices, the consumers), which is tantamount toimposing new indirect taxes. (3) Modern society works thanks to functional specialization, and these responsibilities do not correspond to the functions of the corporation. (4) The "invisible hand" does - indirectly- a better job in procuring the desired effect than does direct corporate social responsibility. (5) Corporate social responsibilty reduces shareholders' profits and does not take their interests into account.

In contrast, the economics-related arguments in favor of corporate social responsibility are the following. (1) Since it shapes public trust in the corporation and its good image and also improves the social environment where it operates, corporate social responsibility leads to long-term profits and can thus be considered a form of investment. (2) Social responsibility partly corrects the social problems and costs caused by corporations. (3) It uses resources and capacities that are often available only to corporations in order to address social problems that would otherwise be difficult to solve. Moreover, it is not necessary to understand functional specialization as if it consisted of creating totally separate fields of action. (4) It is a way of stating and accepting that maximization alone does not ensure corporate viability. (5) Since in actual fact the economic system does not optimize the use of social resources (contrary to what the theoretical ideal maintains), accepting social responsibility is the corporation's way of correcting this deviation. (6) Social responsibility is a way of responding to shareholder demands because ensuring maximum profits for them involves preserving invested capital (and therefore ensures a long-term vision that takes the entire corporation into account). And (7) shareholders do not always expect profits alone, they also expect the corporation to pursue socially desirable ends. They are not only shareholders but also consumers, citizens, and members of a community and also have interests as such.

The arguments focusing on management[22] refer to Management's view of its own functions in the corporation and its management of corporate resources. Here we find the following arguments against corporate social responsibility: (1) It creates internal confusion in companies because it often transmits diverse objectives and criteria for action and also disperses energy. (2) Those who form part of a corporation are not trained or prepared to resolve social problems and therefore have no capacity to make decisions in this area or correctly gauge what is expected of them in this respect. (3) The problem lies not in promoting corporate social responsibility because corporations

---

[21] See: Boatright, 1993; Carroll, 1989; Donaldson, 1982, 1988; Frederick, et al., 1988; García E., 1980; Steiner & Steiner, 1988; Walters, 1977.
[22] See Carroll, 1989; Frederick et al., 1988; Goodpaster, 1983; Jones, 1980; Mintzberg, 1983; Stone, 1975; Walters, 1977.

themselves cause many of the problems that they should supposedly resolve: whatever their social responsibility consists of is made possible or prevented by the very structure of the corporation, and it is precisely this that should be the matter under discussion.

In contrast, Management's arguments in favor of corporate social responsibility are the following: (1) The capacity for both individual and corporate self-regulation is indissociable from the capacity to manage and make decisions, and thus any expansion of the scope of business regulation reinforces the capacity to manage in a more complex context. (2) Management has some capacities and know-how that are lacking in Government (which, moreover, has revealed itself incapable of resolving many social problems): the issue then is to give the corporate world the opportunity to address these problems because it is more efficient than Government and can resolve many problems with lower costs. (3) Focussing on social responsibility makes corporations act in a more pro- active way, rather than being re-active, because they must be aware of and anticipate social demands. (4) Managers are probably not prepared to attain social objectives, but since the social and political impact of corporate actions is inevitable, they must consistently accept this fact.

Political arguments[23] refer to the way in which the interrelation between the business and political worlds is understood. Here the following arguments against corporate social responsibility have been put forward: (1) It would give companies too much power (in addition to the strictly economic power they already have). It is therefore necessary to keep watch over all institutions to ensure that they don't exceed their particular sphere of action. (2) If companies aim to take on social responsibilities, we will discover that there is no way to call them to account for what they do in these areas, because - unlike the case of the political arena - we do not yet have institutionalized mechanisms to do so. Thus corporate social responsibility could be considered an anti-democratic approach which subverts the political process and could lead to some sort of corporate tyranny. (3) If companies become involved in this area, Government will soon respond with more regulations. (4) The law does not permit companies to take on this kind of responsibility because managers are simply employees whose actions are dictated by company shareholders.

On the other hand, we find the following political arguments in favor of corporate social responsibility. (1) If companies are socially responsible for their actions, Government will not need to intervene with more regulations because by avoiding or solving social problems companies will contribute towards preserving social pluralism. (2) Apart from excess government regulation, the other danger caused by social non-responsibility of companies is an increased attraction to Socialist ideology among the population. (3) Social responsibility cannot be separated from politics, which means that it opens the doors to a greater cooperation between Government and Business (which, incidentally, benefits them both in the long term). (4) The law follows society and does not anticipate it. Consequently, legislation cannot be expected to determine the need for corporate social responsibility.

---

[23] See Boatright, 1993; Carroll, 1989; Donaldson, 1982; Frederick et al, 1988; García, E., 1982; Jones, 1980; Mintzberg, 1983; Steiner & Steiner, 1988; Stone, 1975; Walters, 1977.

Socio-cultural arguments[24] refer to the way corporate social responsibility transforms society's valuation of companies. The following arguments against corporate social responsibility have been advanced: (1) Emphasis on social responsibility fosters excessive expectations towards companies.

Companies cannot live up to these expectations, and their inability to do so ends up turning against the companies themselves. (2) Social values should not be determined or interpreted by companies as this would be tantamount to turning them into a socially dominant institution, such as the church, the army or the nobility were in the past. (3) It is not necessary to have so much trust in corporations: the discourse about corporate social responsibility is no more than rhetoric aimed at improving corporate image. (4) In a social context of axiological pluralism, the problem is not only the lack of a minimal consensus about what corporate social responsibility actually involves, it is also that pluralism itself inevitably produces various interpretations about how to understand who is socially responsible and who is not.

On the other hand, the socio-cultural arguments in favor of corporate social responsibility are the following: (1) It responds to social and cultural changes, thereby leading to increased approval and legitimization of what corporations do. This is needed because society is more and more aware of corporate power and less and less inclined to accept groups and institutions that do not make responsible use of their power. (2) It seems clear that the industrial society faces some social and human problems that are synonymous with big corporations. This implies that companies should make an effort to solve these problems, or at least reduce them, since corporations – particulary large - are not entities that are separate from society. On the contrary, they are a core element whose activity contributes towards shaping society. (3) Corporations are social institutions and must live in accordance with social standards: if society's expectations and demands of companies have changed, then companies must react accordingly.

Lastly, I will mention the ethical-moral type of arguments,[25] among which I include everything that explicitly refers to justifications of ethical or moral character. The following arguments against corporate social responsibility have been presented: (1) It replaces individual responsibility with corporate responsibility. This makes no sense (inasmuch as only individuals can have responsibilities of a social or moral nature) and is unacceptable because it encourages individuals to relinquish their own responsibility, transferring it to the corporation. (2) There is no consensus - nor can there be any - about socially desirable values and therefore corporations lack something that is essential to accepting corporate social responsibility. (3) What is at stake in corporate social responsibility is the exercise of rights and freedoms, since what the corporation ultimately does is violate the rights of ownership and association.

In contrast, we find the following ethical - moral arguments in favor of corporate social responsibility: (1) It is a form of enlightened selfishness since it promotes the company's long-term interests in a broader, more viable, more open, contextualized way. (2) Ethical and moral criteria have ultimate priority over their economic counterparts, and corporate social responsibility is the practical recognition of this. (3)

---

[24] See Carroll, 1989; Frederick et al., 1988; García, E., 1982; Jones, 1980; Mintzberg, 1983; Steiner & Steiner, 1988.

[25] See Boatright, 1993; Frederick et al., 1982; Donaldson, 1982; García E., 1982; Mintzberg, 1983; Walters, 1977.

Managers, even when acting as such, do not cease being citizens or members of a society. When exercising their profession they cannot decline the opportunity to contribute to developing and improving the society and the world in which they live; this should then be made part of the criteria by which companies are managed. (4) Even in economic relations not everything can be reduced to the right of ownership and contract demands: the right of ownership is not an absolute right and does not justify everything (moreover, it cannot be reduced to the relation of the owner with the company, but must include the relations with others that inevitably take place through ownership of the company). (5) A rationality which only calculates and maximizes can deal with the basic rights and the legal principles in terms of cost/benefit, and whether or not they should be taken into account. (6) The market not only excludes certain behavior, but also includes -and must include - some minimal moral values that cannot be overlooked (7) In their actions, corporations and managers should not consider only their objectives, but also the ethics involved in the means they use and the impact they have.

4.7.   Corporate social responsibility: a diversity of concepts

Although many of these arguments deserve examination (and have a decisive importance in understanding the meaning of corporate social responsibility), in my view it is not in the discussion of these arguments that the core of the question lies. It is true that many of these arguments must be taken into account at some moment or another, if one wants to talk meaningfully about corporate social responsibility. But ultimately their plausibility depends very directly on the conceptual framework in which they are situated, which actually means that a single argument can be used for several different purposes.

Corporate social responsibility has a certain diversity of meanings, as I indicated at the beginning of this section.[26] But it always amounts to adopting the viewpoint that one must "consider his (or her) acts in terms of a whole social system"[27] and therefore thinking about the consequences of specific corporate acts in the framework of the system also involves seeing the corporation from the standpoint of its real power in society and interpreting this power.

Perhaps the best perspective would be one that allows us to visualize corporate social responsibility in such a way that it takes into account the largest number of parties affected by corporate action.

If we adopt this perspective, which progressively expands the number of groups taken into consideration, we will better understand the different ways corporate social responsibility has been conceptualized. There are two general approaches to the need for corporate social responsibility. One can be described as the negative way (which

---

[26] "The term means something, but not always the same thing, to just about everyone. To some it conveys the idea of legal responsibility or liability; to others it means socially responsible behavior in an ethical sense; to still others the meaning transmitted is that of 'responsible for' in a causal mode; many simply equate it with 'charitable contributions'; many of those who embrace it see it as a mere synonym for 'legitimacy'; a few see it as a sort of fiduciary duty. Even the antonyms, socially 'irresponsible' and 'nonresponsible', have multiple interpretations." (Zeniseck, 1979, p. 359).

[27] Carroll, 1989, p. 26. "Social responsibility refers to the need for business to be concerned about the social effects of its actions." (Davis, 1976, p. 19)

acknowledges social responsibility basically by denying that companies should be driven only by economic criteria). The other can be called the positive way (which affirms the positive features of corporate social responsibility by making a distinction between social responsibility per se and social responsiveness. It is in the framework of each of these conceptualizations (which we should not conceive of as separate off from one other, but as the expression of a progressive gradation) that the different arguments presented above can be put in order and take on meaning.

The negative way of affirming social responsibility is characterized by denying that the corporation can be reduced to the purely economic function of maximizing profits. In fact, this is the course usually taken by arguments which are diametrically opposed to Friedmanite approaches. Thus one can consider the negative way as transition between these approaches and those that are characteristic of corporate social responsibility. Indeed, the negative way maintains that it is essential to view what the corporation does and how it does it in context. Consequently, it proposes a broader and more complex view of the corporation as an institution and adopts a specifically organizational perspective. Nonetheless, this discourse does not go much further than simply stating and justifying the need for corporate social responsibility.

The issue then is to adopt a strictly organizational perspective that is not limited to the views owners and shareholders might have. Obviously, this does not mean giving up demands for profitability, which are linked to criteria of efficiency and effectiveness (essential if you want to survive in the market). But it does not confine itself to this and does not exclude the question about how this profitability is attained and with what social, rather than only business, cost. Thus, another perspective has gradually emerged, according to which the company per se has a social responsibility in addition to its economic responsibility. It should assess its activities from all angles: in terms of economic performance and in terms of social performance. Relations between corporations and their environment and society in general are the core of the debate on social responsibility.

Nonetheless, what characterizes attempts to conceptually explain corporate social responsibility is precisely the aim to pinpoint what we have now "generally" affirmed. The issue is to transcend the one-dimensional character of profitability and economism, and start shaping an understanding of the corporation that explains its complexity from an organizational standpoint, taking into account all the factors that converge in it. In short, the idea is that the corporation is not a neutral institution or organization and therefore it is not independent of the structure of society. The corporation is inserted in this society and has an influence on it. But its influence on society is not limited only to the services that the corporation offers or may offer to society. Indeed, the corporate structure itself, its power structure and evolution, have a strong influence on society. No one will deny that, apart from its socio-technical and economic structure, the corporation has a serious influence on the model of society which it is attempting to develop. It is in this sense that the corporation is not neutral in relation to its social environment. I therefore feel that the various conceptualizations of corporate social responsibility are no more than a more systematic and explicit explanation of this non-neutrality in positive or integrated terms, rather than a kind of optional addition.

When the question of corporate social responsibility is raised in these terms, Carroll considers that "the basic issue can be framed in terms of two key questions: Does business have a social responsibility? If so, how much and what kinds?"[28]. The answers to these questions are based on making a distinction between corporate social responsibility and corporate social responsiveness. Corporate social responsibility "relates primarily to achieving outcomes from organizational decisions concerning specific issues or problems which (by some normative standard) have beneficial rather than adverse effects upon pertinent corporate stakeholders. The normative correctness of the products of corporate action have been the main focus of corporate social responsibility."[29] From this perspective the fundamental objective is to discern all types of social expectations and demands which are addressed to the corporation, affect it and cause changes in the results of corporate action. Thus "social responsibility implies bringing corporate behavior up to a level where it is congruent with the prevailing social norms, values, and expectations of performance. Social responsibility does not require a radical departure from the usual nature of corporate activities or the normal pattern of corporate behavior. It is simply a step ahead of time - before the new social expectations are codified into legal requirements. By adapting before it is legally forced to, a corporation can be more flexible in its response pattern, achieve greater congruity with social norms and therefore legitimacy at a lower social and institutional cost."[30]

In contrast, social responsiveness refers "principally to development of organizational decision-making processes whereby, consistent with the limitations of incomplete and imperfect information, corporate decision makers collectively anticipate, respond, and manage the total ramifications of organizational policies and practices. The concept, accordingly, is decidedly process oriented."[31] From this standpoint, the fundamental objective is developing processes in order to determine and evaluate the company's capacity to anticipate, respond, and manage the questions and problems emerging in the face of various internal and external stakeholders' demands and expectations. "The issue in terms of social responsiveness is not how corporations should respond to social pressures, but what should be their long-run role in a dynamic social system. The corporation here is expected to anticipate the changes that are likely to take place in the system in the future."[32]

Nonetheless, I think that what is most important with regard to BE is that social responsiveness places a greater emphasis on the process of responding than on the content of the response per se. This shift from action and acts (responsibility) to corporate processes (responsiveness) marks a line that is in full harmony with my proposal that BE be understood as an internal dimension or moment in corporate

---

[28] Carroll, 1989, p. 25.

[29] Epstein, 1987b, p. 104.

[30] Sethi, 1975, p. 62.

[31] Epstein, 1987b, pp. 104-105. Frederick has proposed looking specifically at corporate social responsiveness not only in conceptual terms, but also emphasizing the practical aspects and aspects of evaluation: "In general, CSR advocates have urged corporations to eschew philosophic questions of social responsibility and to concentrate on the more pragmatic matter of responding effectively to environmental pressures. One way to do this, they say, is to develop the various tools of social response - social forecasting, social auditing, issues management - and to integrate social factors into corporate strategic planning. Another way is to increase the corporation's involvement in public policy matters. (Frederick, 1986, p. 131). Along similar lines: "The management of social issues in a socially responsive corporation is integrated into the strategic planning process, instead of being handled as an ad hoc reaction to specific crises." (Boatright, 1993, p.390).

[32] Sethi, 1975, p. 63.

dynamics. Seen from this angle, business conduct can be described as an ever more embracing three-tier phenomenon based on an expansion of the idea of legitimacy. Sethi has summarized the three perspectives in a chart that illustrates the evolutionary process. [33]

A Three-State Schema for Classifying Corporate Behavior

Dimensions of Behavior	State One: Proscriptive Social Obligation	State two: Prescriptive Social Responsibility	State Three: Anticipatory and Preventive Social Responsiveness
Search for legitimacy	Confines legitimacy to legal and economic criteria only; does not violate laws; equates profitable operations with fulfilling social expectations.	Accepts the reality of limited relevance of legal and market criteria of legitimacy in actual practice. Willing to consider and accept broader - extralegal and extramarket - criteria for measuring corporate performance and social role.	Accepts its role as defined by the social system and therefore subject to change; recognizes importance but includes other criteria.
Ethical norms	Considers business value neutral; managers expected to behave according to their own ethical standards.	Defines norms in community related terms, i.e., good corporate citizen. Avoids taking moral stand on issues which may harm its economic interests or go against prevailing social norms (majority views).	Takes definite stand on issues of public concern; advocates institutional ethical norms even though they may be detrimental to its immediate economic interest or prevailing social norms.

---

[33] Sethi, 1975, p. 63

Dimensions of Behavior	State One: Proscriptive Social Obligation	State two: Prescriptive Social Responsibility	State Three: Anticipatory and Preventive Social Responsiveness
Social accountability for corporate actions	Construes narrowly as limited to stockholders; jealously guards its prerogatives against outsiders.	Construes narrowly for legal purposes, but broadened to include groups affected by its actions; management more outward looking.	Willing to account for its actions to other groups, even those not directly affected by its actions.
Operating strategy	Exploitative and defensive adaptation. Maximum externalization of costs.	Reactive adaptation. Where identifiable internalize previously external costs. Maintain current standards of physical and social environment. Compensate victims of pollution and other corporate-related activities even in the absence of clearly established legal grounds. Develop industry-wide standards.	Proactive adaptation. Takes lead in developing and adapting new technology for environmental protectors. Evaluates side effects of corporate actions and eliminates them prior to the action's being taken. Anticipates future social changes and develops internal structures to cope with them.
Response to social pressures	Maintains low public profile, but if attacked, uses PR methods to upgrade its public image; denies any deficiencies; blames public dissatisfaction on ignorance or failure to understand corporate functions; discloses information only where legally required.	Accepts responsibility for solving current problems; will admit deficiencies in former practices and attempt to persuade public that its current practices meet social norms; attitude toward critics conciliatory; freer information disclosures than state one.	Willingly discusses activities with outside groups; makes information freely available to public; accepts formal and informal inputs from outside groups in decision making. Is willing to be publicly evaluated for its various activities.

Dimensions of Behavior	State One: Proscriptive Social Obligation	State two: Prescriptive Social Responsibility	State Three: Anticipatory and Preventive Social Responsiveness
Activities pertaining to governmental actions	Strongly resists any regulation of its activities except when it needs help to protect its market position; avoids contact; resists any demands for information beyond that legally required.	Preserves management discretion in corporate decisions, but cooperates with government in research to improve industry-wide standards; participates in political processes and encourages employees to do likewise.	Openly communicates with government; assists in enforcing existing laws and developing evaluations of business practices; objects publicly to governmental activities that it feels are detrimental to the public good.
Legislative and political activities	Seeks to maintain status quo; actively opposes laws that would internalize any previously externalized costs; seeks to keep lobbying activities secret.	Willing to work with outside groups for good environmental laws; concedes need for change in some status quo laws; less secrecy in lobbying than state one.	Avoids meddling in politics and does not pursue special-interest laws; assists legislative bodies in developing better laws where relevant; promotes honestly and openness in government and in its own lobbying activities.
Philanthropy	Contributes only when direct benefit to it clearly shown; otherwise, views contributions as responsibility of individual employees.	Contributes to noncontroversial and established causes; matches employee contributions.	Activities of state two, plus support and contributions to new, controversial groups whose needs it sees as unfulfilled and increasingly important.

This perspective, which has a more evolutionary character, emphasizes that there can be gradations in the various areas. This makes it possible to pose the question not so much in normative terms as in constructive ones: in corporate social responsibility the type of corporation that one wants to establish is expressed through the options being taken in the various relevant areas of action.

In my opinion, however, this understanding of corporate social responsibility, with its various emphases, should be completed with a more analytical understanding, such as the one Wood so accurately formulated. Such an understanding allows us to integrate, conceptually at least, everything I stressed when discussing corporate social responsibility. Wood talks about a model of what he calls corporate social action which refers (1) to the principles that motivate it. 2) to behavioral processes and 3) to observable results of corporate and managerial actions vis-à-vis the company's relations with the outside world. I would define corporate social action as the company's establishment of the principles of social responsibility, the processes of social responsiveness and the policies, programs and, to the extent that they are linked to corporate social relations, the observable results. These things thus become almost a guideline or program for making social responsibility materialize. One of the reasons for this – and one which I consider decisive, is that it is based on the assumption that we should not "isolate corporate social performance as something completely distinct from business performance."[34]

This integrated distinction between principles, processes, and results enables us to situate the issue of corporate social responsibility in the framework of a BE based on a concept which is much more compatible with my proposed approach. It enables us to see the corporation as a whole because it explicitly clarifies the content of corporate social responsibility in each area and, at the same time, allows the specific features of each area to be addressed.

In short, the progressive development of the concept of corporate social responsibility has revealed its practical importance, its relevance from the standpoint of corporate management, and its methodological significance (since it has led us to reflect on the corporation as such from an axiological perspective). But it has not always been possible to establish a link between the concept of corporate social responsibility and BE.

4.8.   The place of corporate social responsibility in the framework of BE

The relationship between discourses on corporate social responsibility and BE has not always been clear and indeed the two have often been confused. In fact, we have already observed that as BE as such has become progressively systematized there has been a parallel decline in the discourse on corporate social responsibility. We should not completely disregard the fact that a tendency in management theory (and above all in the themes proposed in business schools) contributed towards confusing adaptation to social and economic changes with fashionable terminology. Still, the truth is that the family resemblance between corporate social responsibility and BE, as well as the imprecise and indiscriminate use of both terms, has caused them to be frequently

---

[34] Wood, 1991, p. 693.

employed as equivalent concepts. In short, "many executives confuse business ethics with social responsibility",[35] without giving sufficient thought to "the fact that a corporation or executive responds to social pressure or anticipates a community need does not necessarily indicate that any ethical dilemma is involved"[36] One should indeed bear in mind that corporate social responsibility as well as corporate social responsiveness (to the extent that it involves an anticipatory attitude) do not presuppose the need or demand for any reflective or analytical moment involving ethical considerations.

Carroll reveals this risk when he considers that "a definition of social responsibility to fully address the entire range of obligations business has to society, must embody the economic, legal, ethical, and discretionary categories of business performance."[37] Economic responsibility is social insofar as society demands that companies produce goods and services in an efficient and profitable way. Legal responsibility is also social insofar as society has allowed corporations to take a productive role in the context of the social contract and therefore expects them to adhere to the laws. Ethical responsibility is social insofar as society expects corporations to act in the framework of certain values that are not, nor can they be, demanded of or included in the foregoing sections, but that are socially acknowledged; and, therefore, corporations are expected to take them into account. Finally, discretional responsibility (either voluntary or philanthropic) is also social insofar as society wants corporations to - voluntarily – engage in activities that benefit society, although they are neither economically nor legally required, nor can they be expected of companies from an ethical point of view. As Carroll puts it, however: "The major danger in presenting this model is that the impression may be left that the four components are separate and independent. Nothing could be further from the truth. Not only are the four responsibilities interrelated, but also they create tension for the manager as he/she attempts to simultaneously achieve them all. The separation is for conceptual purposes only."[38] Thus, "each responsibility is but one part of the total social responsibility of business, giving us a definition that more completely describes what it is that society expects of business: The social responsibility of business encompasses the economic, legal, ethical, and discretionary expectations that society has of organizations at a given point in time."[39] This approach to social responsibility includes ethics, but only insofar as ethics is identified with the dominant (moral) values of a society to which its members are expected to adapt. Is this sufficient?

To put it in the terms that I proposed earlier: the non-distinction between ethics and morality as well as the non-distinction between an ethics of maximums and an ethics of minimums prevents us from acknowledging that some of the demands that can be placed on organizations and their practices are based on a reflection that is explicitly

---

[35] Cooke & Ryan, 1989, p. 30. I think that this is true not only of managers, but also of consultants and teachers.
[36] Cooke & Ryan, 1989, p. 30. It seems important to me to note what this observation entails: that one can perfectly well adopt the corporate social responsibility discourse without explicitly adopting an ethical perspective.
[37] Carroll, 1979, p. 499.
[38] Carroll, 1989, p. 32.
[39] Carroll, 1979, p. 500.

ethical in character and not on an adaptation to empirically existent social demands.[40] In my opinion, corporate social responsibility is very valuable because it facilitates the transition in organizational life from preconventional approaches to conventional ones. But the identification or confusion between corporate social responsibility and BE amounts to an identification with or confusion between conventional and postconventional perspectives, and, therefore, the loss of all possibility of experiencing an internal moment of a postconventional character.

Although corporate social responsibility has undeniably made important contributions, it is also necessary to acknowledge its limitations in relating to BE. It is even more necessary to do this in view of the increasing social and economic complexities in which corporations are operating. I believe that one of the biggest limitations is that it can concentrate all attention on "social" questions, thus preventing any analysis of economic activities, which would cease to be an object of reflection, or would be one only to the extent that they can include the social dimension. Corporate social responsibility can contribute to reinforcing the assumption that "social" is different from "economic", and that economic issues cannot be considered in social terms.

On the other hand, from the standpoint of BE, corporate social responsibility opens the door to the possibility of reflecting on the corporation from an axiological perspective. This makes possible an ethical discourse about organizations as well as an organizational discourse that would incorporate an ethical dimension. But this possibility is only viable in a plural and interdependent context if social values, demands, and expectations are taken as a starting point on which to construct an organizational project rather than being taken passively as a kind of homogeneous and unquestionable datum. In this organizational project, responsible attention to the consequences of actions goes hand-in-hand with an awareness that such responsibility only makes sense in relation to the principles regulating the action and the values guiding it. And it further involves the awareness that such responsible attention to the consequences of actions is only viable through the concrete and contextualized constitution of the responsible subject. This means, in short, that one cannot talk freely about corporate social responsibility without rethinking an ethical understanding of the corporation, one of whose fundamental dimensions must be social responsibility.

As we have progressed in our consideration of corporate social responsibility and gradually increased its implications, we have not only increased its content but have at the same time seen its horizons change before our eyes. What has become more and more apparent is that corporate social responsibility is not a final destination. Rather it

---

[40] I propose to restate this analytical model in the following terms:

Affected parties	Economic dimension	Legal dimension	Ethics of maximums dimension	Ethics of minimums dimension

leads to a change in mentality, to a change in concept, and to a change in the frame of reference for a theoretical and practical understanding of organizations.

What happens at the end of the examination of corporate social responsibility is that the ethical dimension that exists in all human actions is shifted from individual ethical responsibility to a more institutional approach. Corporate social responsibility, then becomes, the organizational expression of a conventional perspective. Both the success and the limitation of corporate social responsibility are that it acts as a catalyst, triggering an organizational leap from a preconventional to a conventional approach. However, because it fails to go any further, it reveals its capacity to take critical a distance from its own reality. It also reveals its limitations when it is called upon to confront practical problems that are too complex to be resolved using only a conventional approach.

On the other hand, the need for greater integration in the organizational ethics approach points up the need to recognize the interdependence between organizational and personal processes. The development of corporate social responsibility must be conceived as something inseparable from executive development and, ultimately, from the development of maturity in everyone belonging to the organization. For this same reason reconstructing corporate social responsibility from an ethical standpoint should also lead us to raise the question as to which processes of learning and organizational and personal development the organization favors and how they are systematically addressed.

I think that this clearly reveals the possibility of taking another step forward, a step that involves ceasing to consider corporate social responsibility in a fundamentally passive way.

The issue is no longer responding to the environment, but spurring organizations themselves to construct their own responsibility.

It seems, therefore, essential to end this chapter by concluding that the fundamental problem "is that judgments of responsibility can be ascribed according to two schemes that are superficially distinct, if not in outright opposition. The first sense of responsibility, Responsibility 1, emphasizes following the law - abiding by the rules of one's social office: carrying out the authoritatively prescribed functions of a prosecutor, judge, soldier, or citizen. The second sense, Responsibility 2, emphasizes cognitive process, and, in a way almost diametrically opposed to Responsibility 1, puts a premium on autonomy, rather than rule obedience. Which of these two notions of responsibility - that which emphasizes following rules or that which emphasizes cognitive process, with some allowance for autonomy - would we ideally want to implant into corporations? The answer is both. For where it is feasible to design relatively unambiguous rules for corporate behavior - not to include nonskeletal meats in frankfurters - all we want is the responsibility of the rule-following, role-adhering sort. But as I have stressed throughout, there is also a large range of cases where rigid rules are increasingly ineffective, and perhaps even counterproductive, as instruments of corporate control. To meet the problems in those areas the responsibility that is needed - whether we are talking about corporations or persons - is a responsibility of the "mature" sort, emphasizing cognitive processes, rather than blind rule obedience."[41]

---

[41] Stone, 1975, p. 113, 115.

My opinion is that today the issue at the root of the discussion about corporate social responsibility is whether organizations are directed towards this second kind of responsibility, which is much more susceptible to being understood also in constructivist terms and in terms of human maturity. But what is hardly ever proposed, within either the framework of corporate social responsibility or BE, is the need to go even further and adopt a theoretical and practical perspective that talks in terms of corporate social Copresponsibility. This is, in my opinion, the core of the challenge posed to ethics when it tries to understand our age as a technological civilization and as a society of organizations. What is needed, then, is to think about corporate social responsibility not as personified by isolated actors, but by interdependent agents whose actions cannot be understood outside their network of relationships. And, thus, it is a part of their responsibility to see themselves in the context of this network.

CHAPTER 5

STAKEHOLDERS: WHO ARE THEY AND WHAT ARE THEIR INTERESTS?

I will use the model proposed in Chapter One to reconstruct an organizational ethics. I will begin by establishing a connection between the understanding of BE as an ethics of responsibility and the different approaches to corporate social responsibility discussed in the foregoing chapter.

In Chapter 4 I stated that the whole debate about corporate responsibility was based on a shift that can be summed up in two phases: from property to management and from the market to society. Nevertheless, I would like to insist that it is every bit as important to be aware of the management perspective as to be aware of the social perspective inasmuch as both views are correlative in terms of corporate social responsibility. This correlation becomes apparent in a theoretical and practical view of the corporation, which is usually the one taken when we try to acknowledge and actually apply corporate responsibility. This is the stakeholders' standpoint. This standpoint, however, implies recognizing the power of the corporation, since without power there is no responsibility. In short, corporate responsibility is a response, among other possible responses, to a prior acknowledgement of the power of corporations and organizations in our societies. The starting point is therefore not one of pure reflection, but the reality of power. Ultimately, we should not forget that one of the essential elements of the specificity of any ethics of responsibility is precisely its attention to the consequences derived from the exercise of power. In short, talking about corporate social responsibility as correlative with the reality of power enables us to also adopt a perspective that is not resigned to merely talking about the system, but seeks to say something relevant about the actors in this system.

5.1.   Power in the corporation, power of the corporation

When examining corporate power it is important to start by recognizing power as an intrinsic component of any organization or institution. Although acknowledged and understood as such, it should certainly be accounted for. Power is inevitable for many reasons, not least of which is the fact that it is a constituent part of any organization: "The modern phenomenon of the corporation only becomes comprehensible if it is situated at the intersection between technical rationality (the "how") and political rationality (the "what" and "why") as irreducible forms of rationality. Renouncing either of these two forms of rationality would mean relinquishing the possibility of giving an account of the reality of the modern corporation."[1] It is equally important, then, not to forget that the reality of corporate power is not some kind of raw fact, but is inseparable from the particular and complex rationality embodied by the modern corporation.

Nonetheless, when one deals with the reality of intra-organizational power, this rationality might not be recognized or consciously accepted by the specific actors in an

---

[1] Marzal, 1983, p. 32.

organization. On the contrary: the reality of power within an organization can channel different sorts of dynamism and compulsions which are clearly irrational. Thus, it is important to distinguish between the practical exercise of individual power and the organizational institutionalization of power, and to further distinguish between the various forms power can take. All this must be understood before entering into an analysis of stakeholders and the responsible recognition of one's own power which is implied in this analysis.

As concerns power within organizations, it is perfectly plausible to ask whether an organization can be understood as a political system and, therefore, whether "politics and politicking may be an essential aspect of organizational life, and not necessarily an optional and dysfunctional extra."[2] The sources of power within an organization are various and plural (as opposed to the cliché hierarchical pyramid structure). Thus, apart from being a necessity, the conquest of power can become the most important motivation among managers.

But we should avoid confusing the idea of power as a predominant tendency in any organization with the tactical reality of power as something characteristic of any organization. "We can analyze organizational politics in a systematic way by focusing on relations between interests, conflict and power [...] In talking about "interests" we are talking about a complex set of predispositions embracing goals, values, desires, expectations, and other orientations and inclinations that lead a person to act in one direction rather than another [...] Conflict arises whenever interests collide. The natural reaction to conflict in organizational contexts is usually to view it as a dysfunctional force that can be attributed to some regrettable set of circumstances or causes [...] Conflict is regarded as an unfortunate state that in more favorable circumstances would disappear. If our analysis is correct, however, then conflict will always be present in organizations [...] Power is the medium through which conflicts of interest are ultimately resolved"[3]

Thus the power-related issue in management is how conflicts are confronted and resolved in such a way as to express dynamic organizational development.

The reference to power can also have this function in the organizational context: one assumes that the good manager does not seek power for personal aggrandizement but for the good of his organization. But the hypothetical good manager will have to take into account the fact that contemporary organizations can hardly be unitary, that they are more and more pluralistic. That is to say, it is not realistic to suppose that everyone in an organization wholeheartedly identifies (or should identify) with the organization, its values and objectives. Hence what must be recognized is that conflicts of power are not only the result of functional structuring, but that a diversity of interests, identifications, and, in short, personal values and motives also take part in these conflicts.

As I have already pointed out, organizational power has seldom been the object of specific analysis in a BE context. Obviously, if one wants to talk about corporate social responsibility and about stakeholders, one is compelled to deal with corporate power. But, despite this, power is not one of BE's top priorities. I think it is very important to

---

[2] Morgan, 1986, p. 142.
[3] Morgan, 1986, p. 148, 149,155,158.

recognize that the issue here is not to analyze the mythology that may surround corporate and business power. Nor do we need to examine the relations of the corporation with a social system, or the variety of possible forms of corporate power and their relation to all their functions in society. When one discusses the power of the corporation, what is ultimately at stake is "the fundamental democratic belief that no institution should be capable of dominating societal decision-making processes."[4]

Epstein distinguishes between power over social participants and power over social processes and events. Power over social participants refers to the capacity to determine or influence the behavior of others. This can be either intentional (when A is able to produce the desired effects in B in accordance with the objectives of A) or consequential (when A produces in B's actions some effects that A did not plan or did not set out to directly achieve). Power over social processes and events, on the other hand, refers to the capacity to influence the orientation of social life through normal business activities. Surely, in real life these two types of power can overlap (Epstein, 1973).

These two types of corporate power can be analyzed by looking at the different areas of power. According to Epstein, the areas of corporate power are as follows: (1) Economic power: this would seem to be the most obvious form of corporate power, but it in itself already entails a considerable complexity, which goes beyond its technical or economic aspects to affect the nature, quality, and conditions of production, prices, investments, industrial location, employment, relations with clients and suppliers, etc. Because this sphere of power is so obvious efforts to limit corporate power have almost always focused on their economic dimension, independently of the recognition of the non-economic functions of corporations. (2) Social and cultural power: this manifests itself in corporate power over the activities of other social institutions as well as in the power to influence values, customs, and life styles. This seems evident, considering the goods and services they offer and the way in which they are offered. But it is also necessary to take into account the habits they foster, as well as their criteria in terms of hiring, promoting, training, and mobility. (3) Power over individuals: while corporations can exercise considerable power over individuals, they also have an impact on the character of individuals. It is not by chance that the development of character, which Riesman (1950) described as out-directed, should be correlative with the spectacular development of big corporations. Nor should we forget that identification with corporate values and practices has made a decisive contribution towards fragmenting our life styles and identities. (4) Technological power: nowadays technological and organizational development are intimately related, to the extent that one cannot be understood without the other. Hence corporate power has significance in technological terms since corporations have a decisive influence on technological innovation and development, in the direction and rhythm of technological change, and in the repercussions of technological change on economic and social development and quality of life. (5) Environmental power: this concerns the management and allocation of resources as well as impact on regional economical development. (6) Political power:

---

[4] Epstein, 1973, p. 10. I believe that it would be possible to try out a version of Walzer's approaches (1983) which consists of reconstructing his analysis about the diversity of goods and the spheres of justice in terms of organizations and institutions.

precisely because it is not possible to clearly separate economic and political power, it is necessary to bear in mind that corporations (separately or jointly) seek to influence political decisions[5] and that they compete with other interest groups with the objective of giving priority to their own interests.

At any rate, we should take into account that "first, corporate economic power underlies the other five spheres of corporate power. Corporations manifest the remaining aspects of power in the course of either performing their economic functions or structuring an environment conducive to undertaking these functions. Second, although for analytical purposes, six distinct spheres of corporate power have been identified, each sphere is inextricably related to the other. Corporate power in one sphere has reciprocal consequences for the others. Finally, corporations do not all possess the same degree of power. The corporate community is not monolithic [...] The power of a particular firm in each of the six power spheres can be determined only after an analysis of its specific situation."[6] I believe that this is precisely the analysis one seeks to carry out when one analyzes an organization taking the various stakeholders into account. Indeed, taking the various stakeholders into consideration is a consequence of analyzing the reality of the power of the corporation. But this consideration goes beyond an analysis of the network of corporate relations. No matter how hard it tries, stakeholder analysis is never merely analytical or descriptive. It always includes an evaluation: precisely the one that takes this network of relations to be a relevant consideration. The confirmation of corporate social responsibilities thus implies the integration of an ethical dimension. Therefore, the issue is not only to show the power *of* corporations, but above all to reflect on what this means in ethical terms.

5.2.   Stakeholders, an understanding of the corporation

In my opinion, stakeholder analysis is a particularly good way to build mediation between power and responsibility, because "power cannot be viewed in isolation from responsibility, and it is this power-responsibility relationship that is the foundation for calls for corporate social responsibility."[7] In short, if we decide to talk about stakeholders, then we are not confining ourselves only to a reflection on corporate responsibility or to showing only the reality of corporate power. I think that the most relevant thing is that talking about stakeholders represents a first attempt to construct a well thought-out, practical understanding of organization management linked to some kind of ethical foundation.

"The word stakeholder first appeared in 1963 in an internal memorandum at Stanford Research Institute. Since then, it has become incorporated in our common vocabulary and a challenging concept in the business community. Stakeholder theorists call for a change in the basic definition of modern corporations from a stockholder perspective to a stakeholder perspective."[8] This change of perspective - from

---

[5] I am not referring only to the moment of decision, but to the entire process, from setting the agenda to assessing the outcome.

[6] Epstein, 1974, p. 32.

[7] Carroll, 1989, p. 17.

[8] Wang and Dewhirst, 1992, p. 115. It is worth noting, however, that the original term has expanded in many directions, so that some authors now consider a precise definition impossible. (Freeman & Reed, 1983).

stockholder to stakeholder - was based simply on the recognition that there are a number of groups without whose support the organization would cease to exist. Nonetheless, the development and diversification of the concept has given rise to a distinction of the stakeholder concept on three levels: as a management theory; as a process for practitioners to use in strategic management; and as an analytical framework."[9] Obviously, it is very difficult to pretend that the three areas are strictly separate, but as I will discuss somewhat later on, I do believe that they represent different accents or emphases.

First, however, we should clarify to whom we are referring when we talk about stakeholders, having pointed out that the term embraces more than just corporate shareholders. A more positive approach (and one that explains the phonetic similarity between stockholder and stakeholder) would consider stakeholders everyone who has something at stake in the organization and in its viability. It is worth noting that this approach was the basis for a subsequent, more systematic conceptualization. Sacconi (1992a) took the first step towards this systematic conceptualization when he proposed that this "stakeholding" includes what he calls the principle of interdependence. In other words, corporate success depends on the actions of the individuals or groups of individuals whose interests are at stake in the management of the corporation.

The idea of something being at stake was expressed in more consequentialist terms by Frederick et al.: "When business interacts so often and so closely with society, a shared community of interest develops between a company and its surrounding social groups. When this occurs corporate stakeholders are created. Corporate stakeholders are all the groups affected by a corporation's decisions and policies."[10] It is obvious that "being affected" and "staking" something imply, to say the least, two non-coincidental perspectives. A company that sees stakeholders as "affected parties" puts itself in the their place, seeing the consequences of corporate decisions from the viewpoint of the affected parties. But here one could object that the accent on interdependence is lost, given that one talks only passively about the affected parties. This is reflected in Freeman's classical definition, according to which "a stakeholder in an organization is (by definition) any group or individual who can affect or is affected by the achievement of the organization's objectives".[11]

We see here that "affecting" is a two-way process. But we also see an ambiguity: one must clarify the extent to which the criteria and the points of reference used to define them are the objectives of the organization; i.e. as defined by the organization itself. Were this the case, we would lose the capacity to adopt the viewpoint of others, be it that of the affected parties or that of those producing the effect. Mitroff (1983) seems to propose a synthesis starting from the bi-directional consideration of affecting and being affected, but in relation to corporate actions, behavior and policies. I think that this broader reference permits a kind of analytical and practical development like the one proposed by Arthur Andersen (1992), which makes a distinction between the viewpoints of the individual, the organization, and the system and stresses that there are different specific stakeholders in each category. But inevitably the more complex the

---

[9] Freeman & Reed, p. 91.
[10] Frederick et al., 1988, p. 82.
[11] Freeman, 1984, p. 54. Quoted in Goodpaster (1991).

analysis of this differentiation, the more complex the understanding of what is at stake in each case. For this reason Carroll (1989) does not reject the dominant approach but recommends that we distinguish between property, interests (individual or shared), and rights (legal or moral). In short, it is necessary not only to ask what stakeholders there are but also, and more importantly, what makes them stakeholders in a particular situation.

We see then that the stakeholder perspective (be it theoretical, strategic or analytical) can only be adopted if it goes beyond a simple definition. Indeed, it is not a matter of simply noting organizational interdependencies and interrelations, nor is it a matter of drawing up a list of possible affected parties. The point is rather that we cannot talk about stakeholders without making explicit the criteria and concepts which cause us to consider them -and rank them hierarchically - as such and cause us to consider - or not consider- them all equally. As mentioned earlier, Friedman might not refuse to talk about stakeholders, but he would have been in radical disagreement with the usual list of stakeholders as well as with its operational consequences. For Friedman the problem would not be the existence of stakeholders, but the list of those one should consider as such. And this depends on business values and options, not on a descriptive analysis.

It becomes evident then that consequentialist approaches are operationally insufficient unless one assumes that they become operational only when principles, criteria, and values are incorporated. The stakeholder theory cannot even concretely systematize its analytical claim if it does not bear in mind the following: the network of relationships in which the corporation is implicitly or explicitly embedded involves thinking about what interests and powers will be taken into consideration, in what areas it is considered pertinent to talk about the capacity to affect and be affected, and how one defines both what one understands by success and what one understands by performance. In terms of consequentialism, the apparent clarity - and utility- of stakeholder analysis cannot hide its shortcomings unless it is limited to no more than a list of interrelations.

At this juncture, I think it would be useful to discuss some specific contributions to the understanding of stakeholders. This will enable us to see that it is a necessary approach, but not sufficient to construct an ethics of organizations.

5.3.   Stakeholders: An analytical classification

How many types of stakeholders are there? And who are they? Stakeholder analysis assumes that we are in pluralistic societies, with pluralism being understood here not in ideological or cultural terms, but in terms of the distribution of power. Taken to its extreme, this position can lead us to an excessively fragmented perception in which we would only find groups that occasionally coincide, according to the interests or strategies they pursue. But this perspective allows us to see the corporation as a knot in a network of relationships, and consequently as related to all kinds of groups and in interaction with them. This view of the corporation almost as a point of intersection between various groups is what stakeholder analysis attempts to systematize.

At this point, Freeman and Reed propose two definitions of stakeholder which they characterize respectively as wide and narrow. In a wide sense they refer to "any identifiable group or individual who can affect the achievement of an organization's objectives or who is affected by the achievement of an organization's objectives. (Public interest groups, protest groups, government agencies, trade associations, competitors, unions, as well as employees, customer segments, shareowners, and others are stakeholders in this sense.")[12] And, in a narrower sense they refer to "any identifiable group or individual on which the organization is dependent for its continued survival (Employees, customer segments, certain suppliers, key government agencies, shareowners, certain financial institutions)."[13] What I want to emphasize here is the delimitation of two levels of stakeholders, which under different formulae have become commonplace. And I will not go into whether the proposed double list of stakeholders is due to the criteria adopted, which would make some stakeholders relevant and others not, rather than to simple empirical corroboration of the interrelations.

Mitroff (1983) distinguishes between internal and external stakeholders and therefore situates the dividing line at the walls of the company. But he observes that this division itself can only become operative depending on the concept of the corporation. As an example, he points to the contrast between what he labels the "traditional" view (according to which the corporation would only be the mediator between two stakeholders: shareholders and customers) and what he calls the "wider" view (which results in a list very much like the one discussed above). Cavanagh and McGovern (1988) also distinguish between internal and external stakeholders: they consider managers, workers, and stockholders internal, whereas government, customers, the local community, the environment, and the international community would be external.

Assuming that it is necessary to consider the relations between corporation and society as an interactive system, Frederick et al. propose to distinguish between primary commitments or bonds and secondary ones. The first include "all the direct relationships necessary for [the company] to perform its major mission of producing goods and services for society:[14] workers, shareholders, creditors, suppliers, competitors, distributors, and so on. Secondary commitments are "the result of the impacts caused by the company's primary business mission or function:"[15] local communities, governments (state, regional, and local), foreign governments, social movements, mass media, corporate support groups, the general public, etc.

Finally, Carroll suggests that one should only consider those approaches that acknowledge the distinction between primary and secondary stakeholders. Not every approach that takes some stakeholders into account should be included, but only those that recognize the double category of stakeholders in its full complexity. For the same reason Carroll takes a distance from what he and Freeman (1984), call the production approach (which only takes customers and suppliers into consideration) and the management approach (which only considers customers, suppliers, owners, and employees). The management approach is concerned only with primary stakeholders, whereas secondary stakeholders include consumer associations, environmental associations, political groups, interest groups, local communities, mass media, and society in general. Perhaps we could synthesize all this in the following way: if we want

---

[12] Freeman & Reed, 1983, p. 91.
[13] Freeman & Reed, 1983, p. 91.
[14] Frederick et al., 1988, p. 78.
[15] Frederick et al., 1988, p. 78.

to consider the corporation from the perspective of stakeholders, we need to make explicit all the interrelations in which it is involved and distinguish between those interrelations that stem from the corporation's standard ordinary activity and those due to the implications and consequences of this very activity.

It is in the operational and analytical aspects that we note that, in terms of power, stakeholder analysis ultimately becomes almost superimposed on corporate analysis. It is this superimposition of the two analyses that sustains the issue of corporate social responsibility. We can see this in the matrix proposed by Epstein (1973) to analyze the reality of power in the business world, a matrix closely related to the distinctions I presented earlier:

Level Area	System	Sector	Company	Individual
Economic				
Social and cultural				
Individual				
Technological				
Environmental				
Political				

With this matrix, Epstein aims to depict an approach that systematizes the reality of corporate power on each level; a reality that can be analyzed in relation to the six areas that Epstein considers relevant. This analytical approach is what Carroll (1989) reformulates, substituting the stakeholder for the possible areas of power and replacing analytical levels with the levels he attributes to corporate social responsibility:

Stakeholders	Economic Responsibility	Legal responsibility	Ethical responsibility	Voluntary responsibility
Shareholders				
Employees				
Customers				
Suppliers				
Local community				
Mass media				
Consumer associations				
Others				

Carroll calls this the stakeholders-responsibility matrix and considers that clarifying the content of each box would enable us to develop a type of management which would take into account everything that is at stake in business activity.[16]

---

[16] Here we will not enter into the approaches that aim to be more precise in the use of this analytical and operational tool: the issue is now not so much to see the extent of the stakeholders' perspective, but rather its possible integration in an ethics of organizations.

Frederick et al. (1988) propose a very similar diagram arrangement, but put more emphasis on the process of constructing stakeholder analysis and therefore give it a more management-oriented slant. This approach considers that "stakeholder analysis helps the manager identify each stakeholder, each stakeholder's interests, and the changes in stakeholder perceptions of issues and in the balance of influence over time".[17] I believe that the following steps are necessary to accomplish this:

(1) drawing a map of stakeholders, starting from a list as complex and detailed as possible of the groups and individuals that interact with the corporation, have an influence on it, and affect or are affected by it; (2) drawing a map of stakeholder coalitions, because one shouldn't forget that in practice stakeholders are never an aggregate; they are or can be interrelated; (3) discovering each stakeholder's particular interest because these interests can have different meanings and degrees of importance for the corporation. Once they have been acknowledged, the corporation can address them in different ways; (4) discovering each stakeholder's power and how it connects with the interests involved in its relations with the corporation; (5) constructing a table of priorities in relation to stakeholders because, once all the information is collected, the corporation has to decide on its line of action; (6) starting with decisions already made and checking to determine whether there are changes in stakeholder coalitions.

It is clear that we have gone beyond a simple analysis of stakeholders here. Some proposals for action have been constructed on the basis of this analysis, although no matter how exhaustive it may be, stakeholder analysis definitely does not give us either criteria for action or the lines of articulation that link the corporation with the various detected interests at stake. If we recall the distinction made earlier between stakeholders as corporate analysis, as corporate theory, and as corporate strategy, it becomes evident that this model can be an element for analyzing an ethics of organization, but if we want to make it operational we will need to add other elements, which a simple stakeholder analysis cannot provide. Let us examine this in more detail.

5.4.   Stakeholders: Beyond Analysis

Those who suggest an approach to the corporation based on understanding stakeholders do not always succeed in separating the what from the what for. They often confuse them or assume that the what for is already included in the what, since it is customary to present analytical proposals as norms. For this reason I believe that if we want to evaluate the contribution of the stakeholder approach to an ethics of organizations, we must first consider its analytical, theoretical, and strategic dimensions.

From an analytical point of view, drawing a map of stakeholders is no more than an exercise in description which all that needs to be specified in detail is the network of relations in which the organization is embedded: the groups and individuals that affect it or are affected by it; the interests, demands, and expectations that are at stake in each case; and the real power held by each member of this network of relations. But this does not go beyond a simple perception and analysis of a situation. Therefore, an organizational approach cannot be based on a mere description of stakeholders.

---

[17] Frederick et al., 1988, p. 84.

But neither is the analysis - and this is the most important thing for us- self-sufficient in terms of ethics (contrary to what often appears to be, or would like to be, the case):[18] "To be informed that an individual or an institution regularly makes stakeholder analysis part of decision-making or takes a 'stakeholder approach' to management is to learn little or nothing about the ethical character of that individual or institution. It is to learn only that stakeholders are regularly identified – not why and for what purpose. To be told that stakeholders are or must be 'taken into account' is, so far, to be told very little. Stakeholder analysis is, as a practical matter, morally neutral. It is therefore a mistake to see it as a substitute for normative ethical thinking [...] stakeholder synthesis offers a pattern or channel by which to move from stakeholder identification to a practical response or resolution".[19] And this step is the result of a synthesis, and not only of the simple analytical description of stakeholders. This step requires something more than just this analysis, as becomes evident when one adopts a more theoretical and strategic approach.

The theoretical and strategic approaches are so closely interrelated that stakeholder theory is not actually considered a business theory, but a theoretical extrapolation of what is simply a strategic approach. But I feel that one cannot ignore the fact that the stakeholders' viewpoint represents a particular comprehension of the corporation. Ultimately it conceives the corporation from a management standpoint: stakeholders do not make sense unless one accepts that corporations and organizations must be managed and directed, and that it is therefore necessary to understand them from this perspective. "Stakeholder theorists attempt to explain and assess the company as a balance between individual and group interests, stakeholders, and as an instrument for their aims and projects."[20] We thus encounter a change of concept that emphasizes management - and managers- or, as Chandler (1997) put it, that replaces the visible hand of the market with the invisible hand of management.

Now that we have accepted that there are two different groups of stakeholders (whether we call them internal and external, or primary and secondary), "the main lessons that emerge from this interactive model are the following ones: a) In making decisions, business shares power with all primary and secondary groups. Shared decision making has become more and more typical of all businesses, large and small. b) The managers of business firms need to become skilled in the social and political factors involved in their secondary relations, as well as in the economic and financial aspects of their primary relations. Neither skill alone will suffice. c) A business firm's acceptance by society – its legitimacy as an approved institution – depends upon its performance in both the primary and secondary spheres."[21]

---

[18] In my opinion, Carroll (1989) is the clearest example of the risk involved in rashly holding this belief since his proposal for ethical management and opening the corporation to society is essentially founded on the treatment of stakeholders.

[19] Goodpaster, 1991a, p. 57.

[20] Sacconi, 1991a, p. 153.

[21] Frederick et al. 1988, p. 81. We therefore see that one can defend the stakeholder approach by focusing on a better quality in decision making, a more adequate comprehension of management, and a consideration of the need for legitimization. Talking about stakeholders does not automatically include an ethical perspective. In my opinion, it instead allows a certain ethical re-reading of the approach, but this is precisely what one ought to do, rather than taking it for granted.

Goodpaster (1991a) nonetheless insists that duties and commitments towards shareholders are different from those towards other stakeholders. Incidentally, he makes this observation recalling the traditional view of the corporation, but in so doing he indirectly raises an issue that we will discuss later, albeit in a very different sense: if one takes all interests into account, does this imply that they should all be taken into account in the same way?

This question is crucial in terms of ethics if we accept that, from the theoretical point of view, "an organization may be thought of as the entire set of relationships it has with itself and its stakeholders."[22]. For the same reason, Mitroff has stressed that the importance assigned to stakeholders represents the translation into organization theory of the awareness of the growing complexity of our world and of its interdependent relations. In other words, in taking stakeholders as a reference it is not only the problem of social legitimacy that is at stake, but also the need to respond to the challenge of managing in a context of permanent change. Thus, in taking stakeholders into consideration, considerations of strategy, legitimation and ethics converge, all three of them having the same theoretical and analytical basis in relation to understanding the organization. This is precisely what I think requires more clarification.

From the strategic point of view, if one adopts the stakeholders' understanding of the corporation, one also adopts an ostensibly global vision of management that can be taken into account at every stage of a new strategy, from design to evaluation. But the strategic process implies paying attention not only to the diversity of stakeholders, but also to the approach to the relations between each of them. Since it is also a part of business options, this interrelation can be different in each case, and simply acknowledging stakeholders is not enough. From the strategic point of view, the question is then twofold: who are our stakeholders and what do we want our relations with them to be (Carroll, 1989). And for the same reason, "to manage these interdependencies, corporate managers need both a conceptual understanding of the relationships and practical skills for responding."[23]

In short, drawing a map of stakeholders enables us to determine business responses and, consequently, the criteria and purposes that allow them to be established. "Effective strategic management involves the guidance and direction of the whole business enterprise. Therefore it requires an understanding of two important concerns: a)Where and how the organization is going to change, develop, and operate in the present and in the future. These issues comprise the corporation's strategy, or basic plan, for relating current decisions to future goals and objectives. b) What general managers (as opposed to managers with narrow or technical responsibilities) do in integrating all of the interests and considerations into current decision making. The way managers perceive their environment, organize and order their thinking about those factors, and weigh the various interests of stakeholders in making decisions are all relevant factors. Managers must balance two sets of concerns simultaneously: current short-term business needs and long-term survival and growth needs."[24]

---

[22] Mitroff, 1983, p. 22. From my point of view, the step taken in this conceptualization, which talks about the organization and not only the corporation, is very important because, in fact, any organization can-analytically- draw a map of its stakeholders.

[23] *Frederick et al.,* 1988, p. 77.

[24] Frederick *et al.*, 1988, p. 99.

Marzal (1983) has rightly observed that if the stakeholder approach is taken to its limit, it can become a process of formalization and abstraction, by virtue of which the corporation would end up being (conceptually, of course) a function without a subject. Managers would become the personification of a formal process that seeks to strike a balance between the various interest groups. However, we cannot forget that the stakeholder approach is one that gives pre-eminence to management, even affirming normatively that the managerial function involves taking a balanced account of stakeholder diversity.

Thus, if we want to consider the managerial function as the way to manage relationships with the various stakeholders, we should address criteria and considerations that go beyond mere analysis. This becomes evident when we re-think the problem in terms of decision making. The question then becomes: "The best possible decision for whom? The question completely ruins the painstakingly constructed classic analysis of the corporation. But the question is not trivial, let alone irrelevant. It is tantamount to asking if there is only one best possible decision or several best decisions; as many 'best decisions' as there are interest groups to which these referred, and which come together objectively and with sufficient power within the corporation itself."[25] This question, however, is not usually raised when one emphasizes the significance of stakeholders, among other things because simply acknowledging them is insufficient to make a decision.

For this reason, I pointed out earlier that considerations of strategy, legitimation and ethics converge or can converge in the consideration of stakeholders; and all three of them have the same theoretical support in terms of understanding the organization. But one thing is that they may converge and quite a different one is whether they in fact do. If we bear in mind the conclusions we have reached in analyzing corporate social responsibility (which is linked to stakeholder analysis because it is in relation to them that such responsibility is exercised), we will recall that one of the conclusions we considered most important was that corporate social responsibility was an essential feature of an ethics of organizations and that, at the same time, it was neither automatically identified or confused with it.

Thus we should assume that "social responsiveness considerations permeate both the formulation and implementation of an organization's strategy. The strategy of a business involves basic decisions about its mission, purpose, and reason for being. These are value-laden decisions, affected by the values and ethics of management, the interests of various stakeholders, and the web of social issues and problems that are a vital dimension of the environment. In other words, a business strategy that will effectively guide an enterprise over time cannot possibly be formulated without taking management, stakeholder, and societal interests into account."[26] In other words, organizational strategy aimed to effectively guide a company over time certainly requires stakeholder analysis, but it also requires an analysis of the values and social questions implied. I would conclude then that the consideration of stakeholders is a necessary, but not sufficient, condition for an ethics of organizations; and I would then pose the question about how it can be integrated in an ethics of organizations.

---

[25] Marzal, 1988, p. 27.
[26] Frederick et al., 1988, p. 103.

5.5. Stakeholders in an ethics of organizations

We cannot then agree with "the suggestion that introducing 'stakeholder analysis' into business decisions is the same as introducing ethics into those decisions. To make this plain, let me first distinguish between two importantly different ideas: stakeholder analysis and stakeholder synthesis."[27] That is, what we should do is disclose - and differentiate - what is implicit in the construction of an analysis and the configuration of a decision or an orientation, and the consequences this has for an ethics of organizations.

I believe that this differentiation becomes clear when we recognize that stakeholder analysis entails describing the various interests at stake, but does not consider the quality (or hierarchy) of these interests. One usually gives more importance to simply taking them into account and even seeking a balance that works in terms of the corporation's objectives than in reflecting on their quality. Paradoxically, "the stakeholder theory does not sufficiently explain the meaning of the idea of ' being essential' or 'being vital' to the survival and success of a corporation. Nor does it explain what it means for a stakeholder to have an interest 'at stake' in the management of the corporation."[28] For this same reason it has been said that it is not possible to talk about stakeholders without simultaneously raising a question whose answer is quickly taken for granted: for whom- and for whose benefit - is an organization managed? It is therefore necessary to avoid confusing stakeholder-oriented management with the ethics of organization: "The inevitable task of management is not only to deal with the various stakeholder groups in an ethical fashion, but also to reconcile the conflicts of interest that occur between the organization and the stakeholder groups. Implicit in this challenge is the ethical dimension present in practically all business decision making where stakeholders are concerned." [29] But if we raise serious questions about the ethical dimension, the answer cannot consist only of talking about stakeholders: "the theory of strategic management based on the equilibrium of various stakeholder interests does not specify the weight which should be given to the various interests at stake in order to determine the form this equilibrium must take. But the essence of all moral discussion about meeting corporate obligations to stakeholders is naturally not the equilibrium per se, but the weight the company's strategic choice assigns these various interests and whether this weight reflects a morally justified behavior criterion. [...] Stakeholder theory aims, above all, to be a better description of corporate strategy than the one based on the existence of a single objective (maximizing the interests of a single stakeholder: the owner). But the fact that it is a better description of a company's strategy does not mean that it also has the moral duty to strike a balance between the aspirations of the various stakeholders. This latter requires a specifically ethical principle. But, from what

---

[27] Goodpaster, 1991a, p. 55.
[28] Sacconi, 1991, p. 151. My opinion is that it does not give a sufficient explanation because it cannot do so: consequentialism needs value criteria to be able to operate and we cannot grasp the creation of meaning from consequentialism alone. In my opinion, responsibility is not like a raw datum, as if it were intelligible independently of the configuration of the responsible subject and of the construction or acceptance of values and criteria that identify the subject's responsibility. It seems to me that the literature and proposals about stakeholders are seldom aware of this.
[29] Carroll, 1989, p. 20.

normative argument does it follow that only a strategy that reflects an equilibrium between stakeholder interests is justified?"[30]

Thus if we take one more step, we can conclude that, in addition to these questions being impossible to answer without ethical and axiological references, these references are in fact already present in the analysis performed. "The identification of stakeholders is a way of getting at assumptions. Most persons cannot readily name assumptions. They are too vague, too hazy, too hidden from view. Asking people to list the actors or parties involved or affected by one's actions, however, is concrete and do-able."[31] Now if we are conscious of this twofold level (that the description of stakeholders is not conceivable apart from the assumptions on which this description is based), then we must raise the following questions: from what point of view does one define the existence of a stakeholder? And from what point of view does one define the interest in considering a stakeholder as such? And not only that: we must also acknowledge that problems are perceived differently depending on the particular type of stakeholder taken as a reference.

In my opinion, the contribution of those who stress the importance of stakeholders is that it postulates that the actions of organizations should take into consideration the parties affected by these actions. And its limitation - or ambiguity - is it is generally confined only to this postulation. Indeed, in the various approaches that we have reviewed, once we set aside the nuances and variations of emphasis in the definitions of stakeholder, we could not determine whether the goal was -normatively- to include all the affected parties or only those who can also have an influence on the corporation. In other words, it is not clear whether they want to include all those with an interest in the company or only those who have the power to make their interest count for something; whether stakeholders are considered solely from the organization's standpoint or whether the perspective of the stakeholders themselves is taken into consideration; whether the interests at stake are considered as equivalent or whether they are ordered hierarchically and given priority of some kind. In short, to put it in my own words, similar to those of dialogical ethics: the various treatments of stakeholders have no difficulty in accepting them as affected parties, but they hardly recognize them as interlocutors.

At this point, "the question is evident: what advantage do the parties involved in an agreement have if consensus must also include people who are only 'externally' affected by negative secondary effects, and cannot contribute any strategic counterbalance?"[32] In other words, what can one say, based exclusively on stakeholder analysis, about considering the interests of the powerless affected parties? (It is here where one sees how the treatment of stakeholder interests connects with the treatment of power).

The limitations we have pointed out in the stakeholder model become evident when we note how exceptional are the claims that a distinction must be made between whether stakeholder interests or (moral) rights are at stake. And, even in these cases, the

---

[30] Sacconi, 1991a, p. 158-159.
[31] Mitroff, 1983, p. 28.
[32] Ulrich, 1990, p. 26.

distinction does not usually have a practical application: more often than not, interests overwhelmingly impose themselves as the point of reference.

In my opinion, only through the awareness of this distinction can the consideration of stakeholders become the condition that makes what Mitroff calls "reflective management" possible. This type of management overcomes the fragmentation resulting from considering each particular stakeholder without any integrating reference.

Connecting stakeholder theory with the issue of corporate social responsibility leads us to suspect an important correlation: whereas corporate responsibility, as noted above, tends to adopt prevailing social values, stakeholder theory pays little attention to the issues raised from the perspective of moral rights. I believe that it is in this sense that Boatright stated that in the – by no means unusual – case that treatment of stakeholders is accepted as including the recognition of the rights that are at stake - -which is by no means common -, then "the stakeholder theory remains a very promising version of the managerial view. The concept of a stakeholder is a valuable device for identifying and organizing the multitude of obligations that corporations have to different groups. At the present time, however, the theory is only a framework to help us get started on the very difficult task of deciding exactly what obligations of corporations come under the heading of corporate social responsibility."[33]

This question has been raised time and again by those unsatisfied with the mere acknowledgement that interested or affected groups exist; that is, by those who inquire about the quality of these interests as well as the consequences for the affected parties. Thus, Freeman & Reed (1983) claimed that it was necessary to ask not only – analytically - what influence stakeholders have on corporate operations, but also – normatively - what kind of participation they should have. But having accepted this, we should also accept Mitroff's observations: "I have also deliberately emphasized each step in the process because the method, if there really is just one, of working on complex problems is above all a behavioral process for allowing persons to see their differences in perceiving stakeholders (who is involved, who should be considered), in naming assumptions (what the stakeholders are presumed to be like), and in mapping (what is important and what is felt to be known)."[34] In short, when one adopts the stakeholder approach one realizes that what is understood as business success does not have a single, exclusive and excluding meaning. Therefore, one realizes that the question is to propose the construction of a "just process so the various stakeholder voices in these matters can be heard and have some influence on the decision."[35]

This, however, is an open question which cannot be answered by the stakeholder theory alone because, as has already been shown, it cannot be considered as an ethically self-sufficient construct. And, incidentally, this issue is inseparable from the examination of what in the previous chapter I labeled the social co-responsibility of the corporation. A detailed analysis of stakeholders seems to me a necessary condition for an ethics of organizations in terms of both the ethical demand to answer for the consequences of one's own actions and the construction of responsibility.

---

[33] Boatright, 1993, p. 406.
[34] Mitroff, 1983, p. 29.
[35] Bowie, 1991, p. 64.

"Ethically responsible management, it is often suggested, is management that includes careful attention not only to stockholders but to stakeholders generally in the decision-making process."[36] But for this management to be ethical it needs to examine how it sets its own particular criteria and values, and needs to deliberately address the configuration of a responsible subject. All this is also included in the way relations with stakeholders are handled. And only if this is clearly explained will we be able to talk about organizations as forming a new subject.

Just as we saw that everything that comes under the heading of consequentialism does not embrace everything that I labeled "the hermeneutics of responsibility", we now see that what constitutes the (co)responsibility of an organization does not originate only with a non-reflective relation with its stakeholders. It also demands the establishment of regulatory values, criteria, and corporate norms, as well as the configuration of the goods and values that identify the organization. These are the questions that I will analyze in the next two chapters.

---

[36] Goodpaster, 1991a, p. 53.

CHAPTER 6

CORPORATE CODES: CONSTRUCTING CRITERIA AND GOALS?

In recent years drafting corporate codes has been one of companies' favorite ways of explicitly stating values, criteria, and business standards. It should be kept in mind, however, that "corporate ethical codes have roots in early professional codes"[1] Analysis of corporate codes hardly ever acknowledges that they take professional codes as models, although often not explicitly and sometimes even unconsciously. It is important to realize this because it will help us better understand both their limitations and failures.

Professional codes warrant a brief reference for another reason. As I pointed out in Chapter 2, my thinking on ethics is grounded in the methodological distinction between system, organization, and individual. Developing an ethics of organizations is thus only possible if we take the organization as a specific object of ethics and do not limit ourselves to mechanically projecting onto it the results of our ethical thoughts about individuals or the system. But I also noted that this methodological distinction does not mean that there are three isolated realms. Furthermore, some approaches are only credible when they are situated at the intersection of two of these realms. For the same reason, and contrary to general opinion, I consider any analysis of corporate codes insufficient if it does not view them in relation to professional codes.

6.1.   Professional codes as a point of reference

Indeed, it seems evident that the justification of a professional ethical code is based on one's understanding of a profession in general and on one's position as to whether a particular profession actually needs a code of professional ethics. This understanding would lead us to consider the possible interrelation between the professional activity and the process of drafting an explicit ethical code. As regards whether professional codes of ethics are needed, we should ask ourselves whether professional managers need to identify themselves through an ethical code.

Although there is no absolute unanimity, there is a certain agreement on some basic traits that enable us to establish what a profession is. Thus, according to Hortal's thesis, professions are "occupational activities a) in which a service is rendered to society in an institutionalized form, b) by a group of people (the professionals) who steadily devote themselves to these activities earning their livelihood therefrom, c) forming with other professionals (colleagues) a collective that obtains or seeks to obtain a monopoly over the exercise of the profession d) and accede to it after a long process of theoretical and practical training on which the accreditation or license to exercise such profession depends."[2] Along similar lines, González has summarized what he defines as a "professional paradigm"[3] a) it is a unique, definitive, and essential service to society; b)

[1] Stevens, 1994, p. 64.
[2] Hortal, 1993, p. 207.
[3] See González 1994, p. 26ff.

it is considered a "vocation"; c) it is based primarily on knowledge and intellectual techniques for rendering the service or performing the task at hand; d) it requires a period of specialized training; e) it claims autonomy in the exercise of the profession; f) it implies taking responsibility for the judgments and decisions made; g) the emphasis is more on the service offered than on the profit earned (this does not prevent motivations from being pecuniary, but this is not a criterion of professionalism); h) there is a self-governed organization of professionals in the field.

Both authors agree on the basic traits, even though it is worth noting that they do not explicitly address the need for professional ethics. In this approach, the ethical dimension would be specifically acknowledged at a later date. i.e. when reflecting on the profession itself.

In the context of BE the dominant tendency is to understand professional ethics as one more element among those that define the profession. No doubt here we find again the echoes of the U.S. tradition that takes the individual as the main subject of moralization in social life. But I think that we also once again find the tendency, noted in my earlier analysis of BE, to understand ethics fundamentally in terms of conventional morality, i.e. as the acceptance of commonly recognized values. This acceptance does not, however, imply that there is any postconventional reference which would provide ethical grounds for this acceptance.[4]

Before discussing this point, however, there is one thing which should be noted as it will directly affect our understanding of professionals and, by extension, professional ethics. I am referring to the fact that definitions of what a profession is usually do not take their organizational context into consideration. Today most professional practices are exercised within the framework of organizations. Therefore, their point of reference is the organization rather than individual professional practice.

Furthermore, we should be cautious and avoid defining professions on the assumption that "the paradigms of the professions are the medical and legal professions."[5] We should also avoid assuming that we live in culturally stable societies with a shared idea of the good life and the common good which would allow us to situate and understand the contribution of particular professions. That is to say, we should acknowledge that we live in a society where professions have been diversified and become more complex (like society itself). Consequently, more than sharing a pre-established set of values, professions must learn to develop a responsible system of self-regulation in a cultural context marked by uncertainty and pluralism and in an organizational context.[6]

Obviously, in saying this I do not mean to detract from the importance that professional ethical codes might have in conventional terms because it is true that professional ethics refers to a reconciliation between values and techniques that is

---

[4] My hypothesis is that development of a professional ethics should involve investigating the correlations given within each profession between corporativism and its legitimization through "professional ethics." In fact, Solomon (1993) suggests that the ideologization of professionalism very often does not aim to do anything more than protect the profession from competition. Stevenson (1989) affirms that the aim is to ensure that only members of the profession define what is good for customers or society.

[5] De George, 1990a, p. 383.

[6] "Codes are made from the presuppositions of autonomy and independence in the professional exercise, which on many occasions do not correspond with reality. Professions are exercised today primarily in corporate contexts" (Hortal, 1994a, p. 60).

inherent to some practices. But here the usual distinction between ethics and professional deontology becomes relevant. Deontology deals with the formulation of duties and obligations inherent to a particular profession. Ethics, on the other hand, makes a broader reference to the good inherent in professional activity, its social context, and the principle of humanity.[7] The ambiguity we find in codes stems precisely from the fact that they can accentuate deontological aspects to the detriment of their ethical counterparts and can ultimately reduce professional ethics to a set of norms, adherence to which would automatically qualify the professional as an ethical person.

It should be remembered here that "because members of professions are moral beings first and only secondarily professionals, professional ethics cannot appropriately relieve one of the general moral obligations that apply to all people.[8]

In other words, if we don't want to cut off professional deontologies from their ethical basis, we should not turn the lack of coincidence between person and role into a norm. This lack of coincidence is characteristic of advanced societies inasmuch as they are societies of organizations. In sum, what is ultimately at stake in any professional ethics is whether or not it is approached from a pre-critical standpoint, a question that is rejected by the separatist paradigm.[9] Through their practices, professionals are inevitably transformed into agents that articulate values, and this is what ethical codes should express and formalize. But, in addition, their formulation should not be the result of seeing the profession only from the inside and their articulation should not ignore the horizon of consensus among all the parties involved and affected by the professional action.

Thus ethical codes can express the mediation (in the professional field) between individual and society. However, the need for professions to generate trust and social legitimization means that statements of professional ethics risk becoming corporatist, rather than a foundation of legitimacy.

6.2.   Codes and their ambivalence

Since I begin with the assumption that "corporate ethical codes have roots in early professional codes",[10] I consider it important to sum up the evaluations of the advantages and disadvantages of such codes. If this assumption is correct, corporate codes might have automatically inherited the advantages and disadvantages of professional codes.

In De George's view (1990a), the characteristics of a professional code are the following. It must be regulatory (and therefore must distinguish between the formulation of ideals and the explicit determination of what can be sanctioned). It has to protect the public interest and the interest of those who receive the services of the profession. It should not serve the profession with a corporatist aim. It must explicitly

---

[7] Deontology speaks of what is binding to all. Ethics takes care of the remaining open and plural spaces that the good can occupy. Ultimately, ethics refers back to individual conscience while deontology remains rather in the field of what is approved by a collective (Hortal, 1994a, p. 57, 58).

[8] De George, 1990a, p. 395.

[9] "An important component of the separatist thesis, then, is the idea of professional role autonomy. The idea is that each profession is to be defined in terms of its own aims and procedures, and each therefore has its own criteria of value and its own inherent moral justification. " (Gerwith, 1986, p. 284).

[10] Stevens 1994, p. 64.

refer to professional practice and not limit itself to recalling everyone's moral obligations. It has to be controllable and controlled. Here the practical difficulty of distinguishing between professional ethics and professional deontology is already apparent. Given that professional deontology is implicit in professional ethics, this means that a professional ethical code has to include the dimensions of a deontological code. But it also has to go beyond this: it has to include dimensions other than the strictly deontological. In short, a profession's code of ethics is perhaps the most visible and explicit assertion of its standards. A code embodies the collective conscience of a profession and testifies to the group's recognition of its moral dimension. But taking our cue from Frankel (1989), we can identify three types of ethical codes. A code of aspirations is the explicit statement of the ideals that the profession's members should strive to reach. An educational code aims to reinforce understanding of its proposals with extensive commentaries and interpretations. A regulatory code includes a set of detailed rules to guide professional conduct. Although these three types of codes are conceptually different, any particular code may well include aspects from all of them.

In my opinion, this plurality of registers is inherent to every professional code (because, though often forgotten, this plurality is inherent to the ethical understanding of all professional practices). Thus I think that, in practice, not only can a code combine the different aspects, but that it must do so. In order to systematize what the contributions and limitations of professional codes are, I will distinguish their internal functions from their external ones.[11]

As far as their internal functions go, codes contribute the following: a) they stress that professionalism includes a reference to values and not only to technical competence and in this sense they can express a group culture; b) they allow professional self-regulation, even as regards sanctions; c) they allow a distinction to be made between the minimum standards of conduct that professionals should observe (or avoid) and the aspirations that they can share; d) they can have an educational function and guide professional training; e) having a formulated code means having a reference that makes it easier for professionals to recognize ethical problems; f) codes can facilitate socialization of members of the profession.

On the other hand, and still in terms of internal functions, codes have the following limitations: a) they can reflect or express the profession's commitment to ethical conduct, but cannot create it; b) the expression of ideals might lead to the cynicism of considering them impossible in relation to reality; c) however, they might also be too minimalist and uninspiring; d) they might encourage professionals to be too rigid in relation to the norm, and might justify sacrificing one's own moral autonomy to abiding by the established code; e) they do not in themselves create the necessary capacity of discernment, since what predominates in professional reality are conflicts of values; f) affirmation or acknowledgement of a code might be confused with its application; consequently, application might be taken for granted while the instruments to make it effective are neglected; g) to facilitiate agreement codes might be too imprecise and thus embrace practices that are very different from one other.

---

[11] For the development of the synthesis I propose, see Berham, 1988; De George, 1990a; Frankel, 1989; Leining & Zhang, 1993; Kultgen, 1983; Ladd, 1989; Newton, 1983; Prandstraller, 1991; Reeck, 1982; Shaw & Barry, 1989; Solomon, 1993; Stevenson, 1989.

Regarding their external functions, codes contribute the following: a) in a more complex society they express what can be expected from a profession (also on what issues and why they can be trusted); b) they are like social barometers that signal the areas in which professionals must be alert to social demands; c) they manifest society's inherent structural need for responsibility in the exercise of all professions.

In contrast, and still in terms of their external functions, the limitations of codes are the following: a) they might make it easier for professions to escape public scrutiny and convert professional status and privileges in ends in themselves inasmuch as codes - and professions - are considered a monopoly of professional groups; b) they might artificially generate trust as a public relations tool and a way to rationalize professional practices; c) they might remove professions from their social context (and its problems) since they reduce questions of professional ethics to the most internal or strictly professional ones; d) they do not usually raise questions about the society in which they act and about which social order they support, and they can often ignore the criteria of justice; e) they can be the expression and legitimization of a professional ideology that disguises its corporate interests with rhetoric; f) they consolidate the typical asymmetry of any professional relation and the paternalism that might ensue from it.

This brief consideration about professional ethical codes allows us to see the ambiguities and, above all, to anticipate the core questions that we should pose when we deal with corporate codes of ethics. I feel that this is important to note because insofar as corporate codes mirror the aforementioned ambiguities we should ask about the advantages and limitations of ethical codes for an ethics of organizations. But more importantly we should ask about the extent to which it would be necessary to attempt to restate these codes in the context of the new cultural, economic, and organizational realities.

In short, analysis of professional ethical codes reveals that the most important issues in terms of corporate ethical codes are the following: who should participate in formulating them and what procedure should be used; how they should combine the expression of corporate ideals with the regulation of particular organizational practices and, therefore, whether they should be a statement of ideals or of the limits beyond which certain actions are not accepted and are possibly penalized; whether they should affirm the goods (and the telos) that define the activity of a particular corporation or establish the principles that govern it; whether they should emphasize their internal functions, their external functions or whether they should strike a balance between the two; whether they are primarily declarations or whether they should explicitly list the steps that lead from a declaration of ethics to institutionalization of the code and its practical implementation; whether they should foster the social legitimization of the corporation or the development of corporate social (co)responsibility.

Certainly, the things I have just mentioned are not a list of mutually incompatible alternatives, but they do reveal the tension between emphases that do not necessarily coincide. This in turn reveals that, insofar as we recognize it as an organizational construct, a code is not an established formula (with certain requirements that permit it to be considered as such), but an ethical option. Ultimately, the question we should raise is whether a corporate ethical code is directed primarily towards regulating and controlling preconventional behavior, affirming conventional demands and identities, or developing a postconventional capacity in the life of organizations (and, if it aims to incorporate all three of these dimensions, how they fit together).

6.3.   Management as a profession: a significant absence

Perhaps it would be more reasonable to base the transition from thinking about professional ethical codes to thinking about the function of corporate ethical codes on the considerations that have been made about the professional ethics of managers and executives. Symptomatically, however, BE has scarcely addressed the issue of corporate management in terms of a profession or, consequently, in terms of professional ethics.[12] In any case, to put it briefly, one talks more about professions in corporations than about what managers and executives do as professionals. One reason for this is that there is still considerable discussion about whether the exercise of executive functions can be conceived as a profession. Nonetheless, corporate management is usually accepted as a marginal or emergent profession, as a job on the way to becoming a profession.

Earlier I listed the characteristics of a profession. If we look back to them now we can see that the clearest differences between management and other recognized professions are the training needed to enter the management field and the absence of a self-regulating professional group. It is worth noting that BE sometimes tries to resolve this question itself without giving an actual answer to it; i.e., affirming that what is most important for business management cannot be taught[13] or that the aim must be personal, not only executive, development. From my point of view, however, discussion about managers' and executives' professional ethics can take place with relative independence of the question of whether management is or is not a profession. It is, in contrast, more difficult to dissociate it totally from the development of an ethics of organizations: what is expected of executives and what it is demanded of them (in all respects) depends very directly on one's ideas of what an organization is. Nevertheless, the demand for professional ethics among managers and executives has been motivated more by awareness of their responsibility than by awareness of management's function as a profession. I think this is due to the lack of a systematic and specific reflection about what the internal good of the management profession is and therefore about the practice that characterizes it. This gives rise to a question which is not always sufficiently taken into account: in contrast to all other professions, that of the manager is not intelligible unless the organization itself is understood.[14] The difference is that, although to a large

---

[12] Managers'ideas and moral beliefs have been analyzed and the issue of developing moral justice has been raised. But no significant attention has been paid to analyzing the possible professional ethics of managers or executives.

[13] Salomon (1993) echoes a recurrent theme: we can teach finances, marketing, or accounting; but can we academically teach people to accept reasonable risks, create new projects, or lead and motivate ?

[14] Moreover, there are different axiological approaches. Sinclair (1991) summarized the subjects of various studies in the following chart:

Professional Values	Managerial values
Cosmopolitan (identification with professional values)	Local (primarily identified with the organization)
Assessment by colleagues	Activity is objectively measured
Autonomy and discretion	Supervision, planning and control
Technical skills	Managerial skills
Power and status based on experience	Power to meet objectives

extent lawyers, physicians and engineers work within organizations, it is perfectly possible to think about their practices without thinking about their organizational context. But there is no managerial practice without an organization. For this reason I propose as an internal good of organization management: a) making viable the ends (and goods) the organization aims to achieve, and b) making viable the organization itself as an end.

A "professional" ethics of managers (that could be formally expressed in a code recognized as such) would not then depend fundamentally on a prior definition of management as a profession, but on the need to think about the ethical import of managerial functions and responsibilities. It would also depend on the need to avoid the danger of thinking about managers as mere bearers of manifold capacities which are subject to the demands of the organization. In other words, making the "professional" ethics of management explicit is a necessary condition for being able to affirm managers' autonomy in terms of ethics. It is also necessary in order to affirm that what society expects of them does not take a back seat to what the organization expects of them.[15]

6.4.   Corporate codes of ethics: a descriptive approach

Although the first references to corporate codes can be traced back to the beginning of the century, the boom in such codes runs parallel to the development of BE, which I discussed in Chapter Two. Thus, "during the 1960s, a number of proposals concerning general or industry-wide codes of conduct were discussed. As a result of revelations during the Watergate era regarding incidents of corporate misconduct, such as illegal or questionable payments at home and abroad and falsification of corporate books and records, public attention to business practices has increased. The business community has shown interest in company-specific codes of conduct as a means of setting and communicating standards of behavior."[16]

Brooks (1989) synthesizes the historical development of corporate codes of ethics in a change of perspective and in the coincidence of six factors. The change of perspective emphasizes that corporate ethical codes cannot be understood without a change in our understanding of the corporation. In this case, the decisive change consists in seeing the corporation from the viewpoint of management and in understanding it from the viewpoint of stakeholders. The factors that Brooks points to as underlying the growth in interest in business ethics are: the crisis in confidence in corporate activity; peoples' increased expectations in terms of quality of life; society's recognition that, if necessary, managers should be severely sanctioned; the growing power of interest groups; and a change in emphasis in corporate control, whose objectives are no longer limited to simply maximizing profits.

Service quality	Cost, efficiency and effectiveness
Means	Ends
Ethical responsibility	Corporate efficiency

[15] "For the most part, ethical problems occur because corporate managers and their subordinates are *too* devoted to the organization." (Murphy, 1989, p. 81).

[16] White & Montgomery, 1980, p. 80. Once again we find an origen of a reactive kind.

This concern translated to an increase in the number of corporations that drafted corporate codes and, consequently, in the appearance of studies analyzing the extent and content of existing codes. In my opinion, Weaver's (1993) is the most complete quantitative study of these codes.[17] According to his study, the evolution would be approximately the following:[18]

YEAR	POPULATION	RESPONSES	CÓDES
1980	Fortune 1000 and 1000 executives	673 (aggregate)	77%
1986	Fortune 1000	279	93%
1987	2100 companies	300	76%
1990	Not specified	Not specified	56%[19]
1992	1900 companies	264	83%
1992	Fortune 1000	229	93%

The first thing these data show is the need to make an analysis of corporate ethical codes similar to the one carried out by Hosmer (1985). In a systematic study of what was taught as BE in business schools, Hosmer asked what "the others" did; i.e., he asked about the schools that did not respond, which were the majority of them. No similar study has been done in relation to codes. Although the information contained in the table above has a certain interest, it is not enough to enable us to draw conclusions about the weight and significance of ethical codes in corporate practices. "Consequently, there is much still to be learned regarding the extent of code usage in relation to organizational histories, task environments and structures, and the overall character of society. Prior code studies generally have not systematically unearthed and explained the factors related to the adoption of ethics codes by either individual firms or groups of firms."

In fact, almost all studies on corporate ethical codes have been predominantly quantitative. Likewise, analyses of codes are fundamentally reflections based on this quantitative evidence. These studies were primarily concerned with two types of information: one referring to types of codes and one referring to their content.

Regarding types of codes, all authors use their own terminology, although, aside from the words used, the basic lines converge. Donaldson (1989) shows that codes

---

[17] Other studies that analyze quantitative aspects of corporate ethical codes include Benson, 1989; Cressey & Moore, 1983; center for business ethics, 1986, 1992; Chatov, 1980; ethics resource center, 1980; Robertson, 1991; Sacconi, 1991a; Stevens, 1994; the conference board, 1988; Warren, 1993; White & Montgomery, 1980. But none of these has as many sources or is as internally coherent, faithful to data and well-synthesized as Weaver's study.

[18] The figures refer to the total number of companies: 77% of the largest companies had corporate ethical codes.

usually end up expressing a mixture of technical, prudential, and moral imperatives. Stevens (1994) feels that it is important not to confuse corporate ethical codes, professional ethical codes, and missions. He sees corporate ethical codes as a management tool that seeks to have an impact on the conduct of workers; for professional ethical codes he relies on Frankel's analysis (1989) which I mentioned earlier; and he considers the mission as an element of strategic management. But though he warns that confusion should be avoided, he admits that in practice the three types of codes are often confused and overlapping. Brooks (1989) also distinguishes three models of codes: those that take stakeholders as their reference (and establish principles, objectives, and policies for each of them); those that take strategic policies as their reference (the company's guidelines for action with an indication of Management's purposes, objectives, policies, and ideas; and those that have the corporate mission as their reference. Arthur (1984) considers that codes can be distinguished according to their level of specificity: they can affirm values or principles in very generic terms; they can propose guidelines for internal and external action; or they can set out detailed regulations for particular fields of action. Raiborn and Paine (1990) conclude that one can find four levels of formulation in corporate ethical codes: theoretical (which reflects the highest levels of good and morality); practical (which reflects the orientation that leads to moral conduct); normal (which reflects the behavior that society considers moral); and basic (which reflects the acceptable minimum and the letter of the law). Weber (1993) identifies three types of codes according to their orientation: those of constitutive obligations (which express the company's commitments to the various groups it serves); those of professional responsibility (which present a set of corporate general principles that must be followed); and those of corporate mission (which do not explicitly govern employees' conduct but instead state corporate objectives). Finally, we must take into account those approaches that stress that codes are unintelligible unless they are considered in relation to corporate procedures (De George, 1983) or corporate culture (Trevino, 1990).

In short, here again we find the same plurality of registers we saw when we discussed the various types of professional ethical codes: there are those that express generic values and those that are tied to the network of corporate relations (stakeholders); those that are more regulatory and those that are more inspirational and provide guidelines; those that are more in tune with an ethics of minimum standards and those that advocate maximum standards. In my opinion, recognizing that there tends to be a mixture of dimensions should lead us to the following conclusion: drawing up a code is a corporate option which involves deliberately choosing to fit together various dimensions (and therefore can no longer be considered as isolated or independent from the rest of corporate life). Therefore, in answer to our earlier question about whether corporate ethical codes are primarily aimed at regulating preconventional behavior, affirming conventional demands and identities or developing the capacity to adopt a postconventional approach to organizational life, one must acknowledge that the first function is almost always present in codes, that the second tends to be fulfilled (not always explicitly) and that codes rarely fulfill the third function.

This is confirmed when we examine analyses of the content of corporate ethical codes. Here we must take into account the fact that these codes "have shown the frequency with which specific ethical issues are addressed in codes, but it remains unclear why some issues are singled out for attention in codes, and why others are either intentionally or unintentionally ignored."[20] It is fair to say that the various studies can hardly be regarded as homogeneous, given their diversity of methods, universes studied, and even their presentation of results. But I don't consider it necessary to discuss that in detail here. I simply want to underline the subjects addressed in most of these studies. White and Montgomery (1980) point out that, apart from presenting general considerations, the most regulated aspects are those that refer to employees' legal obligations, handling conflicts of interest between employees and the corporation (clearly and explicitly stating behavioral prohibitions), and use of corporate goods. In contrast, codes contain comparatively very little about the issues that affect corporate economic activities that can give rise to conflicts; i.e. issues such as corrupt practices in foreign countries or political contributions. Cressey and Moore also point out in their study (1983) the disproportionate amount of attention paid to anti-corporate conduct, which they find in all codes, and also the emphasis on regulating conflicts of interest. Moreover, their main conclusion is that codes of employee conduct treat the issue of a possible decline in profits vaguely and warily. For example: codes pay more attention to illegal or immoral conduct which is likely to lead to a certain decline in corporate benefits - conflicts of interest, misuse of funds - and much less attention to illegal or immoral conduct that would enable profits to be increased. Benson (1989) also acknowledges the great diversity of codes and contrasts the usual emphasis on relations between employees and corporation with questions like the environmental impact of corporate actions. He also compares the detailed regulations on gifts one can give or receive with the tolerance with which such things are treated outside the United States. Singh and Lefebvre (1992) point out that, with regard to actions taken in the name of the corporation, priority is given to relations with clients and suppliers and the acceptance of gifts or bribes (much less importance is attached to giving gifts and bribes than to receiving them). In contrast, very little importance is given to environmental issues, questions of security, and product quality. But Singh and Lefebvre also stress that, comparatively speaking, more attention is still paid to regulating anti-corporate conduct (particularly when it involves conflicts of interest). Finally, Weaver (1993) discusses in detail the most frequent themes in corporate ethical codes. It is clear from Weaver's list that codes dealing with employee conduct are the most numerous, followed by codes that refer to corporate actions in the marketplace. At the end of the list are codes that address responsibilities towards society. In short, the impression is that matters referring to internal issues are much more frequently addressed than corporate relations with the outside world.

To these considerations should be added others which, in my opinion, are very important: who takes part in drafting codes and how their application is supervised. The data are clear on this point: corporate codes of ethics are fundamentally a senior management affair. This is perhaps the most important difference between corporate and professional codes where the responsibility for the writing process almost always devolves upon a committee created specifically for this purpose, and almost never falls to the president or managing director of a professional association. The explicit involvement of senior management is, however, an essential condition for the

---

[20] Weaver, 1993, p. 44.

effectiveness of any corporate ethical code since only this involvement can transmit to the entire company the message that the code and its content are something that must definitely be taken into account. In practice, however, this involvement tends to translate to a predominance of senior management's points of view. Management views are given a great deal of attention while the views of other members of the organization are taken less into account. This is not merely a problem of form or procedure: what underlies the tendency to make senior management into the basic protagonist of corporate codes is that "the executives who authored the codes tended to consider themselves, not the society or even a part of it, to be the conscience of the corporation."[21]

After an exhaustive analysis of existing codes, Manley (1991) produced a summary of the wide range of elements that codes can take into account. He proposes that when drafting corporate ethical codes, the following points should be considered: (1) The company's general manager should lead the draft process. (2) Under his supervision, the company's key objectives should be identified and used as background when writing the code. (3) Although many people can contribute, it is advisable that the first draft be written by a small group which includes someone from the legal department. (4) The code should include a preface which explicitly states why it is needed, the expected standards of conduct, how the code should be interpreted, and the corporate position in terms of support, decisions and sanctions. (5) It should go beyond existing corporate by-laws and must distinguish clearly between ethical and legal requisites. (6) It should demand that employees adhere to all the pertinent laws and professional standards. (7) It should stress the key values of the organization. (8) It should include sections dealing with all the relationships implied in the corporation's activities. (9) These sections should be concise and easy to understand. (10) It should include operating principles that can be used as a reference in day-to-day activities. (11) It should include concrete examples and situations. (12) It should describe the most common conflicts of interest. (13) It should include a declaration stating that the corporation expects its employees to act correctly in all relations. (14) It should specify how problems relating to the code can be addressed and resolved. (15) It should include guidelines for employee conduct. (16) The general manager should carefully review the first draft proposed. (17) This draft should be circulated throughout the company and suggestions encouraged. (18) The final version should include these suggestions.

I think this list is a good example of the approach usually taken when one deals only with corporate ethical codes: this could be called the textual approach. Although it might take into account many facets and effects of an ethical code, it is always based on a consideration of the text, which then becomes the main concern. For the same reason many of the studies about corporate ethical codes have comparatively little significance when it comes to exploring their practical implementation or their effectiveness. In fact, it is symptomatic that these questions are much more clearly addressed when the issue is the institutionalization of ethics in the corporation than when it is the introduction of an ethical code in the corporation. In short, it once again appears that, although the ethics of organizations certainly depend on the points that constitute these ethics, they depend above all on the integration of these points.

---

[21] Cressey & Moore, 1983, p. 53.

In contrast, studies which tend to focus on texts and managers' opinions have been instrumental in pointing out the advantages and drawbacks usually emphasized in corporate ethical codes.[22] Thus, the following are positively rated: codes that avoid the opportunism implied in the view that interpretation of principles and values depends on each individual's subjectivity; codes that explicitly state the expectations and references that should be taken into account by everyone associated with the corporation; codes that reinforce the idea that ethics is a corporate affair; codes that formalize references that avoid having to start from zero every time there is a conflict of values and ensure some kind of minimum common corporate standards which at least make it easier to avoid undesirable conduct; codes that support individuals who want to resist possible unethical proposals from their superiors; codes that help dispel the danger of managers arbitrarily deciding the forms corporate social responsibility should take and help clarify desired relations with the various stakeholders; codes that when made public contribute towards improving the company's moral climate; codes that. can be a catalyst of corporate change; codes that help reformulate the understanding of corporate actions; codes that reflect and strengthen corporate criteria on internal communication and training, personnel selection and transmission of corporate values, and, finally, codes that help integrate values and practices in the case of mergers and acquisitions.

In contrast, the fact that codes are necessarily generic is rated negatively because it permits non-coinciding practical interpretations or even superficiality. Codes that might cause conflict with professional codes are also rated negatively as are codes that don't specify what must be done when there is a contradiction between the code and corporate interests; codes that tend to overlook individual actions and the tension between motivation and prescription; codes that are used primarily as public relations tools; codes that assume that employees have already developed some minimum standards of moral sensitivity; codes that transmit the idea that the actions and areas governed by the code are the only ones the corporation considers ethically relevant and the idea that ethics refers to routine or regulable actions; codes that implicitly free individuals from their responsibilities by acknowledging these responsibilities in codes that appease the corporate conscience, or can attribute the inadmissible action to the "rotten apple"; [23] codes whose rules and norms do not in themselves guarantee anything morally relevant; codes that can be confused with regulations of a legal type; codes that do not really address all the issues that directly affect the corporation's economic performance and which are often written with the implicit idea that adherence to the code is subordinate to profits; codes that reflect a hierarchical stance, even though they are addressed to "all" employees.

---

[22] For further details, see: Bowie, 1982; Brooks, 1989; Cressey & Moore, 1983; Chatov, 1980; Donaldson, 1982, 1989; Luthans *et al.*, 1987; Matland, 1985; Manley, 1991; Raiborn & Payen, 1990; Roberetson, 1991; Sacconi, 1991a; Stevens, 1994; the conference board, 1988; Trevino, 1990; Warren, 1982, 1993; Weaver, 1993.

[23] From this overly simple perspective, corporations would consider that they had met their commitments simply by virtue of having a code which presumably already states what the corporation expects from its employees; thus, the mere existence of the code allows the company to blame all immoral behavior on individual employees. A code of ethics can shift the blame for corporate misconduct to individual employees and can actually be a way for companies to publicly wash their hands of any responsibility for the improper actions of its employees.

Having seen this diversity - and often also this ambiguity - in everything related to codes, can an ethics of organizations possibly take them into account?

6.5.   Codes of ethics: more ethics or more control?

I believe that corporate ethical codes can be one element of an ethics of organizations, providing that one first examines their contributions, the reason why they are drafted and how they are integrated in organizational dynamics. At this point, it is necessary to bear closely in mind the fact that corporate ethical codes are often strongly marked by what we analyzed before: an often reactive origin, which responds to the existence of reproachable conduct and therefore represents a means to avoid it. That is to say, more than a means for developing organizational ethics, these codes are often a new instrument of corporate control and regulation. This is the reason why existing corporate codes have until now primarily emphasized the regulation of internal conduct and especially conduct that is contrary to the interests of the corporation itself. "Intraorganizationally, codes can provide a relatively clean, socially legitimate language for authorizing forms of control and supervision; control for the sake of ethics may prove more organizationally acceptable than control for the sake of profit."[24] It is thus necessary to ask whether corporate ethical codes ultimately contribute more towards fostering ethics or control.

I think that one of the greatest deficits in the focus of corporate codes is that they tend to consider both the design and drafting processes as self-sufficient. What is hardly ever raised is the point that corporate ethical codes "might also realize that employees are likely to be drawn from a diversity of moral backgrounds and cultures, and that a shared perception of ethical issues has to be cultivated in society and then inside the corporation, rather than be merely presupposed to exist ready made."[25]

I think that a more constructivist perspective and one that is simultaneously more respectful of contemporary moral diversity is only possible if the approach to corporate ethical codes is deliberately placed within the framework of what I call "civic ethics". But this is not possible if they are reduced, as is usually the case, to an expression of the conventional rules and prohibitions of a particular corporation or branch of industry The point then is to avoid granting any kind of legitimacy to attempts to turn professional ties into a form of submission or servitude to certain norms and values, expecting them to be surrendered to passively and unquestioningly.

We have seen that senior management tends to consider corporate ethical codes as one more management tool. They are usually drawn up at the organization's summit with the basic aim of regulating - and avoiding - conduct which, from senior management's standpoint, is harmful and dysfunctional. But it is advisable not to confuse the question about the need for ethical codes with the question about what corporate ethical codes can contribute. The specific need to go beyond merely preconventional criteria for action does not preclude the possibility of clearly explaining the ends, goods, and ideals that socially justify the organization's existence and activities. I feel, however, that this is only possible if one goes beyond the approach that gives priority to the merely textual significance of corporate codes.

---

[24] Weaver, 1993, p. 50.
[25] Warren, 1993, p. 187.

First, instead of being the exclusive province of top management, codes should reflect the stakeholders' perspective, taking them into account and possibly including them in the draft process. Analysis of and speculation about corporate ethical codes have been more concerned with the regulations such codes produce than with the people who take part in drafting them. One consequence of this is that BE has an excessive tendency to separately discuss issues concerned with corporate ethical codes and issues concerned with stakeholders. I believe that closer integration of these two kinds of issues would help overcome what I described in the previous chapter as a merely analytical acceptance of stakeholders and what I now see as a reduction of codes to a simple form of control, supposedly justified on ethical grounds.

Secondly, inasmuch as corporate codes should address many ethical issues, we should assume that the format of the code is neither the only way of stating these issues nor the most appropriate for all cases. Earlier, I raised the question of what a corporate ethical code seeks to achieve: whether it is primarily directed towards regulating preconventional behavior, affirming conventional demands and identities, or developing the capacity to adopt a postconventional approach to organizational life (and, in the case that it seeks to express all three aspects, how it does so). Nonetheless, we have seen that Frankel (1989) advocated making a distinction between the codes' educational and regulatory dimensions, as well as their aspirations, and that Stevens (1994) insisted on making a distinction between codes and missions. Finally, we pointed out the wide range of issues addressed in codes (and the dangers they entail). All this should raise the question of whether everything an organization wants to say about itself has to be said in the same way.

I certainly think that an organization must be able to express itself in terms of regulating preconventional behavior, voicing conventional demands and identities, and developing the capacity to adopt a postconventional approach. Accordingly, the success (or popularity) of corporate ethical codes lies in their being easily formalized and in their capacity to respond to the primary necessity of regulating preconventional behavior. However, in my opinion, they are ambiguous in that they might foster the belief that they say everything the corporation has to say about ethics and that whatever the corporation has to say about ethics is subject to its formal code. This is why some importance has been granted to other kinds of statements (like corporate "missions" or "visions") as attempts to express specific organizational proposals in positive terms.

In other words, what we again encounter as a constant in the various studies on corporate ethical codes and their practical application is a problem that our analysis of professional ethical codes had already revealed as fundamental: the danger that codes might contribute to the organization closing in on itself; the danger that they might become mere mechanisms of internal control, often impervious to any consideration which is not related to factors already established in the organization. Continuing the analogy with professional ethical codes, corporate ethical codes run the risk of being more deontological than ethical. They might thus fall into a deontological atomism, which cannot fit into the framework of civic ethics, and which is incapable of taking a dialogical approach.

Returning to my proposal of ethical integration as a frame of reference for BE (the principles of humanity, responsibility and development of persons), we can see that the dominant treatment of corporate ethical codes reveals a sharp break between their deontological dimension and the other two dimensions (responsibility and the development of persons). When corporate ethical codes are not integrated with the other dimensions of organizational ethics, they accentuate a passive attitude towards some standards and values proposed to the organization as a management tool rather than as the result of a process in which the affected parties also have a voice. Ultimately, the following questions are raised in relation to the feasibility of corporate codes: to what extent are they integrated in a broader process of (ethical) organizational development and are they confined to being an isolated moment (or playing an isolated role), suitable only for rhetorical and/or regulatory functions? I therefore think that the need for integration in BE is not only a theoretical necessity, but also a practical one inasmuch as an ethics of organizations can be developed in such a wide diversity of areas. Closer integration - and not merely in terms of methodology - of the stakeholder perspective analyzed in the preceding chapter and the perspective of corporate ethical codes could permit the latter to become an expression of the goods sought by the corporation and the values which make it possible to attain them. Corporate codes could then also become an expression of the corporation's acceptance of the values and rights it shares with society.

Thus, I consider that discussion on ethical codes should not be centered on their textual dimension. It should be centered on whether codes are the expression of a will to control and regulate or the expression of a will to construct an intersubjective framework of shared responsibilities. Just as we earlier raised the question of whether a corporate ethical code is primarily aimed at regulating preconventional behavior, affirming conventional demands and identities, or developing the capacity to adopt a postconventional approach to organizational life, we should now add that a code can and should perform these three functions. For this reason, we should not be limited by the formal conditions of corporate ethical codes as a literary genre. Instead, we should be much more concerned about fostering organizations' capacity to affirm their own intersubjective framework of shared responsibilities (thus understanding corporate ethical codes as one of several ways to create this framework).

Yet if we want codes to be open to a postconventional approach, they will have to explicitly state the procedure they involve. As far as codes are concerned, it will be necessary to accept that "the procedures by which rules and decisions are made are of equal importance to the values expressed in the decisions and rules themselves."[26] Only when we reach this level will codes become more than an expression of corporate self-reflection. They will also become an expression of corporate self-regulation as they will "recognize that corporate, professional deontological codes and external normative demands are necessary but insufficient. It is important to remember that, even if there is no explicit, well-defined and accepted corporate culture, there is always a corporate culture which serves to justify the decisions taken. One of management's most important tasks is to explain, define, accept, and revise the culture experienced. In other words, the first step in self-regulation is to make this experienced culture objective so that it can also become a culture of thought. But the aim of this exercise is not to achieve a merely cosmetic or decorative effect. The aim can be nothing other than being

---

[26] Donaldson, 1989, p. 133.

able to continually revise the culture experienced, making it more creative, more cooperative, and more responsible."[27]

What I propose, in short, is that those aspects of corporate ethical codes that deal with norms, express values and present guidelines should be integrated in the corporate code rather than presented separately: the text of corporate ethical codes cannot be dissociated from the context of corporate life and dynamics. This is why I have continually stressed that any discussion of corporate ethical codes must necessarily include an understanding of organizational cultures in ethical terms. Moreover, I believe that corporate ethical codes become unintelligible - and unfeasible - outside the context of the organizational culture.

Before proceeding to examine organizational cultures from an ethical perspective, I should, however, point out that this chapter has presented another of the elements necessary to shape an ethics of organizations: We should now have reached the point where we want to think carefully about and define the shared responsibilities in an organization and publicly express the criteria, values, and ends that identify them. In short, what is at stake here is the practical, explicit, and logical acknowledgement that all organizations express their values through their very activities and practices.

---

[27] Cortina, 1994c, p. 118.

CHAPTER 7

CORPORATE CULTURES: MANAGING VALUES?

In recent years, organizational culture has become one of the most popular subjects of management theory and practice.[1] According to Morgan (1986), understanding organizations as cultures has two particular strengths: it focuses attention on the symbolic meaning, or mystique, of many of the most rational features of organizational life, and it demonstrates that organizations are based on systems of shared meanings and frameworks of interpretation that create and re-create these meanings. This approach has introduced a whole new language in organizational studies - symbols, meanings, interpretative frameworks, etc.- a language which, at least initially, does not address the issues one assumes should be addressed when studying organizations: performance, efficiency, effectiveness, and the like.

Studying culture is by no means new to organizational research. It is a subject that is addressed in a good number of the classic descriptive studies on organizational behavior. However, it was not until the end of the 1970s that organizational culture became a subject of study in its own right. In other words, increased interest in organizational culture developed pretty much in parallel with BE's firm establishment as an academic discipline. Still, despite the amount of time that has elapsed since scholars of enterprises and organizations began focusing on the subject, no general consensus has been reached on the definition and use of the concept of organizational culture. To cite one significant example: Schein (1985) gives five reasons for writing a book on organizational culture, the second of which is there is confusion about the subject. He feels that the authors who write about corporate culture use different definitions and methods to establish what they understand by culture and different parameters to assess the way in which culture influences companies.

It should be noted that discussions on organizational culture basically revolve around the epistemological issues that underlie all organizational theory. Viewing organizations as cultures is novel in that it does not reduce them to their formal and rational dimensions. Instead, it leads us to seek another type of rationality. It is no longer a question of basing all decisions solely on economic objectives and quantitative techniques, but of also examining alternatives in terms of their consistency with organizational values. It is an approach that goes beyond the normal interpretation of Weberian tradition which sees certain organizational forms as an expression of rationality and focuses instead on the informal and non-rational features of organizational life that cannot be explained by "the paradigm of formal organizational structure".[2]

Smircich stresses that describing organizations with such well-worn metaphors as "machine" and "organism" has led to a deviation in both theory and practice:

---

[1] Note that according to "an analysis of the most popular management books published in 1990 the key buzz words for the early part of the decade are corporate culture, holistic, ethics and ecologically conscious management" (dierke and zimmerman, 1994, p. 533).

[2] Ouchi & Wilksins, 1985, p. 468.

"organizational theory is always rooted in the imagery of order [...] and development of organizational theory is a history of the metaphor of orderliness [...] What we see in the link between culture and organization is the intersection of two sets of images of order: those associated with organization and those associated with culture".[3] What then is the problem? That "prevailing theories assume that the coordination and control of activity are the critical dimensions on which formal organizations have succeeded in the modern world. This assumption is based on the view that organizations function according to their formal blueprints: coordination is routine; rules and procedures are followed and actual activities conform to the prescriptions of formal structure. But much of the empirical research on organizations casts doubt on this assumption".[4]

This approach then considers that formal structures and procedures actually work more like "myth and ceremony" (Meyer and Rowan, 1977) which clothe, legitimate and give meaning to certain practices with which they do not necessarily agree. Morgan (1986) has pointed out that modern organizations are sustained through a system of beliefs that underscores the importance of rationality, so that their legitimacy often depends on their skill in demonstrating the objectivity and rationality of their actions. If to this we add the impact on the organization's life of the influence of the socio-cultural context in which it operates, perhaps we will be better able to understand the increased attention now being paid to organizational cultures. In short, the aim is to more accurately explain the complexity of contemporary organizational reality.

7.1.   Some questions about the concept of organizational culture

Smircich proposed that the issue be systematically researched along five lines which boiled down to one basic alternative: considering culture as an organizational variable (whether independent or dependent, external or internal) or considering it as a metaphor for conceptualizing organization. The option was clearly expressed in the main question posed in her work: Do organizations have a culture or are they a culture?[5]

In terms of an ethics of organizations, the essential question is whether organizational culture is or is not another variable and, in consequence, if it can or

---

[3] Smircich, 1983, p. 341.
[4] Meyer & Rowan, p. 342.
[5] According to Smircich (1983, p. 342), research programs can be broken down by converging ideas on culture and organization, as follows:

Concept of culture (anthropology)	Research programs on organization and management	Concept of organizations (organization theory)
Serves human needs (functionalism)	Transcultural or comparative management	An instrument for fulfilling functions
Functions as an adaptive-regulatory mechanism (structural functionalism)	Corporate culture	Organizations which exist by virtue of their transactions with their environment
A system of shared Cognition (ethno-science)	Organizational cognition	A knowledge system
A system of shared Symbols and meanings (anthropology)	Organizational symbolism	A matrix for symbolic discourse
A projection of the Infrastructure of theUniversal unconscious Mind (structuralism)	Unconscious processes and organization	A manifestation of unconscious processes

cannot be accepted in a practical sense of managing values. One of the approaches which views culture as a variable considers individuals primarily as carriers of external cultural traits which they introduce into the organization. Another approach that sees culture as an organizational variable acknowledges that, in addition to contextual influences, organizations as such generate and develop socio-cultural features. Here culture "expresses the value or ideals and the beliefs that organization members come to share social. These values or patterns of belief are manifested by symbolic devices such as myths"[6]. But in the final analysis, the understanding of culture as a variable focuses on what can be done with and within a culture.

In contrast, the approach that affirms that culture is a metaphor for the organization and not an organizational variable "leaves behind the view that a culture is something an organization has, in favor of view that a culture is something an organization is.[7] Whether this is expressed as a concept of the organization which underscores its role as a generator of shared knowledge and images, as a concept of the organization as a matrix for symbolic discourse (which generates the symbols and myths of the organization itself), or as a concept of the organization in which organizational forms and practices are the manifestation of unconscious processes, this approach sees the organization not so much in terms of the results it obtains but in terms of the meanings it produces.

Be that as it may, I feel that the most important thing is that "whether one treats culture as a background factor, an organizational variable or as metaphor for conceptualizing organization, the idea of culture focuses attention on the expressive, non-rational qualities of the experience of organization. It legitimates attention to the subjective and interpretative features of organizational life".[8] It is therefore necessary to also incorporate a dynamic vision (Schein, 1985) which underscores not only the fact of organizational culture, but also the processes that comprise it, so that the discourse on corporate values legitimated by this approach is not reduced to a perspective that is merely analytical or instrumental.

To this end, Schein's approach provides us with several instruments which enable us to focus more closely on ethics.[9] Schein (1988) describes culture as a model of basic assumptions - invented, discovered or developed by a particular group determined to gradually learn how to confront its problems of external adaptation and internal integration - that have been influential enough to be considered valid and consequently taught to new members as the correct way of perceiving, thinking about and experiencing these problems. Schein focuses on leadership as the key factor in understanding and influencing corporate dynamics. Without dismissing his approach, I nevertheless feel that it is more important to explore corporate culture in the context of organizational processes (which obviously include leadership) because this provides a broader and more global view of the organization.

One then inevitably begins to wonder about the role of corporate culture in creating cohesion and guiding organizational change. But it is not a question of addressing

---

[6] Smircich, 1985, p. 344.
[7] Smircich, 1983, p. 348.
[8] Smircich, 1983, p. 355.
[9] Schein's work is considered among the most fundamental references. See also Bourcier (1988); Brown (1990); Drake and Drake (1988); Morgon (1986); Price- Waterhouse-Cranfield (1992); Weber (1993).

corporate culture according to the old paradigm that was primarily concerned with formalization and control, but to realize that "when we question whether or not 'a cultural framework' is a useful one, we need to ask more precisely, "Useful for whom and for what purpose?"[10] I feel that it is here that we can begin to link organizational culture with ethical thought: in the final analysis, talking about corporate culture always involves talking about a group, a content (values), certain (shared) borders, and a relationship between them, a diagnostic method and a training process that transmits this culture.

According to Gagliardi, this makes the task of creating and maintaining symbols of organizational culture perhaps one of the most important features of management. We should view "the creation of culture as a dynamic learning process"[11] on the basis of which both cultural values and their underlying assumptions are shaped, accepted, transmitted and possibly transformed. In this way, "the process by which a value system is born and consolidated can be explained on two levels: the psychological and the organizational and social"[12] which are interrelated to such an extent that it has been claimed that "any organization of work can be described as a 'psycho-structure' that selects and molds character"[13]

Thus, a distinction should be made between organizational processes that refer to the core of cultural identity (which tends to be enduring and difficult to change) and those that deal with expressions of this culture (which are easier to deliberately change). Change processes have traditionally been viewed as a matter of technological and structural change, employee skills and motivations. Although this vision is partly correct, genuine change also involves changing the images and values that guide actions. Change programs should therefore pay careful attention to the kind of corporate character required by particular situations. Assuming that the organization is based on shared frameworks of interpretation, the view of organizations as cultures makes it increasingly important to explore the changes in corporate culture that can facilitate organizational viability. This link between organizational and cultural change has led certain authors to stress that organizational culture is not only a matter of values but also of ethos.

In short, discussions on organization cultures (in all their dimensions) have ended up proposing an approach to companies and organizations that does not merely reduce them to their technical and formal aspects but also takes into consideration the meanings and values shared through company operations. The challenges (and ambiguities) of interpreting organizational cultures as ethics are underscored when we realize that in many cases corporate culture is understood not as a particular expression of human character and vitality, but as a new form of influence and control.

7.2.   Corporate culture and ethics: an ambiguous relationship

An analysis of the links between corporate culture and ethics can take two directions. On the one hand, corporate culture can be viewed as a fundamental ingredient in

---

[10] Smircich, 1983, p. 354.
[11] Gagliardi, 1986, p. 120.
[12] Gagliardi, 1986, p. 123.
[13] Macoby, 1976, p. 100.

institutionalizing ethics in organizations. On the other, it can be considered the backbone of corporate ethics, to such a point that occasionally the terms ethics and culture are confused.

Studies on organizational culture were quick to promote the idea that "organizational culture had great potential as a means of improving ethics in the organization".[14] Indeed, ethics and culture began to be confused from the moment in which both were able to share a reference to certain common values in an organization, values which supposedly embody basic shared beliefs about what work and the company are and signify for everyone involved in it.[15] In this way, the solution to the problem of the company as an ethical subject is sought in corporate culture: developing corporate culture would be the way to resolve the antinomy between individual and corporative values. In all events, what is definitely true is that "because the shared beliefs include values about what is desirable and undesirable - how things should and should not be - they dictate the kinds of activities that are legitimate and the kinds that are illegitimate."[16] The possibility of approaching organizational cultures from an ethical standpoint thus arises as soon as study of these cultures has verified that many of the thoughts and actions of individuals in organizations are culturally influenced, that individuals can act and operate according to different standards and criteria depending on the context, and that socialization processes in organizations are usually aimed at shaping individuals to fit into a normative structure.

Two approaches have been proposed with the aim of molding organizational culture towards ethical ends: "the first and most popular is the approach of creating a unitary corporate culture around ethical values [...]. The second fosters the co-existence and diversity within the organization of underlying national and racial cultures as well as professional and occupational sub-cultures [...] Each approach defines organizational culture and the nature or process of good ethics differently and each argues a different role for management in the shaping of ethical values"[17]

A unitary culture can be said to exist when the members of an organization share (and not simply give lip service to) certain values - which may involve ethics - to such an extent that they operate within the framework of certain norms regardless of the social or geographic setting in which they are located. In cases like this, the literary genre in which these shared values is publicly expressed is not a corporate code of ethics so much as a "credo" that understands the organization's goals as more than just economic performance. Discussions on this focus stress the danger of it becoming an imposition of management's ideology or outlook that uses an ethical discourse to legitimate its functions. It has also been pointed out that it is not necessarily the strongest cultures that get the best results. This is true only under certain circumstances and can cause a sort of strategic nearsightedness in the organization, making it less sensitive to changes in its environment. Lastly, it has been stressed that strong cultures socialize people in a way that closely resembles indoctrination (Pascale, 1985) so that,

---

[14] Sinclair, 1993, p. 6.

[15] "For a corporation to be morally excellent, it must develop and act out of a moral corporate culture" (Hoffman, 1986, p. 236)"

[16] Beach, 1993. p. 10.

[17] Sinclair, 1993, pp. 65-66.

in the final instance, individual autonomy can be watered down by collective, ostensibly moral, values.

In contrast, a fragmented culture indicates that the organization not only recognizes the existence of different viewpoints but also of different groups to which one can belong. This co-existence of various sub-cultures makes it more likely that the organization will have a certain dynamism and there will be a certain capacity for criticism. However, unless there are integrating features, this can unleash centrifugal forces. Nevertheless, recognizing the existence of a fragmented culture enables management to address the company's cultural dimensions, paying closer attention to process than to static features. "Both approaches contain different risks for business ethics. In the first approach, the risks are that the ethics are those of a managerial elite, out of touch with the environment in which the organization operates, or alternatively that these ethics are not internalized, but just given lip service by much of the organization. The risks in the second approach are that the plethora of competing values of subcultures allows deviant groups to flourish, leaving management unable to find a common basis on which to proceed and an anarchic or paralyzed organization. Each approach offers the opportunity for a different brand of ethics. A unitary, cohesive culture encourages adherence to certain recognized and reinforced standards of behavior. [...] In contrast, the sub-cultural approach eschews imposing standards but vests efforts in nurturing individual processes of self-inspection, critique and discussion".[18]

I feel, however, that both approaches are rooted in the conviction that personal and corporate excellence are closely intertwined and that organizational culture can be understood as the fit of personal dimensions with all the organizational dimensions (technical, economic, social and ethic). Bureaucracies no longer embrace all these dimensions and therefore the management approach needs to be changed: when the development of an organization includes recognition of cultural dimensions, "the role of management becomes a support for culture rather than control of the work force".[19]

This does not mean, however, that attention to organizational cultures detracts from attention to competitiveness. Instead, it means that in a complex society and a changing context corporate culture is also a key competitive factor. In short, due to the complexity of the bureaucratic system and the shortage of individual creativity and motivation, traditional coordination systems are inefficient in terms of integrating people. The idea then is to minimize these shortcomings by getting people to identify with the values and norms that guide their actions. "Ethics is profitable precisely because of its capacity to reduce the company's internal and external coordination costs because coordination takes place through the values of the institution and the individual and not through functional structures".[20]

In other words, ambiguous interpretations of the relationship between ethics and business culture occur when one accepts that "competitive advantage is gained through a dual focus: satisfying customers and developing people".[21] All business can be

---

[18] Sinclair, 1993, p. 71.
[19] Sherwood, 1988, p. 12.
[20] García, E., 1992, p. 40.
[21] Sherwood, 1988, p. 15.

assumed to strive for customer satisfaction, but it is not clear whether developing people refers to developing employees' personal qualities, their professional and organizational ties and commitments, their learning skills or their moral fiber. Thus, attempts must be made to clarify just what companies mean when they include human development as part of their organizational culture. But first and foremost, we need to discover whether or not human development includes recognition of individual autonomy or is limited simply to attempts to motivate and more closely integrate employees in order to ensure the organization's viability. Indeed, developing organizational change processes from the standpoint of organizational culture implies exercising an influence on features of organizational life that are susceptible to being understood in terms of ethics. But this does not mean that they are explicitly understood in this way. In other words, the fact that organizations are viewed as cultures implies using terms and concepts that are common to the field of ethics does not necessarily mean that an ethics of organizations is being developed.

The confusion becomes evident when comparing standard opinions with those of authors like Trevino (1990) who sees the issue as ethical change and development in organizations and feels that the way to achieve it is through corporate culture. "Organizational culture is created and maintained by a complex interplay of formal and informal organizational systems. Formally, leadership structure, selection systems, orientation and training programs, rules, policies, reward systems and decision-making processes all contribute to cultural creation and maintenance. Informally, the culture's norms, heroes, rituals, stories and language keep the culture alive and indicate to both organizational members and outsiders whether the formal systems reflect fact or facade"[22] In other words, the challenge here is to avoid the temptation to almost automatically consider the content of organizational culture as synonymous with "ethics". This temptation must be fought by critically examining the ingredients of the organization's culture and exploring how it relates to an ethical perspective.

What we must determine is the extent to which certain forms of organizational culture have eclipsed the fact that very close individual links with a company put certain aspects of personal development at risk. An unqualified declaration of organizational culture and what it means and entails could end up blurring or diluting everything that has to do with responsibility and individual autonomy. It is true that culture – and ethics – can reduce coordinating costs, but it is equally true that they can be seen simply as a new form of control that is probably better suited to contemporary social realities.

In short, the discourse on organizational cultures can lead one to conclude that the mutual influence of individuals and organizations (in terms of values) can easily lead to a situation in which personal values are colonized by their organizational counterparts. "A corporation is constituted both by its culture and by its individual members. The culture provides the relational framework of shared beliefs and values around which a collection of individuals is identified as a corporation. The morally excellent corporation is one that discovers and makes operational the healthy reciprocity between its culture and the autonomy of its individuals. [23]Still, we must acknowledge that what is usually most threatened by conflict over the discourse on organizational cultures is

---

[22] Trevino, 1990, p. 202.
[23] Hoffman, 1986, p. 235.

individual autonomy (among other reasons, because it is usually not even taken into consideration).

Thus, a superficial or non-critical reading could lead us to conclude that organizational culture makes it easier to make (moral) values an integral part of the things organizations must take into account if they are to be viable. "It seems, then, that one of the essential features of the cultures of the excellent corporations is the respect that is given and the space that is allowed for personal expression and initiative. Rather than the culture snuffing out individual autonomy, the culture itself is actually built on and around such autonomy"[24] Here, in turn, autonomy can be considered at once an organizational value (linked to initiative and development) and an ethical principle: "The nature of the moral corporate culture is the key [...] This moral culture, which gives meaning, identity and integrity to the whole corporate collective, must also value and encourage the moral autonomy of each of its individual members. To deny such moral autonomy is to cut off the possibility of rationally developing and examining the ethical principles of the culture itself and to fail to respect the persons making up the culture itself - both being violations of the moral point of view to which the culture is committed"[25] Is....or should be...committed? Because it is precisely this commitment to a moral stance that is usually lacking – at least explicitly – in the discourse on companies as cultures.

Although BE has not been discussed very often, the paradox of corporate culture is that its "moral" statement can also be an affirmation of individual submission and integration in the corporate status quo. In my opinion, the dilemma implicit in the contrast between affirming corporate values and manipulating people has strongly influenced the business world's recent fascination with excellence. I believe that confronting this dilemma is essential if we are to develop business ethics that are not overwhelmed by corporatist cultures. I believe that my analysis can show how the dilemma implicit in choosing between affirming corporate values and manipulating individuals has greatly influenced the discussions on excellence which have characterized corporate language in recent years.

7.3.   Ambiguities in the search for excellence

In my opinion, Peters and Waterman's (1982) book is first and foremost a sociological phenomenon. The sales figures bear this out. Although it was not very well-received in the academic world, everyone acknowledges that it drew attention to - and enshrined - a certain interpretation of organizational cultures and how they work. This interpretation was widely circulated and examined and this in itself is fairly significant.

Peters and Waterman define excellence in organizational terms and conclude that excellent companies share eight qualities. As Soeters (1986) noted, half of these attributes are not unfamiliar in the field of business management (a close-to-the-customer orientation, a competitive climate within the company, thus encouraging autonomy and entrepreneurship; a dislike of diversification, and a simple organizational structure), "but the other four characteristics concern the social and cultural side of the

---

[24] Hoffman, 1986, p. 239.
[25] Hoffman, 1986, p. 241.

organization".[26]   According to Peters and Waterman, excellent companies are distinguished by the very intensity of their deeply rooted convictions.[27] The most typical feature of the analysis and approach proposed by Peters and Waterman is thus their emphasis on companies as places where certain values are shared.

The other side of this same statement is the fact that neither formal and structural aspects nor rules and procedures are the most important things in terms of ordinary activities in excellent companies. What is more, we could say that the entire book could be taken as an attack on rationalist approaches to management, to such an extent that we could almost say that rationalism is the "enemy" of organizational cultures and value-based management. What Peters and Waterman do not make clear is whether their belligerent stance on what they call the "rationalist approach" is total and radical opposition or whether it is simply the result of realizing that the cultural focus used in excellent companies enables them to more easily obtain the same results as those sought by rationalist approaches. In other words, their discourse would be less innovative than it purports to be if it simply aimed to propose an alternative way to reach the same organizational goals as those set by proponents of the "rationalist" approach. In this case, these goals could only be rejected on grounds of their failure to take sufficient account of decisive organizational factors which cannot be either handled or expressed in rationalist terms. I do not deny the importance of their discourse but only want to point out that if this is their aim then their discourse is less radical than it purports to be because it does not alter the terms of the discussion on corporate aims, social functions and legitimacy.

"Peters and Waterman suggest that in excellent companies the integration of employees is a process of high intensity. As a matter of fact, integration and socialization processes never stop. The employees are constantly encouraged to spend their efforts and energy just for one goal: the company. They do not merely agree with the basic values of the organization, they are possessed by them. The values and norms of the personnel are supposed to be identical with the values and norms of the organization."[28]

Their understanding of excellence is rooted in what could be called normative anthropology. Peters and Waterman not only consider this as obvious but also as a justification of their ideas. Thus they begin by recognizing a very human need: the simultaneous search for self-determination and security. According to Peters and Waterman, excellent companies will be those that understand such important human needs and offer an opportunity to shine combined with a philosophy and a system of convictions that establish transcendent meanings. The culture of excellent companies, then, is what enables them to assert themselves as institutions that allow people to stand out in their jobs and be individually recognized for it, but in such a way that this takes place in the framework of the company's values, in accordance with them and as a result of employee identification with these values.

---

[26] Soeters, 1986, p. 301
[27] "According to P and W the most important task in management is making the employees fully aware of the 'basics'; the central values of the organization. [...] Thus the organizational culture, socialization processes and the integration of employees in the organization play a major role in P and W's analysis" (Soeters, 1986, p. 302).
[28] Soeters, 1986, p. 302.

In my opinion, this cannot be separated from a constant affirmation of the value and central role of employees (or individuals). People have to be treated like adults, or partners, with dignity and respect. They have to be treated as the main source of productivity increases. The basic lesson to be learned from excellent companies sums up as follows: if you want to increase productivity and obtain the consequent financial rewards, you have to treat your employees as your most important asset. Dignity, then, is not a matter of considering people as an end in themselves, but of viewing them as the most important corporate asset.

Leadership plays a decisive role in getting people to identify with corporate values. Apparently the idea is to take the human need to seek meaning and turn it into corporate returns. The mission of the leader then is to take whatever he can from the company's activity and make it into a lasting commitment to a new form of strategic management. In short: the leader manufactures meanings.

Peters and Waterman theorize that this creation of meanings and personal-institutional relations opens the door to the use of moral terms. They talk about leadership born of the human need for meanings, a leadership that creates institutional purpose. This kind of leadership would appear to operate in such a way that leaders and followers elevate one another to higher planes of motivation and morality. Various adjectives are used to describe such leadership: elevating, mobilizing, inspirational, exalting, improving, exhorting, evangelizing. According to Peters and Waterman, transformational leadership ultimately becomes moral leadership because it raises the level of human conduct and ethical aspiration of both leaders and followers and consequently transforms them both. It should be noted here that at some point the authors themselves mention the possibility that, taken to its extreme, this might turn companies into a sort of sect. Soeters (1986) states this outright. In short, this approach is an attempt at (moral) improvement that does not question the ethics of where the process leads or how it is justified.

I believe that the importance of Peters and Waterman's approach lies in the fact that it does not reduce companies merely to their economic operations. However, rather than broadening our view of the corporation by including its social aspects, they broaden it by emphasizing its cultural features. No mention is made of the company's social responsibility, yet excellent companies are considered to be those whose values include ideas on economic health, customer service and meanings for their personnel. But the way this is expressed only appears to confirm the suspicion that excellent companies bear a strong resemblance to sects: a characteristic of excellent companies is "their obsession with service" so that they "cling fanatically to their beliefs about service", which leads them to an "obsession with quality".

Thus, excellent companies' emphasis on listening to individuals, taking them into account, their stress on the importance of communication is all the result of their conviction that this is the best way to achieve the quality and service with which they are obsessed. Obviously, bureaucratic organizations and rational working systems do not lead people to share obsessions. But the fact that many of the best companies really consider themselves to be extended families[29] makes us wonder if this doesn't mean that they go so far as to consider their employees as mere infants.

Before going on to discuss the positive features of some of the ideas on companies as cultures, I feel that we should briefly re-examine Peters and Waterman's ideas in terms of ethics, especially inasmuch as they have been so widely circulated - and embraced. This is particularly important if we acknowledge that culture not only is, or could be, a very effective form of control (when it is taken truly to heart by individual employees), but that the very concept of excellence somehow includes the ideal of assimilating a strong culture and control (Sinclair, 1991). In short, "Peters and Waterman propagate a lot of human interest, but this attention tends to be manipulative. People are viewed as instrumental for productivity, not valued per se. Using symbolic management, legends, myths and so on, the leaders of the excellent companies try to guide their employees exactly in the direction they want".[30]

In other words, when corporate culture or values are self-affirming and need no social context, when they are affirmed as a form of organizational life without ethical justification, when they are affirmed with ethical pretenses while - paradoxically - being reluctant to undergo the winnowing out to which an ethical criticism would subject them, we have a form of management by values where "ethics" and "values" ultimately perform the same functions previously performed by control and discipline without really questioning the understanding of management and the organization. What happens then is that corporate values are first and foremost identified with "everybody cooperating", with group solidarity and adoption of the common project, with sharing group values; in short, with the aim of ensuring standard behavior with no disagreement over anything related to corporate objectives.

The idea, then, is not so much to deny the pertinence of viewing the company as a culture as to question whether this view implies no reference to its ethical and social legitimation. Just to take one example: there is something symptomatic about the fact that the discourse on corporate values has almost never coincided with the traditional concept of the business firm's social responsibility. As Le Mouël (1991) points out, management literature on values has addressed the "how" rather than the "why" so that terms like excellence, motivation, shared business project, values, and so on have become part of a management jargon that frequently serves no purpose beyond the strictly ideological. Worse still, all organizations try to encourage individuals to adhere to them, not by physical force as in the 19th century but by exercising a mental pressure that works the same way as bonds of love, i.e. identification, idealization, pleasure and anxiety.

Thus, adherence to certain shared values becomes part of an attempt to manage by merging the meaning of life and the meaning of work within a business project that reconciles personal interests and goals with their corporate counterparts. The company will attempt to respond to the hopes and dreams of every individual, structuring their mental representations in accordance with corporate culture: adhesion is achieved by linking the company's socio-cultural world with the individual's psychosocial world.

---

[29] The term is not mine. Authors have found that the words "family", "extended family" and "family spirit" are widely used in the following excellent companies: Wal-Mart, Tandem, Hewlett-Packard, Disney, Dana, Tupperware, McDonald's, Delta, IBM, TRI, Levi-Strauss, Blue Bell, Kodak, Procter & Gamble, 3 M.

[30] Soeters, 1996, p. 309. See also Scott & Mitchell, 1986.

The company is not solely a combination of functions destined to satisfy consumers' material needs. It also creates a social group that attempts to respond to a series of questions about purpose and existence. It should be able to give meaning to life in order to become more human (Aubert and Gaujelac, 1991). My aim, then, is to try to discover whether this ability to imbue life with meaning is intended to humanize business organizations or introduce a new form of submission that infantilizes employees and cultivates narcissism. By calling on excellence, the organization proposes that individuals immerse themselves in their jobs as a defense against anxiety, an anxiety the organization itself constantly helps produce.[31]

In the final instance, then, what I am discussing here is not the interpretation of companies as cultures but an overly pragmatic vision of corporate culture that is in fact self-affirmative, ignoring the autonomy and dignity of the individuals who form part of it. To the extent that this is true, we should not be surprised that so many analogies have been discovered between the way excellent companies treat leadership, values and the group spirit and what sociological studies have revealed about sects. But we should also recognize that the empirical discourse of organizations as creators of meaning can have consequences that are not necessarily contradictory in terms of certain ethical criteria.

I further believe that this involves shaping a more complex vision of the organization, whose rules could thus aim to integrate those dimensions in which, like it or not, the company is by nature implicated. The goal would be to integrate economic profitability, ecological awareness and social responsibility and promote a personal balance that respects individual autonomy. Once again, the question of integration appears to be essential, among other reasons because, as we have already seen, each of the different dimensions of BE usually has considerable trouble acknowledging the others. But, above all, it should be pointed out that the issue of integration is at once a theoretical and practical problem of understanding organizations as well as an ethical problem because reflections on the ethics of corporate cultures need not be simply critical in terms of humanity or the affirmation of responsibility. Reflections on ethics can also acknowledge that corporate cultures have made it possible for BE to initiate a dialogue with the Aristotelian tradition which makes it possible to criticize the ethics of a vision that sees the company as a culture while still remaining sensitive to its particular contributions.

7.4.   Opening the door to Aristotelian tradition

BE has traditionally not been very sensitive to the Aristotelian tradition.[32] Nevertheless, organizational culture[33] has opened the door slightly. Still, the results have been ambiguous because organizational discourses involving values or styles of action have sometimes been automatically identified with the Aristotelian viewpoint (or simply with ethics). Thus, certain Aristotelian-based approaches have had to take a distance from

---

[31] I believe that this explains the "admirable" dedication to work which usually goes hand in hand with excellence.

[32] One has only to leaf through business ethics manuals and textbooks to see that their focus is almost exclusively utilitarian and deontological

[33] It is significant that Solomon (1993) chose the title *Ethics and Excellence* for his Aristotelian approach to business ethics. In one of its chapters, he describes organizational culture as an Aristotelian metaphor.

some features of the discourse on organizational culture. To sum up, then, I believe I can safely say that, compared to other lines of thought, the Aristotelian tradition is still in swaddling clothes and continues to be overshadowed by the discourse on organizational cultures. However, I also feel that it is with these very cultures that the tradition might have the closest affinity.

The specific contribution of Aristotelian tradition to business ethics is not a recovery of Aristotle's vision of economic activity, but a change of perspective. Instead of viewing business ethics as an applied deduction of ethical doctrines or as the result of an ethics or philosophy of economics, proponents of Aristotelian-based business ethics consider that "What we need in business ethics is a theory of practice, an account of business as a fully human activity in which ethics provides not just an abstract set of principles of side-constraints or an occasional Sunday school reminder but the very framework of business activity".[34] In other words, this view is critical of business ethics which have traditionally been more concerned with actions than with agents (Klein, 1989)."The problem is not Aristotle' own prejudice toward business, which is in any case secondary to the importance of his theories. The problem is very much like the preference for impersonal policy and the theorist's timidity with all considerations that even hint at the personal. Both deontological ethics and utilitarianism stress the importance of broad general principles, which can then be applied to particular cases. It is the nature of the Aristotelean approach, by contrast, to start with the particular community and context and understand cases (and abstract principles) within that community and context.[35]

The idea then is to "develop a more appropriate focus for business ethics theory, one that centers on the individual within the corporation".[36] However, it is not simply a focus on individuals, but on individuals in the context of the corporation and, moreover, on the corporation in the context of society. Thus this approach implies that all aims must be placed within a context: individuals in the corporation and the corporation in society. Individual good cannot be viewed independently but must be understood in terms of what it contributes to the corporate good and, through this, to the good of society. We thus arrive at a contextualized vision in which the corporation shapes the characters of its members - all its members, not just its senior management personnel.

This alters and enhances the conventional approach to one of the core issues of organizational life: decision making. One cannot speak of management without referring to decision making. Rather than viewing decisions as the outcome of a process that can be understood in terms of strategic or calculated rationality, Aristotelian-influenced business ethics views actions and decisions, be they strategic or ethical, as an expression of individuals' characters and habits in the context of their organizational life. "Simplifying a good deal, the first model of moral choice affirms the primary importance of conscious deliberation while the second emphasizes character".[37] Consequently, this would lead to an ethical view of organizations as instrumental in

---

[34] Solomon, 1993, p. 99.
[35] Solomon, 1993, p. 113.
[36] Solomon, 1992, p. 319. See also Norton (1988) who argues that contemporary ethical issues are born of practical problems and cannot be resolved by resorting to abstract principles, but by asking ourselves what human good is at stake and what understanding of the good life is implicit in the option taken.
[37] Paine, 1991, p. 71. We agree with the author, who immediately goes on to state his conviction that "these two models of choice are not necessarily rival models".

shaping their members' characters. There is, then, a shift in viewpoint which now embraces companies and organizations in terms of their assets (the attainment of which is their objective) and not just in the performance registered or their social function. Making business practice an affirmation of the internal good and a way to cultivate it is not an easy task because neither the market nor companies encourage actions that are guided by intrinsic values.[38] But the ethical view of organizational cultures aims precisely to go beyond the paradigm of rational maximization of one's own interest as the key to interpreting organizational life and approaching it from the paradigm - and the conviction - that "a commitment to moral ideals and principles becomes a part of one's self-interest as an agent, a part of one's identity as a professional [...]. Virtue talk stands in contrast to regulatory ethics mainly because it is as concerned with the agent's being as with his doing. Virtue talk involves notions of character, habit, disposition, inclination. It implies a way of being in the world, a general orientation towards goodness on the part of the self in the living of a whole life".[39]

Still, we must remember that this implies the existence of certain shared beliefs based on certain shared experiences, among which is the idea that the common good contextualizes corporate actions rather than reducing them to the work of an "invisible hand" (Solomon, 1992). Nevertheless, Aristotelian-type business ethics do not always go so far as to consider that "ethical knowledge, like all social knowledge, is created and maintained through processes of socialization and legitimation [...]. Different organizations provide very different experiences of organizational reality, somewhat analogous with the idea of different corporate cultures".[40] Therefore, the possibility of a narrow reading that deviates from Aristotelian tradition corresponds symptomatically with tendencies to always identify corporate cultures with what we earlier referred to as "strong" cultures.

Thus, if, on the one hand, we recognize that " the basic values that guide an organization help to mold the character of the people in the firm (by nurturing certain habits) [and that] moral virtue and organizational values are, therefore, intimately connected"[41] and, on the other that "the culture metaphor has limitations too, and one of them is that it still tends to be too self-enclosed"[42]. It is symptomatic that overcoming this problem has been approached both in terms of a strictly Aristotelian tradition and in terms of embracing a civic outlook.[43] We could say that the aim here is to bring integration and autonomy to the corporation without resorting either to a socialization that focuses merely on adaptation or to subjectively-focused individualism... and, moreover, to do it as a management process.

In my view, here again we have two obstacles to developing the contributions of BE and the vision of the company as a culture. First of all, it is still too soon to analyze corporate cultures in terms of Aristotelian ethics. Secondly, we have the problems

---

[38] Norton (1988) has suggested that they usually tend to almost exclusively encourage rewards that are not inherent in practices themselves.

[39] Jennings, 1991, p. 565.

[40] Philips, 1991, pp. 794-789.

[41] Klein, 1989, p. 62.

[42] Solomon, 1993, p. 134.

[43] "That's what civic discourse is all about. It is about the kind of society we want to have and to build. How do we want to distribute power and authority? To what ends to de want to use technology and professional expertise?" (Jennings, 1991, p. 567).

caused by an excessive contrast between liberal and communitarian approaches. I believe that practical use of the distinction between the conventional and post-conventional approaches and between ethics of minimums and ethics of maximums would enable us to address some of these questions.

I feel that it is important to note that there is room for a critical reading of organizational cultures even within Aristotelian tradition. There is no need to take an exclusively postconventional stance. The vision of excellence, as symbolized in the work of Peters and Waterman (1982), is reduced to (professional) success (Camps, 1990) and to a hollow cliché (Solomon, 1993). It is not a question of accepting a point midway between two extremes and developing it to its fullest, but of reaching the furthest end of one extreme. It is not an excellence that is suited to its subject, but an external demand expressed as a requirement for competitiveness. It is not an excellence that is linked to practice, but one that depends on results which are unconnected with practice.

That is why I believe that we should perhaps join Solomon (1993) in saying that "it is the role of the individual in the corporation (and of the corporation in society) that concerns me, not the individual alone, not the structure of the corporation abstracted from the individuals that are its members (and not the nature of capitalism, abstracted from the character of particular corporations and the communities they serve). That is why the idea of business as a practice is absolutely central to this approach: it views business as a human institution in service to humans and not as a marvelous machine or in terms of the mysterious 'magic' of the market".[44]

Consequently, the Aristotelian approach to business ethics emphasizes specific aspects of corporate life[45] which are integrated in a global vision. I feel that, among them, community should now be stressed as a way of understanding the corporation that makes it clear that our activities (personal and professional) acquire a meaning in the context of our membership in organized groups and not individually or before undertaking professional commitments. This certainly presupposes that organizations are heterogeneous groups, but also that their actions and the actions of their members are understood and justified by their links to their own context.[46] Therefore "the Aristotelian approach to business ethics presumes concrete situations and particular people and their places in organizations".[47] An Artistotelian approach to business ethics always refers to people within their contexts, both when attempting to shape a reflection and when trying to facilitate processes designed to improve morals. This does not mean that it ignores

---

[44] Solomon, 1993, pp. 103-104.

[45] Solomon (1992) proposed as a framework for virtue ethics in business: community, excellence, role identify, holistic integrity and judgement. See other less systematic approaches (which usually include some of the points discussed by Solomon) in Duska (1993, Jennings (1991), Hart (1992), Klein (1989), Malloy & Lang (1993), Norton (1988, Paine (1991).

[46] "Aristotelian ethics takes both the corporation and the individual seriously without pretending that either is an autonomous entity unto itself. Corporations are made up of people and the people in corporations are defined by the corporation [...] Communities are essential units of morality, and corporations are ultimately judged not by the numbers but by the coherence and cooperation both within their walls and with the larger communities in which they play such an essential social as well as economic role," Solomon, 1993, p. 152.

[47] Solomon, 1993, p. 162.

today's diversity of roles and commitments. Quite the opposite, in fact.[48] But neither does it mean blindly accepting it as good, as an unsurpassable and irrefutable fact.

Getting back to what I said earlier, the aim is to link personal belonging and autonomy, which is unquestionably a complex and difficult task. But I also believe that this is a fundamental aspect of the framework of ethical reference proposed in this approach to business ethics.[49] Because it can reach a point where it is of such decisive importance in the complexity of contemporary organizations, moral exemplarity should be given more importance than it is usually assigned by approaches which are less sensitive to the role of context, history and narrations in shaping corporate ethics. Because, when all is said and done, it is through moral examples that the corporation transmits practical knowledge of how one should live. This therefore makes professional careers susceptible to being interpreted and perceived in terms of their exemplarity. Consequently, we can consider the possibility of not limiting our understanding of decision making to an application of strictly rational criteria (which, moreover, does not coincide with the way people really act and decide). Deciding is tantamount to constructing an interpretation of a situation (an interpretation which always takes place within the context of a history and a process). Failure to realize this can be not only a shortcoming in terms of ethics but can also lead to a simplistic understanding of decisions as such because it ignores the importance of character and virtues in developing a practical wisdom that enables one to be discerning rather than merely analyzing the situations that require decisions. In organizational terms, this means having a mental picture of corporate actions as part of the overall scene rather than reducing them to strategic calculations or confrontations. Our complex and interdependent society of organizations appears to require a frame of reference that is holistic rather than individualistic, able to consider the whole and not just the sum of its parts and, what is more, able to understand the role of the parts within the whole. It then becomes possible to view stakeholders not just in terms of the interests at stake or their consequences for the various groups involved in corporate activities but by weaving this set of relations into a more global and all-embracing perception of reality.

7.5.   Final considerations: the outlook for BE

I believe that the possibilities of engaging in a dialogue with Aristotelian tradition in order to link the view of organizations as cultures to the idea of BE are still largely pending development and that there are only preliminary indications of the path that should be followed.[50] It certainly seems difficult to refute the assumption that the vision

---

[48] "Virtues tend to be context-bound, but contexts overlap and clash with one another. In any organization, there are overlapping and concentric circles of identity and responsibility, and a virtue in one arena may conflict with a virtue in another – indeed it may even be a vice [...] We always wear multiple hats and have potentially competing responsibilities. There is no denying the disunity of the virtues. But neither is there any denying the fundamental importance of role identity in establishing the contextual basis for virtue in business." (Solomon, 1993), p.167.

[49] "It is the divided self that makes integrity so important to us, a kind of coordination problem as well as an ideal in ethics" (Solomon, 1993, p. 169). "This would not have surprised the ancients, who recognized *integration* as the first problem of worthy living" (Norton, 1988, p. 57).

[50] See Duska (1993) for an analysis of what the Aristotelian tradition can contribute to business ethics. The author's premises strike me as highly questionable, among other reasons because he links the possibility of this contribution to a non-critical acceptance of certain premises inherent to the postmodern discourse.

of the organization as a culture (and everything this implies) makes a significant contribution towards a de facto understanding of organizations. It also appears difficult to reject the idea that "applied ethics is not just a matter of applying general principles, but also of discovering the internal good which each of these activities should provide to society, what goals each should pursue and what values and habits must be inculcated in them in order to reach these goals". What's more, the consideration of business and organizations could be seen as one of the "social spaces" in which it might be possible to regain a sense of belonging; as a "social space" in which it is possible to forge bonds and create identities in relation to certain ends, and also as a "social space" in which it is possible to create an added value understood and experienced as one's personal contribution - through the organization - to society and the common good. In this way, businesses and organizations could reach a point where they are also "ethical spaces", understood now as the social space where organizational particularities are the basis for shaping "an ethos as a space for innovation, cooperation and responsibility" [51]

When it comes right down to it, this space can only be ethical[52] if attempts are made to develop a post-conventional[53] internal moment as a constituent feature of the corporate culture itself and we do not simply bless with the name of ethics any discourse that talks about corporate culture, no matter how much this discourse might include morally relevant and attractive values. Otherwise, as we have already seen, corporate cultures can end up legitimating new forms of manipulation and control without in any way acknowledging the human condition of their members. I personally believe that ethical thought can provide a critical and innovative interpretation of the possibilities and limitations of the vision of businesses as cultures. This was eloquently expressed by Conill, who wrote, "curiously enough, in the context of modern societies business economics frequently insists on returning to a pre-modern model of ethics as the most appropriate way to empower the business as an institution. This model recognizes the importance of individual satisfaction and self-realization within a company, viewed as a community, in which the individual feels integrated. Because, as is the case with the Aristotelian model of polis, the aims (interests) of the individual coincide with those of the group so that integration in the company, harmony and a spirit of cooperation among corporate members benefits employers and employees alike. The idea, then, is to recover a communitarian model of ethics in order to achieve institutional integration, not to speak of global and complete social integration. This then is the reason for again proposing virtues, attitudes and codes of conduct in which excellence plays an important part. We could then say that in a modern or post-modern context like ours, the model most frequently proposed by the business version of economic ethics is a pre-modern, communitarian model. It seeks

---

[51] Cortina, 1994, p. 96.

[52] Nevertheless, this ethical space cannot be shaped solely on the basis of cultural aspects and this is a significant feature of my approach. Shaping it in terms of corporate culture is a necessary condition (and there is increasing agreement on this) but it is not sufficient (and not enough emphasis has as yet been placed on this). That is why Weber (1993) insists that business ethics that are sensitive to the reality of the company as a culture can be a key factor in corporate viability (and, of course, its profitability), but only if organizational culture in its formal expression (codes, missions, etc.) is linked to well thought out specific training programs and reward systems. Trevino (1990) considers that organizational change processes based on an ethically shaped cultural outlook should address the organization's formal and informal systems equally and cannot be the result of a top-down approach.

[53] I have discussed this issue in detail in Lozano (1995)

cooperation through a community of interests, identifying individual values with those of the business organization, and expects that by virtue of this cooperation the company will become increasingly competitive. However, we must not forget that modern economics is one of the things that has caused social differences and therefore requires an ethical model that is not only communitarian but specifically modern in its rational structure". [54]

When taking the organization into consideration we must attempt to address the totality of persons and their interactions and relations. In this sense I feel that we can speak of ethics as a factor in integrating people in a corporation. But this must not be done from a purely individualistic vision but from a corporate understanding of dialogue because, among other things, integration always has a strong relational component. The idea, in short, is to not confuse integration with standardization but to make it possible for shared diversity to exist in the organization, jointly promoting belonging and autonomy. [55] In the final instance, "the value of a shared mission is not the outcome of the shared agreement itself, but the opportunity it creates for the tolerance of discord, for creative individual expression. [...]. Agreement, in fact, is never identity, and so even the appearance of unanimous agreement is only a comforting fiction". [56] I therefore believe that ethical integrity [and ethics as integration] in an organization must also be linked to dialogue, to the recognition of diversity and to promoting development processes and not be viewed simply as a way to make everyone alike or cut down coordination costs.

This will force us, in the final chapters of this book, to question the extent to which one of BE's most fundamental future challenges will be its ability to promote not only a corporate culture but also to foster a certain human quality while respecting the particularities of each organization and the maturity of its members. Indeed, if up to now it has been true that "designing a corporate culture, like designing a social or political culture puts into play an image of man which is not always clarified." [57], we must now ask ourselves whether one of the core requirements of BE today is not precisely this clarification.

I would suggest that we stop here a moment to review what this chapter has added to our approach to BE. One way to put it would be to say that we have explicitly focused on the moral subject. Incidentally, this is something,, which is still recent in the context of BE, if we recall that in Chapter Four I noted that even when BE is approached as a "tool box" the absence of references to the Aristotelian tradition can be interpreted as BE being insensitive to the moral subject. The open dialogue between views of the company as a culture and the contributions of traditional virtue ethics has facilitated not only affirmation of the moral subject as an essential issue for BE but also affirmation of the need for the business world to develop a set of conventional morals that make the BE discourse meaningful and relevant. And this is valid for all types of organizations, not simply business organizations as is usually the case with BE.

---

[54] Conill, 1993, p. 25.
[55] "When individuals become members of an organization, deliberate efforts must be made to support their autonomy while not sacrificing their membership or their bonds with one another." (Srivastava & Barrett, 1988, p. 305).
[56] Srivastava & Barrett, 1988, p. 308
[57] Cortina, 1994c, p. 115.

But I have also pointed out the need to overcome an ambiguity that is always latent in the idea of corporate culture: the tendency to see ethics and corporate culture as synonymous.. This reductionism is the practical expression of what was already analytically revealed: the tension between business ethics and ethics in business; the temptation for companies and organizations to go beyond pre-conventional approaches, introducing conventional morals that are incapable of achieving a post-conventional perspective; the danger of formulating a business ethics whose moral discourse is insensitive to the principle of humanity. In short, my hypothesis is that without corporate culture there can be no BE, but making BE synonymous with a corporation's culture ultimately leads to the disappearance of ethics as such.

Assuming that my hypothesis is correct and inasmuch as my analysis indicates that BE must be constituted as an ethics of responsibility, an ethics of humanity and as an ethics that will generate a set of conventional morals, the challenge that faces us now is not simply to specifically acknowledge the forms in which organizations translate the different dimensions of ethics (which we have discussed in relation to stakeholders, business codes and principles, and organizational cultures). Indeed, probably the most specific challenge facing BE as applied ethics within the framework of a hermaneutics of responsibility is the challenge of integrating all these varied dimensions.

CHAPTER 8

INTEGRATING ETHICS IN ORGANIZATIONS

After pointing out the various fields in which there has been some progress in incorporating ethics in business life, we need to explore the possibilities of a more integrated global view and to indicate the possible paths towards this integration.

I believe my approach has undeniable advantages because it takes the organization as such as its central object, rather than focussing (as a system) on the treatment of concrete questions - or questions inherent to particular functional areas. No doubt BE as applied ethics needs to develop ways of treating the variety of concrete problems posed in corporate practice. But none of them can be solved unless BE's frame of reference is a global view of the organization that is able to introduce an ethical perspective.

However, the integration we seek should use dialogue to expand the established coordinates of ethical reflection. It is essential to ask whether BE can be an ethics of responsibility, attentive to the consequences of actions; whether it can be an ethics that affirms the principle of humanity, attentive to the dignity of human beings acknowledged as valid interlocutors; and whether it can be an ethics that generates conventional morality, attentive to the development of individual subjects in terms of attaining certain goods through shared practices.

These three dimensions must be integrated in BE because they cease to be dynamic when they are turned into separate absolute references. When this happens, responsibility is reduced to a form of consequentialism, ignoring the criteria and purposes that render it intelligible as well as the principles in which it is rooted, such as the attention to acting subjects. Humanity is reduced to the affirmation of abstract principles; it becomes insensitive to context, indifferent to consequences, and ignorant of concrete subjects. And conventional values are reduced to a cultural identity closed within itself: they become impermeable to criticism, incapable of both self-criticism and dialogue, and they proclaim themselves without considering their responsibilities.

This triple reductionism is especially disturbing in the context of a society of organizations marked by the importance assigned to fast development and scientific and technological innovations. Responsibility is not a mere consequentialist datum; it only becomes significant and operative when it is framed by the principle of humanity and linked to the configuration of responsible subjects. Thus BE will have to show how taking the following aspects into account is viable and significant in organizational terms: (1) the consequences of actions for the affected parties, (2) the principle of humanity, which includes the acknowledgment of others as valid interlocutors, and (3) the need to shape a certain conventional morality that can generate identity with the practices and goods at stake in all organizational projects. Up to this point I have attempted to reconstruct each of these three dimensions of BE in both organizational and management terms.

First, I explored the materialization of BE as an ethics of responsibility through the consideration of stakeholders as affected parties, involved or interested in the organization's activities. This perspective enables us to perceive and analyze organizations taking into account their interrelations with all the affected parties, no matter how minor their roles. But I have also pointed out that this approach involves a tendency to see organizational interrelations only in terms of interests, without acknowledging that others are also affected or are valid interlocutors. I have stressed that overcoming this reduction of interrelations to the organization's interests cannot be brought about only through stakeholder analysis. Morever, I have also pointed out that drawing up a map of stakeholders allows us to view corporate responsibilities in more objective terms and it further allows us to rethink the idea of organizations incorporating this ethical dimension. For BE, then, consideration of stakeholders is crucial, but not sufficient because it does not in itself explain the criteria and values guiding corporate relations with stakeholders nor does it address the quality of the subject who develops in these interrelations as both an individual and a member of the corporation Therefore, stakeholder analysis provides a useful guide for developing a consequentialist perspective, but it does not in itself provide the criteria needed to weigh the quality and hierarchy of the interests at stake or the quality of the subject that is developed by satisfying these interests. I repeat then that considering stakeholders is a necessary but insufficient part of BE. It is necessary because it allows us to construct and reach a considered understanding of corporate responsibilities. It is insufficient because BE still needs a critical frame of reference within which to consider interests in such a way that the goals that drive and channel these interests can be developed internally and contextualized socially.

Secondly, I explored the materialization of BE as an ethics of humanity by exploring the self-regulation processes through which organizations express their values, goals, and criteria for action. I pointed out that this can be done by emphasizing the negative aspects (regulating the limits beyond which one must not go or the positive aspects setting an appealing horizon, which should orient organizational development). I also made two other points. First, in practice negative aspects often prevail over positive ones. And second, organizations do not act directly in accordance with the principle of humanity, but indirectly, when they are filtered by autonomy and the acknowledgment of others as interlocutors who have their own processes for constructing corporate criteria, values, and goals. Since the principle of humanity is customarily adopted indirectly, it is threatened mainly by the possibility of being diluted - and disappearing - in the mediations.

What we could call the reflective-normative moment of an organization is visualized and objectified through the formulation of corporate codes, missions, creeds, principles, etc. Critical acceptance of the principle of humanity as an internal moment of this process (which I have associated with the interiorization of civic ethics) is what allows us to speak of responsible self-regulation, which cannot be confused with the mere exactment of some functional rules of the game for the organization. In short, the issue is to fit together the regulation of preconventional behavior, the acceptance of conventional values and the development of a postconventional capacity without confusing them with one other and without eluding the critical - but also dynamic - function of the postconventional moment. Earlier, I asked whether many corporate discourses (and texts) that talk in axiological terms aim to attain a greater moral quality in the corporation or achieve more control over it. At that time I was simply anticipating what I said later when I talked about the difference between open and closed corporate cultures. This can now be restated as follows: if a corporation's axiological discourse loses its postconventional perspective, it becomes an autistic discourse, which closes the organization in itself and which is used by senior executives as a management tool. Therefore, we can conclude that the reflective-normative moment is as necessary to organizations as it is insufficient. It is necessary because it contributes to the acceptance of the principle of humanity. It is insufficient because, as we have seen, it usually considers neither the incorporation of stakeholders nor the subjects who should accept this principle. Therefore, it can foster a kind of corporate deontological atomism which is less than sensitive to social and personal contexts. Certainly, it is necessary for an organization to build an intersubjective framework of responsibilities and shared aims. But it is also necessary not to reduce ethics to this reflective-normative moment since BE addresses processes. Neither should BE simply follow texts if it is to prevent organizations from using a text about values to cover up a lack of profound personal experience of these values.

Third, and last, the materialization of BE as an ethics that generates a conventional morality has been explored through a reading of different perspectives, which allows us to see corporations as cultures. This has enabled us to see that an organization is also a space where particular goods are attained by engaging in particular practices. This implies taking into consideration the fact that the members of every organization develop certain habits, motivations, and sensitivities; that organizations form a sense of identity and belonging, and that they are guided by a particular understanding of excellence. None of these ethical dimensions is contained in more rationalist and formal approaches, but they do appear in organizational cultures and can be expressed independently of whether or not culture is considered a variable. To put it briefly, this attention to corporate values is based on the recognition that any organizationally mediated action has an aim and that this aim can be interpreted in terms of values. These values should not be understood only as a statement of preferences, but also as the configuration of a corporate ethos, of an ethical space that embraces assumptions and beliefs as well as forms and styles of action.

At the same time, this allows us to address organizational dynamics (without maintaining a static approach) and ask ourselves about the quality of subjects shaped by the organization. From this standpoint it is possible to ask about the development of the person within the organization. But it is also true that when affirmation of a corporate culture is not modulated in a civic and postconventional way, it does not provide the resources to prevent reducing it to a simple internalization or indoctrination of collective values. In other words, a corporate culture personalizes, but does not individualize. And it does so precisely to the extent that it facilitates a merger between the meaning of life and the meaning of work, or, in other words, to the extent that it reduces personal life to professional life. I therefore believe that all dimensions developed through a consideration of organizational cultures are a necessary but insufficient part of BE. They are necessary because they allow us to understand the meaning of organizational practices and give the fullest meaning to the subject´s moral force and constitution. They are insufficient because corporate cultures often affirm values without acknowledging responsibilities or considering stakeholders, and because corporate cultures do not always acknowledge subjects in their autonomy nor do they heed the minimum demands of civic ethics.

(reflective-normative moment)
CODE/MISSION/VISION

Ethics of/in organizations

STAKEHOLDERS   ORGANIZATIONAL CULTURE
(consequentialist moment)   (conventional moment)

   Stakeholders (as referring to the consequentialist moment), codes (as referring to the reflective-normative moment), and cultures (as referring to the conventional moment) have allowed us to emphasize the dimensions of a BE that corresponds to a hermeneutics of responsibility as presented in Chapter 1. We have also seen that each of these dimensions underscores a fundamental aspect which would not be viable or consistently sustainable if it did not integrate the other dimensions.
   I think that the practical significance of my approach lies in these three essential aspects: first, it proposes rules for articulating three dimensions that are usually considered separately; secondly, it enables us to reflect on ethics in strictly organizational terms and on the basis of discourse that refers to the organization as such; and thirdly, it entails an approach not restricted to corporations, but feasible for all types of organizations. Nonetheless, I have so far accentuated the strictly analytical aspects of this approach and, to a lesser extent, static ones, strongly emphasizing the need for integration. What we need to look at now is what this proposed integration would be like, assuming that it must be more than a mere combination of the points I have presented up to now. Thus I will now discuss some of the fields in which this integration could take place.

8.1.   The paths towards integration: decision-making, a fact or a process?

Nielsen (1988, 1989) has insisted that ethical thinking, especially in BE, does not follow the same logic when it is knowledge-oriented as when it is action-oriented. This means that if BE really wants to be an applied ethics of corporations and organizations, it has to be on the scene when actions occur. Moreover, if it is true that action always includes a moment of decision, decision-making becomes omnipresent - figuratively and literally - in the organizational world. As a result, an ethics for decision-making has sometimes been BE's only touchstone.
   There have been many attempts to draw up models that allow an ethical (theoretical and practical) approach to decision-making and whose ultimate subjects are individuals.

But, "in general, the ethical decision-making models divided the postulated influences on an individual's decision behavior into two broad categories. The first category includes variables associated with the individual decision maker. The second category consists of variables which form and define the situation in which the individual makes decisions."[1] From this, it appears that taking individuals as a reference is essential, at least at the outset, since only in relation to them can we talk of a rational use of information, will, and intentionality. But even should we want to confine ourselves to the individual aspect, we cannot overlook the existence of the organization.

Although it is not always acknowledged, decision-making processes tend to formally accept some common minimum points of reference. In short, what this formal analysis does is sequentially dissect the steps that ought to be taken in order to make a decision: identifying the type of problem, analyzing it, making a preliminary decision, considering alternative solutions, evaluating these alternatives, deciding on a solution, planning the action, implementing it and assessing the results. It is important to keep this in mind because most models of ethical decision-making (both those that address decision-makers and those that focus on their situation) accept these steps as a reference, albeit not always explicitly.

It must therefore be pointed out that the various BE proposals based on ethically evaluating one decision accept the model described above, simply adding their specifically ethical considerations. And this is true regardless of whether the proposal is made by a corporation, a theorist or a scholar of BE,[2] and regardless of the moral philosophy adopted.[3] These proposals make us see that decision-making process is an especially appropriate time for incorporating the consequentialist ethical dimension. Furthermore, they allow us to see that it is an especially suitable time to realize exactly what a reflective-normative moment is. Nonetheless, these proposals also reveal that the contextual and constitutive aspects of decision-making are hardly ever taken into account. Likewise, they usually neglect the fact that a way of doing and a style of action are being interiorized in decision-making processes.

But the greatest difficulties of customary approaches are rooted precisely in the fact that they are almost exclusively centered on decision-making. We must recognize that, since decisions are an essential part of organizational life, it is essential to have a method with which to confront them ethically. But taking the formal dissection of the decision-making process as a point of reference can cause us to ignore the real and insuperable limitations in which decisions are taken: the ambiguities inherent in all decision-making; the endless diversity - and complexity - of concrete problems involved in making ethical decisions; all the elements that have a real influence on individual actions; or the limitations inherent to the importance of the context. It therefore seems crucial to start considering decisions as a global process, rather than confining ourselves to the view of decision-making as an isolated moment.

Starting from a formal analysis of decision-making and implicitly transforming it to a normative process, which is what ultimately happens, clashes with the realization that in real life people do not act in accordance with this pattern. Even if they wanted to,

---

[1] Ford & Richardson, 1994, p. 205.
[2] See as an example Arthur Andersen (1992) or Murphy (1998).
[3] See for example three proposals each dated 10 years apart: Epstein (1973), Goodpaster (1983), and Solomon (1993).

they couldn't. Hence, "the realistic value of a clear normative concept of rational behavior lies in the fact that it provides a guide for explaining why people deviate from this concept of rationality."[4] Using the term made popular by Simon (1979), we are faced here with a bounded rationality, which is limited only if one's reference is an ideal of rationality that does not correspond to the facts. For the same reason Jungermann (1983) proposed that the field of management distinguish between pessimists and optimists with regard to rationality. The former underline the short-comings, the judgemental biases, the weight of motivations, etc., whereas the latter consider that the important thing is to take more general processes and orientations as a point of reference rather than considering decisions as isolated elements. But, in any case, the idea is to accept that "since decision-making is a dynamic process, it cannot be understood outside the context in which it occurs. It is affected by considerations about uncertainty, risk, people, materials, machines, resources, and any other issues present, or perceived to be present, at the time the decision is to be made. Ordinary models of rationality are inadequate to describe decision-making in complex organizations, for such models fail to incorporate the context in which the decision is made. Instead, contextual rationality is a term that describes decision-making in the real world."[5]

Thus we see that going beyond an approach limited to the formalities of decision-making understood as a moment or event involves shifting our attention to decision-making's global process and procedure, on the one hand, and on the other, to its context.

In other words, we cannot understand how real decisions are made in organizations if we only take into account their formal elements and ignore cultural influences. We should not reduce - ethically or organizationally - decisions to the events that appear formally as such. We must consider the mental frames of reference into which actions fit and on which they are focused. Therefore, we should never forget that decision-making can be better understood when it is oriented as a continual process within a context.

Thus I consider decision-making as a privileged moment for integrating what I proposed as the constitutive dimensions of BE. But if decision-making is so important to me, it is because I think it should be considered as a golden opportunity to move towards the integration of ethics and organizations. And this is a vital condition for BE's credibility and viability as applied ethics. However, this integration will not be possible if we separate decision-making from organizational processes and from a global view of the organization.

8.2.   The paths towards integration: the organization as a project

BE's acknowledgement that decision-making should be considered part of an organizational process rather than an isolated and decontextualized event has led to an approach that emphasizes a more global understanding of the organization.

In line with this approach, Fritzsche (1991) proposes a decision-making model that introduces ethical values. Fritzsche's proposal is based on the assumption that the ethical approach is one of the many facets of decision-making. This enables him to acknowledge and affirm the undeniably individual dimension of all decisions without

---

[4] Guy, 1990, p. 33.
[5] Guy, 1990, p. 34.

overlooking the fact that this dimension is strongly influenced by organizational culture. Fritzsche thus places ethical values in decision-making within the context of an organizational culture, and specifically the consideration of stakeholders, the organizational climate, and corporate obejctives. It is in relation to these three features that he proposes to point out. the economic, political, technological, social, and ethical dimensions that he believes to be part of all decisions.

Yet when taking the step towards addressing the process and organization in their entirety, you obviously end up raising the question of how you can understand the processes and decisions that guide and shape the organization as such in terms of ethics. This is what Epstein (1987b) did when he established what he called the process of corporate social policy; a process that, in his words, "constitutes a useful integrative analytical framework for scholars and other observers of corporate social performance. Moreover, the Corporate Social Policy Process can assist business decision-makers and their companies to undertake, in the terminology of Charles S. McCoy, the 'management of values' by seeking to define, evaluate and institutionalize within the firm core values drawn both from its past and our collective Western cultural heritage."[6]

Epstein's integration process is based on BE's contributions, corporate social responsibility, and corporate social responsiveness. From BE he borrows his thoughts on moral meanings; from corporate social responsibility he takes his considerations of the consequences of corporate policies; and from corporate social responsiveness he takes the consideration of processes that enable companies to anticipate the expectations and demands of their various stakeholders. Thus Epstein's is a dynamic process in which each element is interrelated with the others.

Epstein believes that the following are fundamental features of integration: analysis of relations with the various stakeholders; definition of the most relevant issues at stake in these relations, especially in the case of mid- and long-term problems or situations demanding more urgent decisions; criteria and values that identify corporate orientation and decisions and place them in a social context; establishment of corporate aims and purposes; decision-making processes that make all these features operational and include adequate arrangements for participation; implementation, which includes attributing ethical relevance not only to the decisions made, but also to the procedures through which these decisions are brought about; and assessment, which insofar as it addresses outcomes and the new questions raised by them, once again triggers the entire process. Epstein also claims that the terms used in his conceptualization cannot be considered arbitrary in any way: the word 'corporation' refers to the actions of the organization in the sense of a single company or a consolidated group; the word 'social' refers to the totality of the economic, political, ecological, social, and cultural results and consequences of corporate actions for all stakeholders; the word 'policy' refers to the principles guiding organizational life; and 'process' refers to a dynamics that systematically introduces - and therefore manages - these elements. It should not come as a surprise that approaches like this ultimately lead to the issue of the relationship between ethics and strategy.

Strategy has been a central feature of corporate management for years - and not always in an unequivocal sense. Since the fifties, the concept of strategy has evolved

---

[6] Epstein, 1987b, p. 102.

towards an integral or global view of the corporation, after having first been marked by a rationalist emphasis which caused certain rigid attitudes towards planning and overlooked the organization's internal and cultural dimensions. However, what always underlies these more precise approaches to strategy is a will to integrate.

It is generally assumed that everything related to strategy is one of the most fundamental management functions. This should come as no surprise since it is part of these functions to define the kind of business in which the company engages or wants to engage and what type of company it is or wants to be. I think it is important to realize that in strictly organizational terms (and without as yet addressing specifically ethical issues), having a strategic view of an organization amounts to clarifying what it is the organizations does and, through this, what kind of organization it is. Obviously, this implies having a long-term view of the organization and, above all, seeing the corporation as a whole and not as an aggregate of separate parts.

Thus, establishing a strategy implies having a view that does not reduce the corporation to a mere matter of economics. It involves setting the purposes and objectives of the company considered not only as an economic institution, but as a social and human institution. Therefore, in strategic approaches references and responsibilities other than strictly economic ones also play a role which can restrict economic absolutization (Ansoff, 1985) and are expressed through formulating the corporation's goals and priorities. This is the reason Andrews includes the values towards which the corporation aims and the recognition of its non-economic responsibility towards society as part of strategy formulation.

According to Di Norcia (1988) this means that corporate strategy has to accept the premise that a corporation is a social institution. This is true on one condition: that accepting it does not mean demanding that the company fill all social needs. But it should demand that the company recognize the social demands and functions in which it is in fact involved by virtue of its specific operations. It is therefore necessary to work towards an integration that is not centered merely on the field of ethical discourse or organization theory, but would be a part of the strategy itself.

Without this will to integrate, exclusively economic (and economicist) values will permeate the entire corporate dynamics. Instead, an integrating approach "allows the planners to (1) anticipate ethical problems, (2) apply social responsibility and ethical analysis tools, (3) determine those corporate values that are most important to the organization, and (4) integrate them into the corporate culture."[7]

In short, the affirmation of the corporation's central values has an eminently practical function, since "core values become the day-to-day guidelines for developing and implementing the strategic plans. They are a filter of sorts through which plans are passed to ensure their ethical content. They balance profit and efficiency values with a concern for ethical and socially responsible conduct."[8] If we really expect them to be operative, these central values must be limited and must eventually shape a corporate culture through which they can be interiorized. Thus organizational learning becomes essential because the idea is not to impose these values, but to link them to a process of

---

[7] Robin & Reidenbach, 1988, p. 32.

[8] Robin & Reidenbach, 1988, p. 40, 41. Moreover, Hosmer (1987) has empirically studied how the pressure for results in strategic planning actually leads to the institutionalization of immoral conduct.

organizational development. To sum up, the point is to find a positive approach to corporate ethics, rather than a merely negative or reactive one.

Consequently, when we realize that the concept of corporate strategy has a strong axiological component, the issue raised is not only how to incorporate social preferences in the development of corporate strategies, but how to address corporate strategy itself as an ethical question. It is not a matter of just recognizing that the choice of strategy has an ethical component, but also "the very fact that business strategy involves choices of both ends and means in the forms of corporate objectives and policies, respectively, shows how inextricably intertwined ethicsl questions are in strategic decision-making."[9] In short, this means taking an integrating approach that turns strategy into the means by which a number of autonomous personal projects are made to fit into in a corporate project.

In fact, although the global view of strategy and personal development in the context of BE have been put forward in terms of a project, the emphasis on this term stems from its relation to the problems of organizational development, which is intimately related to the question of strategy.

In its practical facet, then, the corporate project expresses the organization's raison d'être by stating and developing its corporate mission and a diversity of operational objectives. A restricted view of the project will refer only to this materialization (and is limited to drafting a written text) while a broad view of the project would situate it conceptually as the expression of an organizational process that is more relevant as such than its cyclical objectification. In short, the project is a synthesis of the company's main economic and social priorities; it indicates the ways and means the company should adopt to become what it wants to be. Far from simply stating its aims, it is first and foremost the expression of a shared will (Boyer & Equilbey, 1986).

In the context of my approach, I consider it important to note that we are talking about the will to create the purpose and the goods that are an intrinsic part of an organization's identity. The issue then will be the legitimacy of the procedure used, which should in no way be understood as a mere instrument for developing a project, but as one of its constitutive ingredients. Otherwise, there is the danger that any project might be reduced to only two dimensions: one social and cultural, the other operational. This brings us back to a problem that we already saw earleer when we talked about corporate culture: its ambiguity.[10]

We have seen that adopting a global perspective of the corporation implies accepting what I call the need for integration; integration that ultimately refers to the network of organizational relations, everyone affected by the company's corporate actions, culture, and to the organizational's values, criteria and goals. And this holds true for both both decision-making and strategy. Still, if we bear in mind that the need to address organizational processes constantly appears in all these issues, I believe that it follows

---

[9] Murray, 1986, p. 101.

[10] Today what is looked for is dynamization of the whole and individual mobilization through the participation of everyone in a common corporate project and in the clarification of the company's fundamental values. Corporate projects are at the heart of this reorientation: when individual initiative becomes more desirable than strict obedience, corporate regulations shift from a disciplinary model to mechanisms that favor subscribing to values, participation, getting involved in the community. (Lipovetsky, 1992, p. 268, 280).

from here that developing BE depends less on its ability to speak in terms of "ethics and organization" than its ability to propose ways for organizations to institutionalize ethics.

8.3.   The paths towards integration: institutionalizing ethics

The expression "institutionalization of ethics into business" appeared for the first time in 1979.[11] What is at stake in this approach is, in short, to incorporate what has been called "affirmative" ethics into organizational life (Melé, 1991), in contrast to a "negative" ethics which would be limited to striving to avoid certain reprehensible conduct in organizations. Nevertheless, it was not until the second half of the 1980s that the term "institutionalization of ethics" became an analytical and practical point of reference. In a 1986 survey, the Center for Business Ethics found that the following points should be taken into account when evaluating BE: codes, ethics committees, judiciary boards, ombudsmen, ethics training, social audits, and changes in corporate structure. The Business Roundtable (1988) stressed the need to find assessment parameters rather than merely listing the areas in which the viability of institutionalization is at stake. This seems particularly pertinent inasmuch as six years later, when the issue was raised again, the Center for Business Ethics (1992) noted that, oddly enough, the increase in BE texts, studies, and meetings had not caused a significant increase in the institutionalization of ethics in corporations.

I think that the key to theoretically (and not only practically) understanding the institutionalization of ethics is the recognition that in our world the corporation has become a social place where values are produced and shared. In my opinion, it is important to acknowledge that managers and employees can think in an ethical way about the problems they encounter daily in their organizational life. But we cannot pretend or assume that this capacity is the product of today's social context. It is therefore necessary to specifically develop it. In short, we can only talk about institutionalizing ethics in organizations if we accept that "actors and organizations are not merely the passive recipients of moral forces, but also their originators."[12]

This is precisely what requires an integrative perspective. For if we talk about institutionalization, we must acknowledge that the dynamics of values always poses challenges to our ability to discover new ways to structure these values. Consequently, the institutionalization of ethics implies a permanent break or change in the way of doing things and resolving problems, needs, and situations. Still, in order for this change to take place, someone is needed to perceive, discover, develop and make the idea materialize. And this "someone" cannot be conceived independently from some process of institutionalization. If this process does not take place, the ethical discourse will inevitably end up functioning in parallel to the everyday organizational discourse.

Bird and Waters (1989) have pointed out that when ethics is not an integral part of corporate day-to-day life, managers perceive moral language as a new source of problems. From their point of view, moral language threatens harmony by generating new problems, efficiency by presenting both absolute and imprecise demands, and the image of power and effectiveness due to its idealism. Thus I think that the institutionalization of ethics is indissociable from the need to fit moral discourse with

---

[11] See Weber (1993), where the terms and contents are defined.
[12] Nicholson, 1994, p. 587.

the experiences and expectations of the individuals involved in the organization. Consequently, it is not necessary to understand institutionalization only as a demand for new structures or new formal procedures. It is also a conviction that cannot be fostered in corporate employees unless they are encouraged to talk more openly and directly about such issues. This explains, for example, why some scholars insist on linking the institutionalization of ethics with organizational development and why this link consists of principles of participation, power sharing, and truth (Deaner, 1994). As can be readily understood, this means that institutionalizing ethics is an issue that must be fundamentally approached in terms of organizational processes.

In my view, this takes us back again to analyses of moral development in organizations. In line with my proposals, it will now be necessary to take one more step and ask ourselves whether new organizational and social situations make it plausible and necessary to understand organizations as places of learning and, therefore, also of moral learning.

It is already assumed that "ethical/unethical behavior in practical situations is not simply a product of fixed individual characteristics, but results from an interaction between the individual and the situation."[13] Apparently, then, the institutionalization of ethics should be oriented towards taking an explicit part in this interaction. Not surprisingly, Pascale (1985) has insisted on the importance of the corporate socialization process and, therefore, the need to not leave it to chance. And, similarly, Goodpaster (1991b) has affirmed that the ethical imperatives for corporate leadership are to guide, institutionalize, and sustain.

While one of the essential aspects of every process of ethical institutionalization is the corporate dynamics that make it possible, another refers to the establishment of the organization's purposes and priorities. "Not all values are of the same kind, or of equal importance. How, then, is it possible to assign priorities to values, and which ones can be recognized as important or overriding, which should be regarded as trivial, which should be regarded as 'good' values, and on what grounds?"[14] The problem is not merely one of introducing an ethical dimension, but of accomplishing this through a process that also includes learning how to solve the conflicts of values that inevitably occur in practical situations. Yet, such resolution of conflicts cannot appeal to some kind of stable hierarchy, which often reflects the pressing need to seek a mechanical rule that would free individuals from the responsibility of making decisions.

Ultimately, the processes involved in institutionalizing corporate ethics are indissociable from the development of a kind of corporate autonomy that allows each organization to create its own purposes based on its particular practices. And this leads us to a decisive question: how can corporate success be measured?

This question comes up now because, if we want to institutionalize ethics in an organization, we should establish the identifying criteria that allow us to evaluate their attainment. In short, every organization, whatever the type, pursues success, but one of the fundamental questions that constitutes it as an organization is precisely how it defines success.

---

[13] Trevino, 1986, p. 610.
[14] Donaldson, 1989, p. 187.

The idea then is to clarify which areas should be taken into account if we want to propose an organizational development that entails the institutionalization of ethics. Nicholson (1994) and Weber (1993) are probably the scholars who have made the most paradigmatic proposals for understanding the processes involved in institutionalizing ethics.

Furthermore, these two proposals (which are probably also the most complete and systematic ones) exemplify two ways of theoretically and practically approaching the institutionalization of ethics in organizations. One underlines the formal or structural aspects (Nicholson) and the other the more operative aspects (Weber). I think that by using these two types of models one can make a preliminary classification of the proposals for institutionalizing ethics in organizations. Let us explore, then, the basic traits of proposals for institutionalizing ethics that stress the formal and structuring aspects and those that stress the operational aspects

8.3.1. PROPOSALS FROM A FORMAL PERSPECTIVE

As mentioned above, Nicholson (1994) made one of the most complete proposals of institutionalization from a more formal or structuring perspective. He distinguishes four levels of analysis in order to determine whether ethics is institutionalized: ethical environment, ethical domains, ethical functioning, and ethical process. Ethical environment refers to all stakeholders; ethical domains are all the ways the company is oriented to its context (which includes objectives and strategies); ethical functioning refers to meeting objectives (through rhetoric and informal expressions, structured forms, and institutionalized behavior); and ethical process refers to the way ethical values and beliefs are generated or altered in the everyday working life of the organization's members. He considers that there is still need to do further research on all four levels. But - significantly - he concludes that this research also needs a conceptual frame of reference as regards the organization, and he suggests this can be obtained through a rereading of Kohlberg's levels in corporate terms.

Trevino (1990) has also made a globalizing proposal with the intention of offering a cultural approach in which moral or immoral behavior is conceived as a consequence of the ethical components of organizational culture. Yet he also has quite a broad view of what should be understood as organizational culture. Indeed, from Trevino's perspective "the ethics component of organizational culture is composed of a complex interplay of formal and informal systems that can support either ethical or unethical organizational behavior. The formal systems include leadership, structure, policies, reward systems, orientation and training programs, and decision-making processes. Informal systems include norms, heroes, rituals, language, myths, sagas and stories."[15] Institutionalization will involve taking into account the specific way in which all these elements fit together. If this fit is accomplished, it will be possible to evaluate the extent to which ethics are institutionalized.

Sims (1990) considers the institutionalization of ethics a problem inherent in any kind of organization and not exclusive to business corporations. But he adds that it is necessary to conceive this fit in terms of learning and relearning the values that foster ethical behavior. For that same reason he stresses the psychological contract between

---

[15] Trevino, 1990, p. 195.

individuals and the organization; it is the ultimate expression of shared values and objectives, and should never be considered as something established once and for all. It is from the perspective of the psychological contract between individuals and organization that we must understand structuring, cultural aspects and informal networks of relationships. This implies acknowledging the great importance of organizational processes when it comes to institutionalizing ethics. It also relativizes the approaches that give priority to the formal establishment of ethical or axiological contents. Sims' point of view is that institutionalization helps produce shared meanings between the members of the organization about what is appropriate and fundamentally produces meaningful conduct. The point then is not to forget that when one talks about institutionalizing ethics, the structures as well as all the elements and values that shape organizational culture should not be understood in a reified way. They should be understood in relation to personal psychological processes through which individuals continuously restate their acceptance of their links to the organization.

Stead et al. (1990) believe that there are some constant qualities that make up both the ethics of organizations and ethics in organizations. We must therefore address all of them. These constants are the following: the individual personality and socialization processes, dominant beliefs and philosophies, the history and traditions that shape current ways of doing things, the organizational factors intrinsically linked to ethical issues (management styles, structures and politics, incentives, job descriptions....), external pressure, the stakeholders. Thus they conclude that ethical conduct in corporations is a complex problem with numerous facets which have meaningful situational and individual dimensions. But they insist that the effective management of ethical conduct requires the organization to adhere to ethics, expect ethical behavior from its managers, create ethical groups, measure ethics, make reports on ethics, reward ethical behavior, and if none of that works: make firm decisions.

In short, the organization should create procedures to make the organizations' commitment to ethics visible.

8.3.2. PROPOSALS THAT EMPHASIZE PROCESS

Among the more formal and structuring kind of proposals for institutionalizing ethics, one can highlight those that emphasize process. I speak deliberately of emphasis, since one of the essential elements of any approach that aims to institutionalize ethics is attention to process. There are, however, proposals that give this so much importance that, strictly speaking, they consist precisely of the presentation of a process. Brooks (1989) formalizes a process that has no point of arrival, but is continually remade from the beginning: it is necessary to start by identifying corporate objectives, which include leadership capability and the ability to give direction to and promote dialogue. It is necessary to reformulate these objectives in operational terms, in an integrated way and involving the entire organization. It is also necessary to establish the way to evaluate them in order to avoid reducing everything related to moral and social values accepted by the organization to a simple declaration of intentions. It is at this point that we can start thinking about how to attain the aforementioned objectives, a process in which participation also plays a fundamental role. Finally, the point is to control the result, evaluate its consequences in terms of structure and pay, and thereafter identify corporate objectives anew.

Nash (1983) considers that institutionalization processes feature some empirically verified constant qualities that can be considered as acquired. Among these are the following: you must set a deadline for developing the project and avoid succumbing to the temptation to believe that issues of corporate ethics are characterized by their vagueness. You must create the psychological and physical conditions for shared thought and discussion about what should next be done. You must have someone external to the organization to catalyze the process, accompany its development, and objectify the various approaches. You must get senior management involved. You must make the effort to formulate the ideas and beliefs that appear during the process and are believed to be shared by the organization. You must avoid approaches that are exclusively abstract, generic, or "theoretical," because these processes should also involve learning from experience. Ultimately you must make some decision and put it into practice.

De George (1990a) considers that the senior management team needs to be explicitly involved if moral behavior is to be introduced in the corporate structure. Managers on all levels must commit themselves, starting with their particular areas of responsibility. You need to create channels and procedures for communication and dialogue. These channels and procedures should explicitly include and refer to the stakeholders in all their diversity. You must create an organizational unit (probably a department) which would serve as a reference and board of appeal in everything involving the institutionalization of ethics. You must adapt the system of incentives and sanctions to the institutionalization project.

Finally, McCoy (1988) makes a proposal that seeks to simultaneously institutionalize culture, values, and ethics. This requires developing a capacity to undertake commitment to corporate values so that it is the result of a personal bond, rather than an external imposition. This means institutionalizing ethics by starting with the human resources at your disposal. It means accepting that change in the way of doing things entails change in the meanings invested in these ways. It requires explicit leadership action. It requires making explicit and formally regulating (at least to some minimal degree) the demands that stem from the values thought to be shaping the organization. It requires fitting these values into the corporate policy-making process. It requires creating adequate information systems that make the process of organizational change required by all proposals of ethical institutionalization both visible and operational.

8.3.3. PROPOSALS FROM AN OPERATIONAL PERSPECTIVE

In contrast, proposals of ethical institutionalization which are fundamentally operational in nature give priority to formulating the specific elements that shape institutionalization. As I have already said, I think that Weber (1993), with his multicomponent model for the institutionalization of ethics, is the author who takes the most well-articulated approach. In Weber's model, ethical behavior is reached by starting from a corporate culture which is expressed in an ethical code, training programs, and reinforcement mechanisms, so that these programs and mechanisms are the explicit and conscious orientation of the code. But, in addition, institutionalization is not conceived as some kind of indoctrination; instead it implies being justified in strictly ethical terms. And for this reason, Weber considers that the three categories presented in the model - frames of reference, interrelation among components, and influence on employee conduct- should also work as a guide for organizations seeking ways to institutionalize ethics.

Werhane (1985) proposes a series of external and internal corporate reforms in order to be able to institutionalize the corporation as a moral agency. External reforms consist of creating non-governmental agencies to keep watch over corporate regulation and its fulfillment, carrying out independent social audits and creating incentives for ethical behavior. Internal reforms consist of insuring that corporations themselves draw up social balance sheets, adding social representatives to boards of directors, creating ethics committees (and other similar bodies) within corporations, incorporating morals into the corporate definition of excellence, developing programs to train employees to accept ethical responsibility, drafting codes of ethics or other fundamental texts.

Murphy (1988) aims to pragmatically show the steps companies could follow to introduce ethical corporate practices. Organizing these practices involves acting on the corporate structure (formal aspect) and corporate culture (informal aspect). Executing them involves shaping responsibilities and tasks. You can act on corporate structure through corporate ethical codes, committees, training, and audits. You can act on corporate culture roles, communication, processes, and relations. Responsibilities are exemplified through leadership, delegating, communicating, and motivating. And tasks are carried out in accordance with individuals' specific senses of ethics and acknowledging their diversity. Later (in 1989) Murphy posed the question of how to develop ethical structures and concluded that the most operative way was to work in the three fields he considers the most viable: corporate creeds, which define corporate values and give them direction; ethical programs, where the corporation strives to focus on ethical questions; and ethical codes, which provide a specific guide for employees in functional corporate areas.

After attempting to reformulate the key questions for the BE approach, Donaldson (1989) makes a list of proposals to improve institutionalization. This list includes linking values with strategies; creating and adopting ethical codes (which the various stakeholders take into account) and making them public; incorporating BE not only in business schools but also in internal corporate training; achieving the maximum possible degree of public information in decision-making; reducing to the maximum bureaucratic and hierarchical structures; and promoting study and research on companies´ ethical conduct.

Frederick et al. (1998) consider that the institutionalization of ethics involves two closely linked points: first, developing a strategy that takes into account the various stakeholders; secondly, changing attitudes (above all, those of managers). This amounts to opening corporate culture to ethical criteria, drafting ethical codes, creating committees on ethics, establishing programs in ethical training, and carrying out ethical audits.

In its day the Business Roundtable (1988) aimed to offer some lines of action for all companies intending to develop, improve, perfect, and renew all their efforts to introduce more ethical policies and conduct in their organizations. These lines are the following: the key role of senior management in terms of commitment, leadership, and example; the importance of a code of ethics in clarifying expectations; incorporating ethical criteria in processes of selection, training, communication, incentives, and sanctions; creating a unit that watches over fulfillment of ethical criteria, and suitable forms of assessment and audit; involving all employees in this process.

According to Carmichael and Drummond (1989), putting strategy into practice requires defining the organization's aim, identifying its stakeholders, establishing its objectives, formulating its ethical criteria (through a code, for example), and endeavoring to ensure that these corporate ethical practices are truly accepted by employees. Lastly, Derry (1991) treats the institutionalization of ethical motivation fundamentally in terms of incentives. This would involve eliminating the following practices: remuneration based on quantity rather than quality, the pressure to seek profit above all else, the dissociation between what is proposed and what is done, sanctions for reported ethical violations, uncertainty with respect to ethical standards, promotion of standards that are immoral. In contrast, it would involve supporting the formulation and expression of ethical norms, repeated announcements of policies regarding ethics, establishing channels of communication, creating means of appeal and rewarding ethical conduct.

I believe this brief description of the areas that have been taken into consideration in approaches aimed at institutionalizing corporate ethics (both those taking a formal approach and those that take a more operational approach) complements my descriptions of decision making, strategy-making processes, and corporate projects.

If we compare the various features of these processes (both in terms of their diversity and in terms of those that are successively repeated) with the analytical model I proposed as a reference for reconstructing the organization´s ethics, I do not think that there is any feature that could not be included in my model and this could be a first verification of its suitability. There is, however, something more: I believe that by comparing a variety of concrete proposals with my model, the gaps can be systematically detected.

If we re-examine the various proposals for institutionalization, we will see that they can all be dynamically reordered in the three-dimensional frame of my proposed model: any institutionalization of BE needs to have a consequentialist moment (which we have analyzed in relation to stakeholders), a conventional moment that refers to the configuration of subjects in a corporate ethos (which we have analyzed in relation to corporate cultures), and a reflective-normative moment (which, as we have seen, cannot be reduced to the drafting of ethical codes, but includes the construction of criteria, purposes, and procedures capable of opening the company to a postconventional approach). The need to shape institutionalization processes (with the inherent demand for integration) thus gives content to my model and, at the same time, my model enables these processes to be reconstructed and ethically justified.

Thus we can rearrange the various proposals for institutionalization in accordance to whether they incorporate the consequentialist moment, the conventional moment, and the reflective moment; and also whether they consider the dimension of processes and the structuring dimension. In addition to the operational details that are proposed as the most adequate for the development of each area, it is interesting to note the direction preferences have taken in the various approaches to institutionalizating ethics.

	Consequent. moment	Conventional moment	Reflective moment	Process	Structure
Nicholson	X	X	X	X	X
Trevino		X		X	X
Sims		X	X	X	X
Stead	X	X	X		X
Brooks		X	X	X	X
Nash			X	X	X
De George	X			X	X
McCoy		X	X	X	X
Weber	X	X	X	X	X
Werhane			X		X
Murphy		X	X		X
Donaldson			X		X
Frederick	X	X	X	X	X
Busin.			X		X
Carmichael	X	X	X		X
Derry		X	X		X

This reflection on the institutionalization of ethics has shown that my model is sufficiently suitable from the analytical and normative points of view. But it has also emphasized the need to adopt a more dynamic approach to organizational processes. This need to establish a frame of reference for organizational ethics that takes not only integration but also dynamics into account forces us to ask ourselves what type of conception of the organization makes this approach plausible. In the following chapters, I will propose what I believe to be the most suitable theoretical frame of reference.

Here again, overcoming economism is a requirement for all corporations in the contemporary socio-cultural context, "because the language of money reduces complexity it cannot express complexity."[16] Adopting an ethical perspective implies taking this complexity into account. Thus ethics is meaningful insofar as it helps clarify organizational practices regarding concrete decisions, establishment of goals and strategies, and explicit declaration of values and preferences. Now this "involves

---

[16] Pruzan & Thyssen, 1990, p. 138.

ongoing learning, a search for and discovery of knowledge and ideas through interaction, a sense of interdependence."[17]

This perspective of organizational learning can become a bridge between the perspective of the organization and our understanding of it as a social institution interdependent with its environment. Thus I believe that the very concepts of responsibility and responsiveness should be understood in terms of learning. They include the creation of meanings and an innovative and integrative educational commitment. In short, this is a process that promotes human development in the organization. But it does not hide the fact that this human development is far from easy and that human beings often avoid complexity by creating worlds that limit it and make us more secure in our thoughts and actions.

There has been, then, a progressive awareness that contemporary organizations have to develop learning processes which will allow them to broaden their horizons of reference and, above all, their understanding of their corporate activities. It is not demands this, but the analysis of the place that organizations occupy in the contemporary world. It is here where BE makes a specific contribution. The moment has come, then, to seek a concept of the organization that allows BE to think about these dynamic aspects in operational terms. It is therefore necessary to explore the relation between BE and the organization in terms of both individual and corporate learning. This is the issue I will address in the next chapter.

---

[17] Srivastva & Barret, 1988, p. 296.

CHAPTER 9

HUMANIZATION (ALSO) AS A PROCESS OF ORGANIZATIONAL LEARNING

I concluded the previous chapter noting the need to link my proposal to integrate the hermeneutics of responsibility in organizational processes with a concept of the organization that would be adequate for and coherent with this aspiration. In my opinion, however, it is very important to note that launching this proposal for BE not only requires careful thought on the part of ethics, but also on the part of business. This is precisely what makes integration possible. I also feel that it is necessary to place this concept of the organization in the framework of the social and technological changes that make it plausible and necessary. Thus we can say that the issue of a new type of organization is inextricable from the issue of a new type of emerging society. I will therefore begin by describing the social context of the concept of the organization on which my proposal is based. Secondly, I will endeavor to show why the aim to go beyond the traditional concept of organizations is justified. In Chapter 10 I will describe the concept I believe to be best suited to contemporary changes and to my proposed understanding of BE.

9.1.   The emerging knowledge society

Our society is changing exceptionally fast, as can be seen from even a simple list of the events that have recently taken place. Indeed, King & Schneider's (1991) report to the Club of Rome heralded it as "the first global revolution". But there is as yet no agreement as to the direction this process is taking. If there is agreement on anything, it is on the fact that this process is inseparable from the dominant role of technological innovations and, more specifically, information and knowledge technology. Discussion is still raging about what to call this process of change. Since it is not my intention to enter into discussions on nomenclature, I will use the term "knowledge society" which is, for a number of good reasons, the one that has gained the widest acceptance.

It is usually acknowledged that Bell (1973) has had a great impact on the way this question is approached. In fact, he preferred to speak of a postindustrial society, which he considered a broad generalization that included five dimensions: the transition from a goods-producing economy to a service-producing one; the preeminence of technical and professional classes; the core role of knowledge as a source of innovation and power; the political importance of controlling technology; and the creation of an intellectual technology for decision-making purposes. However, the most significant aspect of Bell's approach is his affirmation that the most important source of structural change in society involves changing the character of knowledge. According to Bell's approach, the possibility of talking about social change rather than mere technological change is grounded in the fact that knowledge is the key resource in a postindustrial society just as land is in a preindustrial society and machinery in an industrial society.

Thus we must consider some specific traits of these technological innovations. According to Thurow (1991), a very broad definition of information technologies includes computer hardware and software of all kinds; communication webs, ranging from ones that connect personal computers to their bigger public or private counterparts; and the growing importance of the integration between computer and communications technology. The new technologies have a capacity to process information that goes beyond a simple storage function and becomes creative, insofar as it is information for knowledge and communication.

It can therefore be said that technological change - and its acceleration - is a factor of social disorganization; but also - and above all - that it constitutes change and innovation as core elements of a social organization. For this reason it is particularly important to realize that information can be neither treated nor understood as a good, at least in the traditional economic and social senses of the word: it is not divisible; it is not lost when it is transmitted; it can be moved instantly; it does not wear out, but improves with use; it is not a scarce resource in the traditional sense of the term; there is no objective way to assign it values since it depends on the value attributed to it by the subject, and so on. Hence, it cannot be treated or managed in the same way as material goods nor with the same criteria.

The real breakthrough, then, is the possibility of applying technology to a field that until now was reserved for human beings: their mental activity. It is as if the first industrial revolution had increased the strength of human beings and animals in production, whereas the second aimed to expand the human mental capacity. Obviously, this expansion must be understood on a social scale, and not merely an individual one. In addition, according to Masuda (1980) this expansion involves three successive phases. The first phase is automation; during this phase the mental work of human beings is materialized by applying technology to telecommunications. The second phase is knowledge creation, which leads to the expansion of humans' mental work. The third phase is system innovation: an ensemble of social, economic and political changes triggered by the first two phases of development. It is clear that the most open discussion focuses on changes in system. However, I think it is very important not to separate this third level from reflection on new technologies. When the Fast report (1986) attempted to study Europe's situation in relation to the newest challenges of the future, it talked about the information society when referring to a society whose nervous system would consist of information. It also used the term biosociety to refer to a society in which biotechnologies (science applied to the biological process) would have a fundamental impact. Such biotechnologies are also inseparable from information technologies and, in short, allow human beings to work directly on life systems.[1] In other words, new technologies require developing the capacity to think about human action in a non-atomized way in terms of its repercussion on the system in which this action is inserted.

If we think about new technologies in the spheres of both axiology and organizations, we should underscore three traits. The first could be simultaneously described as the value of knowledge and knowledge as a value. A society whose livelihood depends on the production of knowledge not only turns knowledge into its

---

[1] It is fair to say that the Fast report raised a third question: jobs and other forms of occupation; a concern that seems essential in a Europe built around the welfare state and it also appears to be a problem that derives from the other two changes.

value, but it also makes it an assessment criterion:[2] individuals become a key resource in all senses since the routes to innovation and creativity will depend on their capacity; space is no longer simply physical or geographical, it can also be mental or virtual, etc.). Secondly, there is a shift from the importance of "facts" or "objects" to the importance of processes: in a context of innovation a change is not a threat, but the condition of its possibility. Therefore, any concept of value or the organization that is linked by regulations to an image of order and stability is liable to see its credibility seriously damaged. Thirdly, networks now take the leading role in human action, so that individual actions are neither dissolved in the group nor viable or conceivable apart from it. Since they are no longer conceivable as "structures" or "masses", but as interrelated networks, these groups must frame their approaches in terms of projects. In short, the competitive advantage in this new stage is knowledge creation.

Although we must acknowledge that there is not yet total consensus on whether we are initiating a supposed knowledge society, there is much more agreement on the fact that we are being plunged into an economy based on information and knowledge. Ultimately, the term "information society" is associated with an economy in which: 1) information is at the center of society's economic needs, 2) the economy and society itself grow and develop around this nucleus: production and the use of information values, and 3) the importance of information as an economic product exceeds that of goods, energy, and services. The importance attributed to knowledge (and to its corresponding technology) in economic growth increasingly leads to the conviction that knowledge will be the key to economic growth in the twenty-first century (Toffler, 1990).

Thus, recognizing that knowledge is the new wealth of nations and their main competitive advantage entails placing it at the heart of economic activity. This then means that it must be understood through explanatory models capable of reflecting its particularity. And it means accepting that knowledge will become the most important factor of production. "The basic economic resource - the 'means of production' to use the economist's term – is no longer capital, nor natural resources (the economist's 'land'), nor 'labor'. It is and will be knowledge."[3] Knowledge is becoming the ultimate resource. Corporations depend more on their knowledge and information networks than on any other resource. In the new society what counts more than anything else is information and knowledge about knowledge. Under these circumstances discussing the issue of the emerging knowledge society is plausible, given that a radical change in the economic situation has social repercussions and consequences.

As the Fast report (1986) observed, technological options are essentially social options. The central problem of technological change is not technological but social. There is no such thing as technological determinism; neither the direction nor rhythm of technological changes is predetermined. If there is agreement on anything, it is on this: technological change is neither viable nor understandable (nor, of course, manageable) if it is only approached in technological terms, disconnected from the social and cultural

---

[2] "We are moving from a system of production of goods to a system of production of knowledge. This transformation changes us from working men to men of knowledge. [...] in the future the wealth of nations will depend on information, on knowledge, on intelligence." (Corbi, 1992, p. 17-18)

[3] Drucker, 1993, p. 7. In this sense, Cortina (1993) has clearly seen that knowledge can be - to put it in terms of Walzer's analysis (1983) - the new "dominant good."

changes it triggers and of which it simultaneously forms part. One thing is that the basic economic result is knowledge and quite a different one is that, in this context, the problem does not consist of determining what is feasible economically, but what is socially acceptable. Therefore, I will briefly refer to two of the changes that most directly influence today's ideas about BE: those that affect work and those that affect learning.

It seems quite obvious that new technologies have radically changed the working world. Not only do technological factors contribute to this metamorphosis, but so do the logic of the market in a global economy, attitudes and values in relation to work, and new forms of organization However, discussions on the debate about the metamorphosis of work can be simplified by reducing it to two points of view: while some scholars stress what is coming to an end (the ideal and possibility of full employment in the framework of a certain "work culture"), others stress what is beginning (a different kind of work and new forms of employment).[4] But, in any case, it is important to take into account that these changes are not only quantitative in terms of the work-unemployment dichotomy and that the effect of new technologies on the characteristics of work and on the environment in which it is performed is equally significant.

Consequently, BE must inquire whether its discourse is well grounded ethically and whether it is adequate as applied ethics, but, more importantly, whether its construction takes into account the problems raised by the new forms of organization corresponding to the changes taking place in the working world. The relations between man and work are changing because the roles of production, distribution and communication are also undergoing considerable change.

This can be summarized as a twofold change: "from work with individual elements to work with systems and from work in a linear chain to work as part of a network (Fast Report, 1986)." This change is crucial to BE because it has caused the dominant principle of the organization to shift from corporate control through command to cooperation in order to bring out the best in people and rapidly respond to change. Hence, BE's discourse must also take this new reality into account.

The other major change affecting organizations is related to education and learning, which are increasingly treated as a dimension of life, rather than simply a stage in life. Lesourne emphasizes this when he observes in our society "two great lines of strength: 1) it is possible that a new society is in gestation: a society saturated with information, impregnated by science and technology, open to the world; a society characterized by a diversity of individual situations rather than by the size of its large social groups, marked by the variety of its rhythms rather than by strict adherence to a particular tempo; a society that is hungry for capabilities and in a state of perpetual renewal and in which a large number of men and women will individually retain a portion of the collective skill...In short, a society that could also be called a society of education or

---

[4] The *Fast Report* (1986) mentioned optimists (who believe that new technologies will represent an unprecedented leap which will again make full employment possible), pessimists (who consider that the link between growth and increase in production, on the one hand, and increase in employment, on the other, no longer exists), fatalists (who consider fundamental not only the places and forms of work that will emerge, but the number of jobs that will be destroyed or become insecure), and those who consider that there will first be a descent before entering a new long cycle of growth.

training [...] 2) A predominant social demand is now becoming even greater than before: an impressive demand for capability that consists of autonomy, adaptability to innovation, the ability to work in groups, acceptance of responsibilities, competence built on attitudes that guarantee the maintenance and renewal of skills, the competence sought by employers but which individuals need in order to manage their personal lives and address their professional futures."[5] In other words, a society that thrives on innovation and knowledge creation does not need to simply institutionalize periods of instruction, but to foster learning processes, capacities, and attitudes that cause integrated and on-going development of persons and organizations.

In fact, because of the mandate given him, Lesourne's proposals center mainly on the educational system. But some years earlier a report to the Club of Rome (1979) had already raised a question that is today a widespread concern. It is not enough to investigate individual learning processes; it is also necessary to investigate group learning, either in society or organizations. Such research involves a task of the first order. How should private and public organizations and society as a whole be structured in order to enable learning processes to take place and create an atmosphere conducive to learning, guaranteeing free expression and acceptance of different alternatives? How will future learning institutions be designed? Therefore, what is at issue is not only the fact that information and knowledge have become decisive factors of economy; it is that, as a consequence, education and learning have become a decisive factor for the development and success of organizations themselves.

Hence, we are becoming more and more aware that the interaction between new technologies and human beings is only viable if it is conceived as an integrated process, marked by the development of all human capacities needed to be able to conduct and comprehend this process. But I think it is necessary to add that what is requested for the individual and society must occur in organizations as well. We must not forget that improvement of those human capacities developed by knowledge can only genuinely take place in the framework of organizational change to which we previously referred: from work with individual elements to work with systems, from work in a linear chain to work as part of a network. For this reason, it has been said that "this is probably the best definition of employees in the post-capitalist society: people whose ability to make a contribution depends on having access to an organization."[6]

The point, then, is not simply to say that countries which invest more in training and education will have the most competitive advantages. This statement also applies to organizations, especially when they plan to create their own learning processes without imitating the mechanisms of traditional formal education. In a society based on developing knowledge, learning should be a link between personal and organizational life. This learning is not content to create specialists, but focuses on developing persons who simultaneously acknowledge the growing individualization of their capabilities and increasing communicative interaction as the only situations in which their contribution can make sense. In this context, "learning cannot be essentially a matter of contents, but, above all, of correct processes. In a society that survives on the basis of innovation,

---

[5] Lesourne, 1988, p. 227-228.
[6] Drucker, 1992, p. 100.

education should not be a matter of rules and regulations, but should involve educating intuition, sensitivity, discernment, responsibility and freedom."[7]

If organizations have become places of innovation and knowledge creation, it would therefore seem that they should also internalize this learning capacity in all its dimensions (and not only in the supposedly operative and instrumental ones). This is something that until recently and in a different economic context would have seemed strange. In short, a knowledge-based economy may demand that organizations accept that learning is an approach, to knowledge and to life, which stresses human initiative. Such an economy involves acquiring and applying the new methodologies, new skills, new attitudes, and new values needed for living in a world in constant change. Thus, learning is the process through which human beings prepare themselves to face new situations.[8] Today, a problem that many organizations have inherited from our recent past is that they reduce learning to the acquisition of methodologies and skills, and content themselves with that.

If we assume that work is no longer performed with things and tools, but with men and women interacting with other men and women (or with individuals acting on information and knowledge that affects other individuals), then we need to consider that the new system of wealth creation can have an impact and consequences as radical as those produced by what we now call the Industrial Revolution.

In an economic context of innovation and creation, change - rather than equilibrium - becomes a central feature of the new paradigm (Boisot, 1994). The flexibility of systems and individuals becomes a condition for possible survival. This does not imply the legitimization of arbitrariness. On the contrary: the point is to find approaches and procedures that permit us to discern the approach we want to give our new responsibilities. We have moved from an age in which tradition was the guarantee of truth to another in which the guarantee is the rapid-fire process of searching for this truth. When the key to survival is not stability but change, many of the instruments used by humanity become antiquated and dulled and are useless as creators of orientation and meaning.

Thanks to this, we can recognize that in a knowledge society the creation of value and meaning is necessarily based on developing human quality. We find ourselves in a context of change and construction, in which values are no longer - nor will they ever again be- inherited. Furthermore, they are neither part of a natural order, an historical leit-motif, nor do they draw their strength from submission to an authority. In this context, then, the responsible and self-determined creation of goals becomes a necessary part of the new processes of social innovation. This, in turn, opens new possibilities for an ethical constructivism that will be capable of creating goals by taking an ethical approach rooted in dialogue and referring back to responsibility, because a knowledge society is one in which "social innovation is equally important and often more important than scientific innovation."[12]; it is a society in which the most exciting progress is not technological but a broader concept of what it means to be a human being; in which "innovation takes place on four fronts: in scientific knowledge, in technologies, in

---

[7] Corbi, 1992, p. 118.
[8] This was pointed out by Botkin *et al.* (1979) twenty years ago.

changes in the structures of work and society, and in the systems of motivation and goals which drive all these activities".[9]

The emergence of a knowledge society entails changes in the way work is conceived and organized, the concept of learning, and the concept of values. The very fact of considering what this means in terms of understanding organizations and the role individuals play in them should immediately lead us to think about the concept of the organization we should adopt if we want BE to correspond with the reality of the times. But there is another - and definitive - reason that concludes and justifies the leit-motiv of our inquiry: the knowledge society is not only a society in which knowledge is the crucial resource; it is also a society in which "specialized knowledge by itself produces nothing. It can become productive only when it is integrated into a task. And that is why the knowledge society is also a society of organizations: the purpose and function of every organization, business and non-business alike, is the integration of specialized knowledges into a common task."[10] No matter how you look at it, a knowledge society is a society of organizations.

9.2.   Transforming organizational paradigms

If the emerging knowledge society is essentially a society of organizations, we need to ask ourselves whether the organizational models and paradigms we have had until now continue to be the best ones. This question certainly exceeds the scope of BE. But BE cannot stop searching for an answer if it truly wants to become legitimized as applied ethics. In short, BE must critically express the realization that organizations are the key phenomenon of our times. Insofar as the organization is a key space for understanding our times, we must ask why discussion of late has been focusing more and more on revising the presuppositions of the paradigm on which both analytical and normative discourses on organizations have been constructed.

Although there have been attempts to take Kuhn's (1962) perspective into account in order to analyze what we could call organizational paradigms, it is difficult to find a sufficiently accepted approach that explores this perspective. Yet, in the contemporary debate about corporations and organizations the question about the frames of reference from which each scholar thinks about and analyzes them is increasingly present, especially when one tries to understand the reality of corporations and organizations in the context of the knowledge society. What is at issue here then is not organizational design, but organizational thought: many organizations are bureaucratized at some level by the mechanist form of thought that shapes our basic concept of the corporation. Hence, the point here is not to delve deeply into the diversity of approaches to the study of organizations, but to ask under what matrix of thought they have been constructed so that we can inquire about their validity in the context of the knowledge society. It is in this sense that analysis of the presupposition of machine bureaucracy has come to be the reference (either positive or negative) when reformulating organizational images or models.

At this point one begins to explore the fundamental traits of the image (Morgan, 1986), the metaphor (Burrell, 1988; Morgan, 1980), the questions (Bonnazzi, 1991), and

---

[9] Corbi, 1992, p. 135
[10] Drucker, 1992, p. 96.

the underlying myths (Meyer & Rowan, 1977) (not to speak of 'the paradigm') that are the foundation for a basic understanding of the organization. It is evident that these kinds of fundamental traits are always related to a practical management model. But although the management discourse can always rest on certain assumptions, it is symptomatic that the assumptions regarding machine bureaucracies are the ones ultimately called into question when anyone asks what type of organization is characteristic of the knowledge society. It seems legitimate that today's acknowledgement of the diversity of approaches to the study of the organization[11] should raise a question about the traits that are characteristic of organizations that form an inherent part of the knowledge society and that this question essentially goes beyond rejection of machine bureaucracy.

I referred earlier to the fact that one of the features of the current situation is what has been called a crisis of contemporary ideologies of mechanism or industrialization. What we need, then, is to realize that the origin of certain basic traits which enable us to understand organizations is contemporary with mechanism and industrialization and to question what obstacles this represents for the conceptualization of organizations today. New technology came accompanied and strengthened by the mechanization of thought and human action. Organizations that used machines increasingly thought of themselves as machines. A symbiosis between the concepts of the machine and the organization gradually took root so that in the first industrial revolution technology and industrial labor were structured around a mechanical image. The labor process and relations in the work place were viewed as similar to the relations between the different parts of a machine. This mechanistic approach to technology and work regards human beings as an extension of machines. They are harnessed to the machine and do whatever the machine is not equipped to do. The workings of the mind are also viewed in accordance with a mechanical image. Thus we encounter what has been called the mechanistic filiation of the model of organization, in which the machine's rigidity affects the very way of conceiving the organization.

Obviously, we should remember here that the difference between industrialization and a knowledge society does not consist simply of using knowledge. The industrial revolution was possible, first of all, due to the application of knowledge to tools, processes, and products; and the subsequent revolution in productivity was possible because it applied knowledge to organizing labor. The fundamental difference is in the fact that what we have today is an application - through organizations - of knowledge to knowledge itself (and to its creation) as the new basic resource. Therefore, the fundamental difference is that " we now know that management is a generic function of organizations, whatever their specific mission. It is the generating organ of the knowledge society."[12] Precisely because of this the pattern for understanding cannot be based on the acceptance of mechanical control and supervision linked to a certain foreseeable stability, but must be rooted in the logic of change and innovation and, even, of permanent destabilization. As we shall see, rather than flexible organizations this requires a flexible understanding of the organization, an understanding that acknowledges the specificity of individuals as subjects of knowledge.

---

[11] Which as Bonnazzi (1991) says, is sometimes used as an endorsement for epistemological "chameleonism".
[12] Drucker, 1993, p. 39.

Hence, given that the issue of industry and bureaucracy coincided in time as fundamental issues and given that throughout history the organization has been virtually identified with machine bureaucracy, what we should ask now is what it is that made this bureaucracy a mental scheme for understanding the organization.

Taking my approach, one can define Taylor's contribution as the first application of "knowledge to the study of work, the analysis of work and the engineering of work."[13] Taylor was productivity-oriented. It is important to note that the mechanistic approach is inseparable from the typical engineer's mentality, which dissects the organization of labor piece by piece, both in collective and individual terms, starting from a separation between hands and brains. Some people organize jobs and others perform them; the person who organizes them does not perform them; the person who performs a job does not organize it. In short, Taylorist approaches maintain that labor should be controlled by the people organizing it and not by the people who actually do the jobs. This is a clearly hierarchical conception of the organization, in which employees are viewed as accessories to machines. From this standpoint, the factory is a mechanism of control; a control that is exercised by separating the work process from the worker's skill, and by ensuring that management has a monopoly on knowledge and on decisions about using it.

The bureaucratic model originally expressed an organization theory that stressed hierarchy, specialization, formalization, and standardization. However, this stress cannot be understood unless it relates to its fundamental assumption: bureaucracies are created to manage stable, routine tasks; this is the foundation of their organizational efficiency. The problem, therefore, does not lie in the systematic rejection of machine bureaucracy, since, in fact, under certain circumstances it can be an adequate organizational form. The problem arises when machine bureaucracy becomes a normative model for the organization or even a matrix for the comprehension of the organizational fact. Then, as the history of organizational thought reveals, the process that unfolds resembles the process described in the preceding chapter when I discussed the rational model of decision-making: all subsequent elaboration has a strong tendency to define itself by largely underscoring what distinguishes it from the normative model; and, as a consequence, this model continues to be, indirectly, the model of reference.

This is significant because machine bureaucracy implies both a model of rationality and an anthropology, which often becomes, strictly speaking, an anthroponomy. The rationality underlying the machine design is what can be described as a "functional" or "instrumental" rationality, derived from the form in which employees and tasks combine to achieve a specific objective. In the bureaucratic system, actions are rational because of their place within the whole.

The legitimization of machine bureaucracy depends on a discourse in which rationality is taken to be the rationality of engineers and mechanics, who, by means of fragmentation, try to eliminate differences, annul autonomy, and promote submission. All this is an expression of a scientific rationality that legitimizes the power of the so-called scientific organizer of labor under the assumption that there is a single and best method to solve problems or perform actions of any kind. In strictly organizational terms, the limitations of this concept of rationality - limitations that go beyond the

---

[13] Drucker, 1993, p. 30.

recognition of bounded rationality - have been sufficiently emphasized. But I think that BE has failed to realize that some of the difficulties it encounters in its development are due to its overlooking the fact that the model of machine bureaucracy is linked to a bounded model of rationality. And when this model is not questioned, it becomes an obstacle to reformulating certain organizational questions in ethical terms, simply because it does not recognize certain uses or dimensions of rationality. It is here that it becomes relevant to engage in a critique of machine rationality as a generator of the myth of organizational rationality.

As Barely and Kunda (1992) have clearly indicated, the two pillars on which machine bureaucracy rests are the legitimacy and morality inherent to a form of "scientific" rationality and a normative perception of human beings according to which they act only under the criteria of maximizing economic rationality. Consequently, we could point to individualism as the underlying principle of machine bureaucracy and to an understanding of organizational order based on strict discipline.

It should not surprise us, for example, when Mintzberg (1979a) concludes that machine bureaucracy is a structure that is specifically obsessed with control. In other words, the efficiency of that machine bureaucracy in some contexts becomes inseparable from its capacity to sustain certain mechanisms of power and control, so that "prevailing theories assume that the coordination and control of activity are the critical dimensions on which formal organizations have succeeded in the modern world."[14] Thus, controlling labor and control itself as a means of organizing labor are at the heart of machine bureaucracy as an organizational system.

I think that this further illuminates and reinforces the points I discussed when analyzing both corporate codes and organizational cultures. It is particularly in line with the idea that it is dangerous to resort to ethics in order to ultimately seek a new form of control, perhaps more subtle and - supposedly – better suited to contemporary socio-cultural reality. In this kind of recourse to ethics two tendencies coincide and reinforce one other: on the one hand, what I call "negative" ethics, understood only as a reaction to avoid censurable conduct; and on the other hand, the urge to control as the core of corporate management, an inviolable tradition passed down as a legacy of the origins of thought regarding the concept of companies.

9.3.   An understanding of organizations that includes acknowledging the value of individuals and individuals as value

All in all, machine bureaucracy requires a stable environment, predictable processes, and a repeatable formalization. That is to say, it is exactly the opposite of the dynamics inherent to the new technologies leading to the emergence of the knowledge society: "The modern organization is a destabilizer. It must be organized for innovation and innovation [...] is 'creative destruction'. And it must be organized for the systematic abandonment of whatever is established, customary, familiar, and comfortable, whether that is a product, service, or process; a set of skills; human and social relationships; or the organization itself. In short, it must be organized for constant change."[15] If, as I

---

[14] Mayer & Rowan, 1977, p. 342.
[15] Drucker, 1992, p. 96.

suggested earlier, we acknowledge that innovation processes are not limited to creating knowledge, technologies, and the organization of labor but that they also include the motivations and goals that govern and drive them, we can conclude that it is essential to rethink not only our concepts about the organization, but also the matrix from which they stem. To sum up, the issue raised here is the need for organizations to be spaces in which freedom and open-mindedness are encouraged because without them there can be no innovation or "real integration of individuals as the organization's driving forces."[16]

When I referred to the debate about the hypothetical appearance of the knowledge society, I pointed out that the central role of knowledge means that change, innovation, and creation logically become essential elements for understanding this society. Furthermore, as I also pointed out, these elements require a capacity to think of human action that, first and foremost, addresses processes and to adopt a view that is capable of understanding processes not as isolated factors, but in the context of their interrelations within systems.

This issue is not one that should be considered relevant only from the company inwards, but should also be viewed as a key to its outward projection. Seen from this angle, in a knowledge-based economy and in knowledge-based corporations, relations with consumers are, or can also be, interactive relations involving information exchange and mutual learning. In this context, all corporate relations are also viewed as learning relations (or with a core component of learning). The rapid speed of change will force management to adopt new policies and new designs. The moment has probably come to prepare for a radical change both within the corporation and its surrounding environment.

This means that it is necessary to accept that organizations not only produce something (goods, services), but that in so doing they produce themselves (Zeleny, 1990): analyses of organizational life have been so mindful of the results that they have often overlooked the fact that the outcome is the organization itself. The capacity to foster integration while respecting diversity (which is a condition of innovation and creativity) is more and more a core element of management in new organizations. The point then is not to try to substitute a new model of organization for the old one, but to clearly explain the traits that constitute a model of organization from which we can understand and focus the very process of creating and constructing organizations.

In my approach to the issue of the emerging knowledge society, I note that the Fast report talked about a double transformation: from work with individual elements to work with systems and from work in a linear chain to work as part of a network. In my own terms, this implies a change that is not only practical or operational; it also implies a change in the mentality from which we understand the organization as such. Various models or frames of reference which would enable us to better understand and address new organizational realities have been proposed (systems, organisms, brains, networks, and so on). However, all these proposed models imply that culture and organizational values can no longer be considered as a means of exercising control through "inculturization". They must be viewed instead as a central part of organization management, once we have accepted that in the new technological, social, and organizational context managers make decisions and execute policies on the basis not

---

[16] Filella, 1994, p. 56.

only of their experience, but also of their assumptions about what constitutes reality. Thus the so-called industrial reconversion is a reconversion of the minds involved in the production processes and not simply a reconversion of obsolete products.

The step from hierarchy to networks is significant because accepting it entails addressing new needs and demands which are an inherent part of organizations and which cannot be handled with conventional conceptual tools. There are, of course, different views on what these needs and demands are. For some people they consist of sharing objectives, experiences, labor, decision-making, time, priorities, responsibility, and recognition (Rockart & Short, 1991). For others, they involve organizational cooperation (including cooperation between competing corporations) and the protagonism of actors (Solé & Bramanti, 1991); or the creation of a community of individuals who work in a cooperative and decentralized way, aware that they are interdependent and sharing a purpose (García-Ramos, 1990); for still others they are companies that are more horizontal and egalitarian than vertical because competence and personality take on more importance (Toffler, 1990); or because the central role of communication makes the individual a more intrinsic part of the organization (Naisbitt, 1983).

Obviously, I am not assuming that networks are the basic form of the future since this would largely amount to presupposing the same uniformity that bureaucracy imposed, albeit on a higher and freer level. But I note that in organizations in which information and knowledge are the backbone of the company it is necessary to accept some governing principles that are appropriate to this reality. These organizations must be places where each person can learn from the others, horizontally, and where each person can be a resource for other individuals and can receive support and aid from many different sources. Furthermore, these organizations must be able to understand responsibility not only in terms of the relation between cause and effect, but also in terms of acknowledging and accepting their place within the system. From this perspective, the link between conventional and postconventional perspectives is not intended solely to be consistent with a particular approach to ethics, it is also a requisite that stems from our acknowledgement that individuals are crucial for organizational viability.

This central role of people is based on accepting that, when knowledge is the decisive factor, all knowledge workers can work only because there is an organization. But at the same time they own the means of production, i.e., their knowledge. So, accepting the premise that knowledge gives individuals a decisive role, individual and organization need one other. While the person is less and less interchangeable, it is more and more the case that "it is always persons who ultimately decide how they will react and what resources they will place at the disposal of the others, in accordance with their view of the situation."[17] The human subject thus ceases to be a function of the organization and becomes a condition of its viability.

This means that priority must be given to working with persons, rather than working on structures; organizational practices should not be taken out of context and individuals should be considered the organization's structuring resource. Thus, a question that first focused on technology becomes a problem of organizing human

---

[17] Filella, 1994, p. 75.

resources, of encouraging communication among them, and of their ability to share new goals and objectives as well as learn new skills and develop new creative and customer service capacities. Hence, it is necessary for organizations to be able to mobilize individual persons around a project that galvanizes their capacities and inclines them towards cooperation and communication. In short, organizations are persons that work together and therefore their greatest challenge is integrating the individual persons who make up the organization.

Organizations must therefore be able to express what mobilizes and integrates their members' contributions and talents by clearly formulating their purposes, their raison d'être. "One consequence of this new relationship – and it is another new tension in modern society – is that loyalty can no longer be obtained by the paycheck. The organization must earn loyalty by proving to its knowledge employees that it offers them exceptional opportunities for putting their knowledge to work [...] Because the modern organization consists of knowledge specialists, it has to be an organization of equals, of colleagues and associates. No knowledge ranks higher than another; each is judged by its contribution to the common task rather than by any inherent superiority or inferiority. Therefore, the modern organization cannot be an organization of boss and subordinate. It must be organized as a team."[18] This has led some people to think that organizational links are also somehow voluntary (since they involve persons who are putting their knowledge on the line), and must be viewed with this in mind. In short, in today's knowledge-based corporations, the best people are where they are because they want to be there. For them, the organization has become a "voluntary" organization in which they choose to integrate because it can allow them to reach their personal objectives better than any other.

Assuming that companies cannot set themselves strictly economic goals, but must have multiple objectives, their products in practice are not simply economic, but also axiological, communicative, and social. This expands the idea of the corporation and becomes tremendously complex because a process of organizational change and innovation cannot take place in any company without a shared vision guiding and orienting the process itself. In contrast, in old-fashioned companies numbers sum up their vision and shape their goals.

The shared vision therefore guides the organization's integration of personal and collective values. And if we take into account both organizations and professionals, this integration includes accepting basic values which can be reformulated in strictly ethical terms: openness, trust, participation, and simplicity; the distribution of responsibilities at all corporate levels, on the assumption that communicating and sharing are key factors for being able to operate in a network; encouragement of self-determination; organizational simplicity, autonomy, and management by culture. In short, no technology can by itself succeed in making individuals cooperate and it is essential that people cooperate because it is only through cooperation that integrated production will be secured. Therefore, in order to achieve integrated production, you need something more than technology. The dominant principle of the organization has changed: it has gone from command as a means of controlling the company to cooperation in order to bring out the best in people and be able to quickly respond to change. The question is,

---

[18] Drucker, 1992, p. 101.

then, what and who guides knowledge and the organization based on it, given that organizing intelligence is equivalent to organizing autonomy, self-regulation, self-control, and self-planning of teams; and given that organizing intelligence also involves motivating and maintaining the voluntary adherence of each and every one of those who possess knowledge.

Approaches like this are not the exclusive property of the academic world. They also exist in the business world. In Spain, for example, one of the most prominent and well-respected business leaders has stated that "the corporation is, as we know, the fundamental structure driving the extraordinary development of our age, and human beings constitute the hard core that inspires and guides it. We should, therefore, turn the corporation into a smaller model in which the people who are part of it become conscious of the pressing need to establish it as the basic cell in order to meet the great challenge of constructing the new Europe, the Europe that will be sustainable in the future. [...] The new corporation should be handed over to a sensitive kind of human beings who exercise freedom with responsibility; i.e., people with a maximum of creative potential because there is no creativity without freedom. Because of their sensitivity, this kind of human being feels the need to foster moral, cultural, ethical, and aesthetic values on a personal and social scale so that these values converge with the values of the amazing material development of our time and do not diverge from them as has been the case up to now. In my opinion then, responsible freedom and sensitivity are, therefore, the basic values that must define the new class of human beings in these new corporations in the new Europe. Human beings who can worthily personify the new humanism, i.e. scientific humanism, and who are able to carry this humanism over into the decisions of the new corporation, imbuing them with the necessary creative meaning and transcendence, overcoming the typical inertia of a society like ours today in which, unfortunately, rejection of creative and responsible risk is normal."[19] Thus, the issue ultimately raised is that understanding organizations in the contemporary social, cultural, and technological context irremediably leads us to ask about the human quality which will make organizations viable in the future, and to ask about the development in organizations of everything referring to potential human quality. And this implies that the subject of the corporation will have to be human beings, and not structures, procedures, or money.[20]

If we adopt this approach, organizations have to be conceived as contexts that facilitate personal development and promote self-regulation. This includes searching for and discovering hidden talents and making an important effort to find the capacities, the creativity, the initiative, and the resources that individuals possess but which are not used, either because they are unaware of their own possibilities, because we limit ourselves to simply giving them orders, or because we cannot develop them in the organizational context in which they work. But it also entails seeing organizations as educators of the individuals who are part of them, providing an education that includes the ethical sensitivity of their members because organizational projects will only be

---

[19] Duran, 1994, p. 7.

[20] Obviously, this does not imply ignoring the importance of structures, procedures, and money. But it does imply that "the human factor continues to be the great 'unknown' or the unsuspected factor that still needs to be discovered in corporate management. It is difficult for us to think, plan, act, and experience organizations from the viewpoint of the human factor" (Filella, 1994, p. 51).

constructed on the basis of this sensitivity. We must stop thinking that an organization has a series of resources, one of which is human resources,[21] and start realizing that persons are of central importance in organizational development.

In other words, a society increasingly driven by change and technological innovation needs all of us to be educated to develop intuition, imagination, ethics, and freedom. New life and production styles lead us to emphasize the necessity of learning how to learn and innovate as one of the basic conditions for the viability of any organization and any social group. In order to do this, we need to emphasize ethical education, which is more important than ever because the tools available to use are ever more powerful. However, this question cannot be resolved if we do not accept that it is inseparable from the change in learning processes that are produced - and can be produced - within corporations. The central feature of a society that lives off knowledge production is its focus on learning. Learning is at the heart of the collective endeavor and it is the basis of all relations between individuals and groups. It is therefore necessary to ask how to learn within an organization, because what is important is to educate in order to be constantly learning. And to do so from an ethical standpoint in which human beings increase their possibilities insofar as they are able to feel that they are travelling along a common path with other human beings.

---

[21] In Spain, we have insisted on this change which, obviously, is not merely linguistic: "Human resources or individuals with resources" (Filella, 1994, p. 72). "Ethically it might not be very correct to think about human resources, because it equates individuals with things and leads us to speak of men and women as possessions. Neither does it seem to me very correct to say: 'The best capital (we have) are our people', simply because people are not capital of any kind. Men and women are persons, and a person cannot be owned. It is persons who own the corporation, not the corporation that owns persons" (Llano, 1993, p. 7).

CHAPTER 10

THE LEARNING ORGANIZATION AS THE MATRIX OF BUSINESS ETHICS

The attempt to rethink business ethics in terms of learning implies assuming that, as far as understanding organizations is concerned, "the fall of the old order has not marked the advent of overwhelming certainties as regards a universal model of organization and management."[1] However, the fact that we - fortunately- lack a universal model does not prevent certain references from becoming increasingly common in the knowledge society. Since the viability of organizations increasingly requires something more than a mere aggregation of specialists, the question of how to educate people within the framework of organizational processes has become more and more recurrent (Srica, 1993), and particularly so in a world in which the challenge has become "learning in a world of learners".[2] It is therefore necessary to recall that the emergence of the knowledge society can run parallel to "a predominant social demand: an impressive demand for capability that consists of autonomy, adaptability to innovation, the ability to work in groups, acceptance of responsibilities, competence built on attitudes that guarantee the maintenance and renewal of skills, the competence sought by employers but which individuals need in order to manage their personal lives and address their professional futures."[3]

It should be emphasized here that the connection between knowledge and learning is a connection inherent to organizational dynamics itself, and that it refers to all fields in which, as I previously noted, knowledge creation should be an issue: science, technology, organization and axiology. For this reason I subscribe to the Club of Rome's definition, which maintains that learning is an approach, both to knowledge and to life, that stresses human initiative. This includes the acquisition and practice of the new methodologies, new skills, new attitudes, and new values which are necessary for living in a world in constant change. Therefore, when we talk about learning we refer to the capacity to activate human potential in all its dimensions. This is what makes the distinction between sustained learning and innovative learning particularly relevant.

Sustained learning enables people to learn criteria, rules, and methods with which to face known and recurrent situations. Problems are thus solved on the basis of problems already experienced and resolved. In contrast, innovative learning puts the accent on enabling people to face unprecedented situations, which are nonetheless the result of human action. It is oriented less to adaptation than to anticipation. This anticipation already plays a role in the very understanding of problems and is therefore necessarily the result of using different approaches in order to tackle problems in all their complexity. In my opinion the issue is not to simply contrast the two models of learning (since both are necessary), but to affirm the need for innovative learning given that one of its tasks is to increase the individual's capacity to find, absorb, and create new contexts, or, to put it more succinctly, to enrich the range of contexts.

---

[1] Belet, 1993, p. 310.
[2] The expression is from Levitt and March, p. 331.
[3] Lesourne, 1988, p. 227-228.

Is it possible then to conceive of organizations as contexts that also favor learning? This ultimately becomes a primary challenge if we accept that learning "may become the only sustainable competitive advantage."[4] Consequently, "any company that aspires to succeed in the tougher business environment of the 1990s must first resolve a basic dilemma: success in the marketplace increasingly depends on learning, yet most people don't know how to learn."[5] The difficulty consists, then, in the need to think of learning - both as an activity and a process - in a way that is suitable for organizations, and avoid a concept of organizational learning that is a simple extrapolation from the learning model that stressed comprehension and is characteristic of educational institutions as well as a conception of organizational learning that is nothing more than a repetition of what is said about individual learning, simply replacing the words "individual" or "person" with "organization". Instead, we must start with the organization, and not with learning, if we really want to understand learning of organizations and in organizations.

It is important to realize that, even if the agents of learning are individuals, organizational learning cannot be reduced to an aggregate of individual learning. Firstly, organizational learning takes place through shared perceptions, knowledge, and mental models. This means that the possibility of change is blocked if all the most important decision-makers are not learning together, if they do not tend to share beliefs and objectives, and if they are not committed to taking the decisions necessary to bring about change. Secondly, learning is constructed on the basis of previous learning and previous experience - that is, on the basis of memory. Organizational learning depends on institutional mechanisms (for example, policies, strategies, and explicit models) which are used to retain knowledge. Relying exclusively on individuals involves the risk of losing the best lessons and experiences when people change their workplace. Therefore, the challenge is to discover new methods and new management tools that accelerate organizational learning, build consensus for change, and facilitate the change process. Thus, organizational learning becomes inseparable from the processes and dynamics of change. In fact, it can be said that concern about learning in organizations and of organizations has been inseparable from concern about managing processes of organizational change in an economic, social, and cultural context that is also changing.

Seen from this perspective, the question is not whether organizations learn (they all do), but whether they learn consciously and deliberately, and how they do so. "The importance of individual learning for organizational learning is at once obvious and subtle – obvious because all organizations are composed of individuals: subtle because organizations can learn independent of any specific individual but not independent of all individuals."[6]

This is the sense in which I want to propose a connection between learning as an organizational process and BE (as applied ethics) the backbone of organizational processes. I think that only from this frame of reference can we cope with the problem of integration: not as a final point to reach, but as a regulating criterion of the organizational process itself, which BE helps define and understand, and to which it is incorporated as a learning process that includes ethical learning.

---

[4] Stata, 1989, p. 64.
[5] Argyris, 1991, p. 99.
[6] Kim, 1993, p. 37.

Although it is possible to map the coordinates of a learning organization, there is no unanimous agreement about what should be understood as organizational learning and, consequently, how it should be evaluated.[7] There is, however, convergence in the consideration of organizational factors as something more than the sum of its members' learning: "four contextual factors affect the probability that learning will occur: corporate culture conducive to learning, strategy that allows flexibility, an organizational structure that allows both innovativeness and new insights, and the environment. These have a circular relationship with learning in that they create and reinforce learning and are created by learning."[8] But this entails realizing that learning cannot be reduced, as is still often the case, to an increase in operational competences. Instead, it must necessarily include the development, through cooperation, of the capacity to work upon one's own mental models in both their personal and organizationally shared dimensions. Ultimately, it is from these that we establish what we understand as effective action.

In short, in a world of change, whose complexity is the result of both interdependence and vast diversity, one of the requirements for human action involves establishing a frame of reference from within which such action is constituted and understood. This must be done because this frame of reference is not automatically established and shared as the result of a homogeneous social context or some axiological references which individuals accept as evident and immutable. I think that in this context it is necessary to understand the benefits of viewing organizations as learning organizations. In my opinion, this would explain why the study of organizational learning in learning organizations has been so careful to include as part of learning the capacity to determine the "how" and "why" of the mental models on which organizational reality is based and shaped.

Argyris has made one of the main contributions to the explanation of organizational learning. He researched the relations between action and learning in the framework of the need for human maturity and elaborated a theory of "organizational learning" that represents a significant evolution in his approach. Argyris ultimately conceives the organization as a "cognitive construction," i.e, a structure in which subjects are not solely agents of action, but also agents of organizational learning. In other words, subjects become agents who contribute actively to changing the way in which reality (cognitive map) is viewed in the organization.

Another of Argyris' contributions is the systematic observation that in the corporate world (in general, but among managers in particular) there is an exaggerated dissociation or inconsistency between the theories that proclaim how the corporation's actions should be, and the discourse and criteria which guide corporate practice.[9] It is

---

[7] For further discussion on this, see: Argyris, 1991; Argyris & Schön, 1978; Belet, 1993; Fiol & Lyles, 1985; Garratt, 1990; Hedberg, 1981; Kim, 1993; Levitt & March, 1988; Marsick, 1988; Nielsen, 1993; Nueno, 1991; Ramírez, 1983, Senge, 1990; Watkins & Marsick, 1993a, 1993b.

[8] Fiol & Lyles, 1985, p. 804.

[9] "Like the rules for collective decision and action, organizational theories of action need not be explicit. Indeed, formal corporate documents such as organization charts, policy statements, and job descriptions often reflect a theory of action (the *espoused* theory) which conflicts with the organization's *theory-in-use* (the theory of action is constructed from observation of actual behavior – and the theory-in-use is often tacit. Organizational theory-in-use may remain tacit because its incongruity with espoused theory is *undiscussable*. Or it may remain tacit because individual members of the organization know more than they can say –

necessary to take into account the fact that the theories that are being used work as true mental maps of organizations and rule their action. We could therefore reformulate our approach so that we always ask whether BE is an espoused theory or a theory-in-use.

All these approaches conceive of learning not as a merely cognitive (or intellectual) capacity, but always as referring to action: learning is a dimension of which action, whether individual or organizationally triggered, is an inherent part.

This means that all organizations always have a theory of action such as the one described above and that learning is always based on activities, not ideals.

This approach to learning, which is rooted in practice but includes reformulation of the frames of reference from which it is understood and oriented, is explained with another of Argyris' terminological contributions: the distinction between what he calls single-loop and double-loop learning. The distinction is rooted in the question about why professionals, who usually accept the need to change and continually improve their performance in order to be effective, are so resistant to change and protect themselves from it by boasting their expertise as specialists. For Argyris the key lies in the way they think and reason about their conduct and the conduct of others and, therefore, in how to foster cooperation in working on their ways of thinking.

According to Argyris, professionals' resistance to certain requirements of change is due to the strong frames of reference from within which they conceive and orient their action, and not so much due to difficulties that involve technical, operative, or organizational capacities. And for the same reason, corporations err in believing that "getting people to learn is largely a matter of motivation. When people have the right attitudes and commitment, learning automatically follows. So companies focus on creating new organizational structures – compensated programs, performance reviews, corporate cultures, and the like – that are designed to create motivated and committed employees. But effective double-loop learning is not simply a function of how people feel. It is a reflection of how they think – that is, the cognitive rules or reasoning they use to design and implement their actions."[10]

The problem, then, is how organizations learn to develop personal and organizational capacities for double-loop learning, a capacity that, in a context of change, is similar to the capacity to develop what the Club of Rome refers to as innovative learning. Therefore, "the desired consequence of this type of learning often is not any particular behavioral outcome, but rather the development of frames of reference or interpretive schemes, new cognitive frameworks within which to make decisions.[11] For this reason, the conceptual distinction between learning within a frame of reference and learning a new frame of reference is of fundamental importance.

I believe that adopting this approach has a high value-added component for BE. It closes the door to any inclination to adopt a static approach - from the analytical point of view - or a mechanist approach - from the practical point of view - to the treatment of elements that we have previously accepted as constituting BE. Putting the accent on persons and the way in which they understand and orient their actions in organizational

---

because the theory-in-use is *inaccessible* to them. Whatever the reason for tacitness, the largely tacit theory-in-use accounts for organizational identity and continuity." Argyris & Schön, 1978, p. 15.

[10] Argyris, 1991, p. 100.
[11] Fiol & Lyles, 1985, p. 808.

terms is synonymous with facilitating the development of learning how to learn through organized structures and processes that correspond with such development.

The accent, then, should be on promoting processes that foster people's capacity to learn and, consequently, on strengthening the cultures and structures that allow this to happen. Both culture and structures are therefore indispensable, but the focus is on processes. "In this sense, 'values' are better understood as those structured processes within which individuals, groups of individuals, and groups of groups of individuals experience meaning and significance;"[12] and they experience it insofar as they simultaneously shape and accept it. Thus, management ceases to regard itself as a function in which control predominates, and instead emphasizes its function as a process galvanizer, to such an extent that some authors have talked about the triumph of process over structure (Garratt, 1990). Nevertheless, "it is very difficult for business people to accept that complexity because many of them need to see themselves as being in control [...] There are at least two beliefs dismantled here. The first is that people can control an organization from on top or at a distance. The second is that you can ever fully understand a system or figure it out."[13] In other words, the world of organizations is accustomed to being concerned about the complexity of accumulated elements and does not really know how to tackle dynamic complexity (Senge, 1990) since this necessarily involves creating an appropriate organizational paradigm.

This assumes that organizational interrelations must be understood in terms of the processes in which learning occurs. Indeed, learning occurs in all organizations; the problem is that there are few systems for evaluating and attaining it and, consequently, one does not always know how to systematically foster it. But it has been mainly due to organizational and labor changes (linked to the technological and social changes referred to previously) that work is more and more closely tied to learning. Because of this, the need to have an organizational paradigm becomes apparent when it is observed that managers value their own worth in terms of the extent to which they control (or believe they control) their organizations, and consider that devoting time to reflection is a nuisance or a waste of time (Garratt, 1990). It is as if collective inquiry were a threat. The consequence is that people close themselves off from learning. But, because one of the main facets of management responsibilities is to facilitate and improve learning of and in the organization, what appears to be on the cards is a new image of how these corporations work"Just because no one is 'in control' does not mean that there is no 'control'. In fact, all healthy organisms have processes of control. However, they are distributed processes, not concentrated in any one authoritarian decision maker."[14]

Having said that, we should also acknowledge that the concept of the learning organization, towards which we are advancing here is probably very vague, as Belet (1993) pointed out. But I think that, as Belet himself indicates, this is, to a large extent, due to the fact that, "it is not a new model of universal management towards which it would be necessary to tend, but rather it is another process and another dynamic of management which constitutes the sketch of a new paradigm of development of human resources."[15] The elements that constitute it cannot, in many cases, be said to be

---

[12] King, 1989, p. 43.
[13] Gaffney, 1989, p. 32.
[14] Senge, 1990, p. 292.
[15] Belet, 1993, p. 316.

absolutely new in terms of theory, and the definitions that have been proposed do not have a single,common meaning. But, if we address certain converging features, I think that Watkins and Marsick's approach is the most systematic and the one that best expresses what is proposed in the framework of learning organizations. Thus, they say: "the learning organization is one that learns continuously and transforms itself. Learning takes place in individuals, teams, the organization and even the communities with which the organization interacts. Learning is a continuous, strategically used process - integrated with, and running parallel to, work. Learning results in changes in knowledge, beliefs and behaviors. Learning also enhances organizational capacity for innovation and growth. The learning organization has embedded systems to capture and share learning. "[16] Watkins and Marsick point out that it is good to take into account the fact that "advocates may differ about specific details, but in general, they agree that the learning organization:(1) Is not just a collection of individuals who are learning – instead, learning also occurs simultaneously at various collective levels within business units and sometimes within an entire company.(2) Demonstrates organizational capacity for change.(3) Accelerates individual learning capacity but also redefines organizational structure, culture, job design, and mental models (assumptions about the way things are).(4) Involves widespread participation of employees, and often customers, in decision making, dialogue, and information sharing. (5) Promotes systemic thinking and building of organizational memory."[17]

I mentioned earlier that organizational learning is not possible without individual learning and that, as a result, the development of learning organizations rests entirely on the development of personal capacities. Now, in the framework of learning organizations it is emphasized that individual learning is a necessary condition for organizational learning, but does not guarantee it. This is particularly so if we bear in mind that learning should not be confused with training (although training is considered part of learning). Indeed, it should not be confused because, as I pointed out earlier, learning in the context of learning organizations includes a process by means of which shared mental maps are also redrawn and these are the maps through which organizations understand and orient their actions. In sum: it is a learning that includes double-loop learning and therefore a learning that is not possible when viewed only in individual terms.

After observing that "when placed in the same system, people, however different, tend to produce similar results,"[18] Senge raised the thought-provoking question of whether this happens because they are prisoners of the system or because they are also prisoners of their own way of thinking. It is therefore important to take into account Marsick's (1988) identification of three fields of learning: instrumental (technical-oriented), dialogic (culture and objectives- oriented), and self-reflective (oriented towards personal change in a social context). As Marsick points out, these three fields are interconnected, but each one represents a broader view than the preceding one. Now, insofar as the dimensions of learning are broadened, the individualist perspective becomes insufficient. For this reason learning organizations empower individuals, but

---

[16] Watkins & Marsick, 1993a, p. 8.
[17] Watkins & Marsick, 1993, p. XII.
[18] Senge, 1990, p. 42.

they rely on groups. Since there is no organizational learning without individual learning, individual learning is a necessary, but insufficient, condition for organizational learning. In short, organizational learning is a process that requires inquiry through collaboration among individual members.

The basic unit of organizational learning and learning organizations is the team, the group. And this is so because what sustains the concept of the learning organization is the assumption that inquiry is a dialogue in which people mutually explore ideas, questions, and potential actions, and that it takes place through conversation. This is a conversation that is able to question the justification and plausibility of the reasoning presented, and in which all the participants share this open-minded attitude.

Thus, "when talk is meant as inquiry, the goal is meaningful dialogue with the possibility of learning from one another in a collaborative, equal manner."[19] This entails developing attitudes for the kind of dialogue one wants to promote: a disposition to listen, be open to other people's views and go beyond a simple exchange of information. Evidently, this does not mean that there should not be arguments or conflicts, but what characterizes a learning organization is not lack of such things, but how they are approached and tackled. It has been emphasized that in a learning context one should not confuse dialogue with argument or debate. "Dialogue can be initially defined as a sustained collective inquiry into the processes, assumptions and certainties that compose everyday experience."[20] The point then is not a simple exchange, but also a shared rethinking. It has therefore been suggested that teams should be defined as individuals that need each other to act (Senge, 1990). It is thus assumed that shared learning processes do not include only joint elaboration of the comprehension of problems, integration of perspectives - which is achieved by going beyond one's own boundaries and by being willing to make them permeable, and resolution of the problems that have emerged. Above all, they also include changing the contexts in which individuals act as a result of the process itself.

Nevertheless, we should recall that neither group activity nor the process of dialogue which constitutes it is self-sufficient. Neither do they circle around themselves or occur in a void. This explains why there is so much insistence on the organization's cultural and structual capacity to shape a collective vision in order to build a learning organization. A learning process that takes place through group dialogue requires a close fit between individual and collective processes. And this is possible only if mental models are shared because, among other things, individuals are involved in reformulating them. The shift from fragmented learning to organizational learning therefore entails shared and explicit construction of the action's meaning and purpose. This is what is reflected in the vision that enables team members' actions to be aligned with one another. A group vision is not the vision of the most dominating individual or the individual with the clearest vision. It is a reality in itself, comprising formal and informal aspects, emotional and planned commitments, and enabling personal capacities and intentions to be affirmed and reinforced. A vision is more than an idea; it is an ideal that is shared, contextualized, and understood. "You cannot have a learning organization without shared vision. Without a pull toward some goal which people truly

---

[19] Watkins & Marsick, 1993a, p. 89.
[20] Isaacs, 1993, p. 25.

want to achieve, the forces in support of the status quo can be overwhelming. Vision establishes an overarching goal. The loftiness of the target compels new ways of thinking and acting. A shared vision also provides a rudder to keep the learning process on course when stresses develop. Learning can be difficult, even painful. With a shared vision, we are more likely to expose our ways of thinking, give up deeply held views, and recognize personal and organizational shortcomings."[21] A shared view encourages experimentation and a willingness to take risks. It also gives an answer to a question that is fundamental for both ethics and the corporation: how can long-term commitment be encouraged? People do not focus on the long term because they have to, but because they want to, and what is at stake here is the construction of a shared commitment.

This does not mean shutting oneself off from everyday life. On the contrary: a vision invariably has its roots in reality. Some authors insist that the important thing is to resolve day-to-day issues, but with a vision (Senge, 1990); that a vision only makes sense in the present (Garratt, 1990); that a vision cannot be dissociated from the day-to-day reality of work (Watkins & Marsick, 1993a). In sum, a vision only generates commitment when it stems from a consideration of the present with all its problems. It is not a discourse about the future (or about ideals) as a self-contained entity. In short, it is much easier to talk about future possibilities because the results are more abstract, less personal, and therefore more comfortable. Today we know that vision is a familiar concept of corporate leadership. But we also know that most "visions" belong to an individual (or group) and are imposed on the organization. In this case, they demand submission, not commitment, whereas a shared view secures the commitment of many people.

Thus an important feature of a vision is its "appeal". It galvanizes people by attracting them, and not by being imposed on them through either rules or structures. Hence it awakens and expresses individuals' interior strength and energy. The affirmation of a vision rests on the affirmation of individuals as such and is therefore linked to ethics' affirmation and acknowledgment of individuals. For "in encouraging personal vision, organizations must be careful not to infringe on individual freedoms. No one can give another "his vision", nor even force him to develop a vision. However, there are positive actions that can be taken to create a climate that encourages personal vision. The most direct is for leaders who have a sense of vision to communicate that in such a way that others are encouraged to share their visions. This is the art of visionary leadership – how shared visions are built from personal visions."[22] Thus, in the context of learning organizations, leadership is of vital importance. This is a type of leadership essentially linked to facilitating and shaping learning processes and processes of organizational change, involving leaders who are committed to the change process and who are coherent in their speech and action. This coherence can also be called ethical congruence or consistence.

The logic of the learning organization intrinsically refers to ethical criteria due to its basic requirements: learning, dialogue among group members, and attention to the social consequences of its actions.

---

[21] Senge, 1990, pp. 209.
[22] Senge, 1990 p. 202.

As regards developing the ethical values inherent to this understanding of learning, it must be recalled that innovative learning is only possible when there is a predisposition to share power and a spirit of participation which allows both personal and shared mental models to be reformulated through a cooperative approach to the problems and challenges that stem from ordinary action. This process implies building relations that are characterized by open-mindedness, so that people are prepared to suspend their own beliefs when encountering those of another and allow themselves to be influenced by the other (Senge, 1990). It is also characterized by a tolerance of error linked to the exploration of various points of view (Morgan, 1986).

As regards development of the ethical values inherent in corporate attention to the social consequences of their actions, the attitude of learning organizations (Hedberg, 1981) is specifically expressed through an interaction with stakeholders that seeks to address problems through co-determination. Because of this, problems are resolved in a way that is satisfactory to everyone and to the community of interests of all the affected parties. This is done through understanding responsibility in systemic rather than merely causal terms: an understanding based on a commitment to a vision and not on simple obedience.

10.1. BE's three "moments" as an organizational learning process

Integration is a key element in regulating this understanding of learning, provided that it is put into practice through an open process rather than through closed structural terms, and embraces objectives as well as structures, relations, and mental models. As I pointed out earlier, learning organizations are characterized by the conjunction and mutual reinforcement of individual learning and a set of collective learning processes. They shift from an instrumental logic which essentially focuses on individual learning and acquisition of knowledge and competences to an integrated approach that conjugates individual and collective development of human resources in the framework of a new management philosophy.[23] At the heart of the development of learning organizations we again find an affirmation of the value of the individual. Taken to its extreme, the emphasis on quality (which is often understood only in terms of procedures and products) broadens its horizons in the framework of a normative affirmation of human quality.

This opens a path towards solving a question that often cannot be solved in the context of BE. The learning organization sees itself as a social institution, which however needs to foster the development of persons at all levels of their capacities. It thus presupposes an acknowledgment that the affirmation of human quality is not viable

---

[23] One can nonetheless mention other characteristics that describe the learning organization. For example (Belet, 1993): planning strategy in terms of learning; involving all participants in formulating corporate policy, new forms of information, accounting systems and a system for monitoring training; internal logic of customer-supplier transactions; a flexible remuneration system; organizational structures that create opportunities for development; collaborators oriented towards the context of the corporation; a system of organizational learning based on exchange with other corporations; a favorable climate for learning based on experience and experimentation; opportunities for the self-development of all employees. And Watkins & Marsick (1993a) mention: a culture focused on learning; a decentralized structure centered on the relations among work groups; an enterprising strategy centered on innovation and learning; integrated use of the technological and economic resources of information systems.

if it is limited only to professional or job-related aspects. It therefore realizes that improving the quality of life in the work place involves promoting the quality of life in all other spheres. And this can ultimately lead to the development of a kind of freedom which goes beyond dealing with organizational commitment in terms of "freedom to" and integrates things like reason and intuition, vision, compassion, and commitment to the corporation as a whole. In short, with this understanding of learning, the people involved in learning in an organizational context see how "their own identity and growth are recognized as integral to that learning."[24]

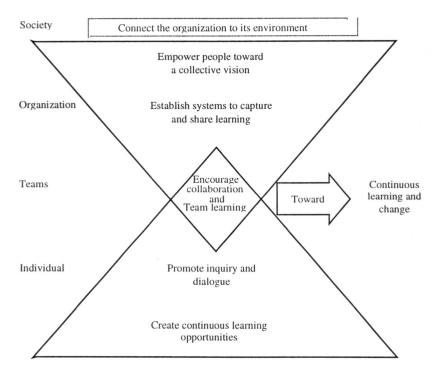

Source: Watkins and Marsick. (1993a)

In a learning organization, learning takes place at successively more complex and larger collective levels: individuals, groups and teams, bigger corporate units and networks, the organization itself, its network of relations with customers, suppliers and other social groups. Learning in the learning organization is highly relational. We must therefore acknowledge that learning organizations aim to integrate four different levels (individuals, groups, organization, society). This integration takes place through

---

[24] Marsick, 1988, p. 194.

organizational mediation and is based on the things that specifically characterize and define the organization's activity. Characterized by an orientation towards continuous learning and change, the learning organization fosters the spirit of inquiry and dialogue in individuals. Moreover, it constantly creates opportunities for learning, encourages collaboration and team learning, grants autonomy and responsibility to people as they work towards a collective vision, establishes systems for acquiring and sharing learning throughout the organization, and connects the organization with its social environment. Seen from this angle, the learning organization is not a normative and universal model of organization, but a paradigm and matrix for understanding any organizational reality. And it is in this frame of reference that I place my conviction that BE's future largely depends on a dialogue with new ideas and with the development of research on learning organizations.

From an analytical and normative standpoint, I think that the view of organizations as learning organizations adds a new basic element to the triple distinction between individual, organization, and society which I consider fundamental for BE's development. This element is the group, held together by shared dialogue and inquiry. I consider this essential to BE because it involves acknowledging a dimension that has up to now been lacking in BE proposals. This has the added value that such awareness is not produced as a consequence of reflections on ethics, but on business. However, it is a reflection that can converge with my approach to BE since the paradigmatic matrix of the learning organization enables us to point to a consequentialist moment in learning (as a responsibility situated in the network of social relations), a conventional moment (which shapes subjects and contexts without reducing this endeavor to a functional aspect of the organization), and a reflective-normative moment (which is expressed in a form more attractive than imperative and which preserves the subjects' autonomy). In the context of the emerging knowledge society, the convergence of BE and learning organizations permits us to accept the claim that innovation is at once organizational and axiological, and also permits us to explain that the proposed orientations respond to both organizational and ethical demands, without confusing them with one other. In other words, it gives us a single language that includes both ethical and organizational perspectives.

Furthermore, the rapprochement between BE and learning organizations is based on something that is fundamental to both: process orientation. Although BE has not yet given sufficient thought to this, the concept of learning in the context of learning organizations only makes sense in terms of process (and project). Similarly, I previously suggested that only a concept of BE as an applied ethics that permeates all organizational processes and projects can successfully avoid a return to ideas of applied ethics of a deductive or inductive type. In my opinion, BE only makes sense (and can only aim for legitimation) as a view of organizational processes that is simultaneously integrated in them. This is why it is so important to realize that, from the standpoint of process, the individual and organizational development advocated by learning organizations can also be understood in terms of moral development.

I therefore believe that my affirmation of the hermeneutics of responsibility should be understood not in static or normative terms but as a process. And for this same reason I believe that in organizations one can speak of humanization as a learning process. In fact, in personal terms, we must realize that an unrenounceable and insuperable declaration of individual dignity and the principle of humanity does not automatically aid in constructing purposes inherent to the person because in a plural society the person is neither given these purposes once and for all nor can it be taken for granted that the person will embrace them as norms within a particular context. Quite the contrary: the individual creates and acquires purposes in the framework of practical life, and professional and organizational dimensions are particularly significant here. It is therefore necessary that this affirmation of the individual be linked to an ethical proposal about organizational mediation, a proposal that should have significance and specificity per se.

As previously pointed out, the hermeneutics of responsibility has three dimensions: a consequentialist moment (responsible), a conventional moment (which shapes contexts and subjects), and a reflective-normative moment (postconventionally framed). But my defense of the heremeneutics of responsibility should be understood as a regulatory approach to and a criterion of a learning process: the process whereby the organization learns how to become what it wants to be. Consequently, the practical elements that constitute each dimension (stakeholder analysis, organizational cultures, codes, etc.) are no longer self-sufficient themes and objectives but have become analytical instruments and practices that become meaningful and useful not by themselves, but to the extent to which they are integrated in the development of an organizational process regulated by the hermeneutics of responsibility. I think that, with this understanding of learning, BE can be plausible today because the demand for responsibility includes a creation of values that is open to the art of separation and discernment, and is a constructivism that does not identify autonomy with some other kind of individualist voluntarism. In sum, I think that from this perspective, BE succeeds in being the organizational expression of shared moral creativity (Valadier, 1987). I think that BE becomes the frame of reference that regulates an ongoing process of organizational learning guided by and experienced from the standpoint of the hermeneutics of responsibility.

REFERENCES

ABBA, G. (1987): Virtù e dovere: valutazione di un recente dibattito. *Salesianum*, vol. 49, pp. 421-484.

ABRATT, J.; SACKS, D. (1988): The Marketing Challenge: Towards Being Profitable and Socially Responsible. *Journal of Business Ethics*, vol. 7(7), pp. 497-507.

ADIZES, I.; WESTON, J. F. (1973): Comparative Models of Social Responsibility. *Academy of Management Journal*, vol. 16(1), pp. 112-128.

ALBERT, M (1991), *Capitalisme contre capitalisme*. Paris: du Seuil.

ALLAIRE, Y.; FIRSIROTU, M.E. (1984): Theories of Organizational Culture. *Organization Studies*, vol.5 (3), pp. 193-226.

AMADO, G.; FAUCHEUX, C.; LAURENT, A. (1990): Organizational Change and Cultural Realities. [Unpublished text].

ANDREWS, K.R. (1971): *The Concept of Corporate Strategy*. Dow Jones-Irwin.

ANDREWS, K.R. (1973): Can the best corporations be made moral?. *Harvard Business Review*, May-June, pp. 57-64.

ANDREWS, K.R. (1984): Difficulties in Overseeing Ethical Policy. *California Management Review*, vol. 26(4), pp. 133-137.

ANDREWS, K.R. (1989): Ethics in Practice. *Harvard Business Review*, vol.67(5), pp. 99-104.

ANSOFF, I. H. (1965): *Corporate Strategy*. New York: McGraw-Hill.

ARCHIER, G.; SÉRIEYX, H. (1984): *L'entreprise du 3e. type*. París: du Seuil.

ARGANDOÑA, A. (1990a): Sentido y funciones del beneficio empresarial. *Ética empresarial*. Madrid: Acción Social Empresarial, 1990, pp. 43-65.

ARGANDOÑA, A. (1990b): Necesidad y 'rentabilidad' de la ética en los negocios. *Boletín del Círculo de Empresarios*, no.50, pp. 15-26.

ARGANDOÑA, A. (1991a): Etica y economía de mercado. *Información Comercial Española*, no. 691, pp. 45-53.

ARGYRIS, C. (1991): Teaching Smart People How to Learn. *Harvard Business Review*, May-June, pp. 99-109.

ARGYRIS, C.; SCHÖN, D.A. (1978): *Organizational learning: a theory of action perspective*. Reading: Addison-Wesley.

ARTHUR ANDERSEN (1992): *Business Ethics Program. Ethics Foundation Presentation*. Arthur Andersen & Co, SC.

AUBERT, N.; GAULEJAC, V. (1991): *Le coût de l'excellence*. Paris: du Seuil.

BAHM, A. J. (1982): Teaching Ethics Without Ethics to Teach. *Journal of Business Ethics*, vol. 1, pp. 43-47.

BAIER, K. (1986): Moral, legal and social responsibility . CURTLER, H. (ed.): *Shame, responsibility and the corporation*. New York: Haven, 1986, pp. 183-195.

BARLEY, S. R.; KUNDA, G. (1992): Design and Devotion: Surges of Rational and Normative Ideologies of Control in Managerial Discourse. *Administrative Science Quarterly*, vol. 37, pp. 363-399.

BAUMHART, R.C. (1961): How Ethical Are Businessmen? *Harvard Business Review*, July-August, pp. 6-19, 156-176.

BAUMOL, W.J. (1991): *Perfect Markets and Easy Virtue: Business Ethics and The Invisible Hand.*

BEACH, L.R. (1993): *Making The Right Decision. Organizational Culture, Vision, and Planning.* Englewood Cliffs: Prentice-Hall.

BEAUCHAMP, T.L.; BOWIE, N.E. (eds.) (1988): *Ethical theory and business.* Englewood Cliffs: Prentice-Hall.

BEHRMAN, J. N. (1988): *Essays on Ethics in Business and the Professions.* Englewood Cliffs: Prentice Hall.

BELET, D. (1993): Le concept d'organization apprenante: vers un nouveau paradigme pour le développement des ressources humaines. *A.G.R.H.*, pp. 310-319.

BELL, D. (1973): *The Cultural Contradictions of Capitalism.* New York: Basic Books.

BENSON, G. C.S. (1989): Codes of Ethics. *Journal of Business Ethics,* vol.8(5), pp. 305-319.

BERGER, P. L.; LUCKMANN, T. (1967): *The Social Construction of Reality.* New York: Doubleday.

BIRD, F.; WESTLEY, F. i WATERS, J. A. (1989): The Uses of Moral Talk: Why Do Managers Talk Ethics?. *Journal of Business Ethics*, vol. 8(1), pp. 75-89.

BIRD, F. B.; WATERS, J. A. (1989): The Moral Muteness of Managers. *California Management Review*, vol.32(1), pp. 73-88.

BOAL, K.B.; PEERY, N. (1985): The Cognitive Structure of Corporate Social Responsibility. *Journal of Management*, vol. 11(3), pp. 71-82.

BOATRIGHT, J.R. (1993): *Ethics and the Conduct of Business.* Englewood Cliffs: Prentice Hall.

BOISOT, M. (1994): Information, Economics, and Evolution: What Scope for a Ménage à trois?. *World Futures*, vol. 41, pp. 227-256.

BOMMER, M.; GRATTO, C.; GRAVANDER, J.; TUTTLE, M. (1987): A Behavioral Model of Ethical and Unethical Decision Making. *Journal of Business Ethics,* vol.6, pp. 265-280.

BONNAZZI, G. (1991): *Storia del pensiero organizzativo.* Milan: Franco Angeli.

BOTKIN, J.W.; ELMANDJRA, M; MALITZA, M. (1979): *No Limits to Learning. Bridging the Human Gap.* Oxford: Pergamon Press.

BOURCIER, C. (1988): Une definition de la culture d'entreprise. *Travaux et recherches.* Grenoble: E.S.C., no. 3.

BOWIE, N.E. (1982): *Business Ethics.* Englewood Cliffs: Prentice-Hall.

BOWIE, N.E. (1986): Business Ethics. DeMARCO, J.P. & FOX, R.M.: *New directions in ethics. The challenge of applied ethics.* London: Routledge & Kegan Paul, 1986, pp. 158-172.

BOWIE, N.E. (1988): Does It Pay to Bluff in Business?. *Ethical Theories ans Business*, Englewood Cliffs: Prentice-Hall, 1988, pp. 443-448.

BOWIE, N.E. (1991a): Business Ethics as a Discipline: The Search for Legitimacy. FREEMAN, R.E. (ed.): *Business Ethics. The State of the Art.* Oxford: Oxford University Press, pp. 17-41.

BOWIE, N.E. (1991b): New Directions in Corporate Social Responsibility. *Business Horizons*, july-aug., pp. 56-65.

BOWMAN, E. H.; HAIRE, M. (1975): A Strategic Posture Toward Corporate Social Responsibility. *California Management Review*, vol. 18(2), pp. 49-58.

BOYER, L.; EQUILBEY, N. (1986): *Le projet d'entreprise*. París: Les Éditions d'Organisation.

BRITISH INSTITUTE OF MANAGEMENT. (1984): *Code of Conduct and supporting Guides to Good Management Practice*. London: BIM.

BRÖDNER, P. (1991): Producción antropocéntrica y eficiencia económica. *Quaderns de Tecnologia. Institut Català de Tecnologia*, vol.4, October, pp. 126-131.

BROOKS, L.J. (1989a): Corporate Codes of Ethics. *Journal of Business Ethics*, vol.8(2-3), pp. 117-129.

BROOKS, L.J. (1989b): Corporate Ethical Perfomance: Trends, Forecasts and Outlooks. *Journal of Business Ethics*, vol. 8(1), pp. 31-38.

BROWN, M. (1990): *Working Ethics. Strategies for Decision Making and Organizational Responsibility*. San Francisco: Jossey Bass.

BURRELL, G. (1988): Modernism, Post Modernism and Organizational Analysis 2: The Contribution of Michel Foucault. *Organization Studies*, vol. 9(2), pp. 221-235.

BYRON, W. J. (1977): The Meaning of Ethics in Business. *Business Horizons*, vol. 20, Nov., pp. 31-34.

CADBURY, A. (1987): Ethical managers make their own rules. *Harvard Business Review*, vol. 65(5), Sept.-Oct., pp. 69-73.

CAMPS, V. (1988): *Ética, retórica, política*. Madrid: Alianza.

CAMPS, V. (1990): *Virtudes públicas*. Madrid: Espasa-Calpe.

CARMICHAEL, S.; DRUMMOND, J. (1989): *Good business. A guide to corporate responsibility and business ethics*. London: Hutchinson Business Books.

CARR, A.Z. (1968): Is Business Bluffing Ethical?. *Harvard Business Review*.

CARR, A.Z. (1970): Can an executive afford a conscience? *Harvard Business Review*, no. 48, pp. 58-64.

CARROLL, A.B. (1975): Managerial Ethics: a Post-Watergate View, *Business Horizons*, April, ppg. 75-80.

CARROLL, A.B. (1979): A Three-Dimensional Conceptual Model of Corporate Performance. *Academy of Management Review*, vol. 4(4), pp. 497-505.

CARROLL, A.B. (1987):In Search of the Moral Manager. *Business Horizons*, March-April, pp. 7-15.

CARROLL, A.B. (1989): *Business & Society. Ethics & Stakeholder Management*. Cincinnati: South-Western Publishing.

CARSON, T. (1993): Friedman's Theory of Corporate Social Responsibility. *Business & Professional Ethics Journal*, vol. 12(1), pp. 3-32.

CAVANAGH, G.F. (1976): Corporate Values for the Future. HOFFMAN, W.M. & MOORE, J.M.: *Business Ethics*. New York: McGraw-Hill, 1984, pp. 509-524.

CAVANAGH, G.F. (1984): *American Business Values*. Englewood Cliffs, New Jersey: The Prentice-Hall.

CAVANAGH, G.F.; McGOVERN, A.F. (1988): *Ethical Dilemmas in the Modern Corporation*. Englewood Cliffs: Prentice Hall.

CAVANAGH, G.F; MOBERG, D. J.; VELASQUEZ, M. (1981): The Ethics of Organizational Politics. *Academy of Management Review*, vol. 6(3), pp. 363-374.

CENTER FOR BUSINESS ETHICS (1986): Are Corporations Institutionalizing Ethics? *Journal of Business Ethics*, vol. 5, pp. 85-91.

CENTER FOR BUSINESS ETHICS (1992): Instilling Ethical Values in Large Corporations. *Journal of Business Ethics*, vol. 11, pp. 863-867.

CLEGG, S. R. (1990): *Modern Organizations. Organization Studies in the Postmodern World*. London: Sage.

COHEN, D. B. (1993): Creating and maintaining ethical work climates: anomie in the workplace and implications for managing change. *Business Ethics Quarterly*, vol. 3(4), pp. 343-358.

CONILL, J. (1993a): Ética del Capitalismo. *CLAVES*, no.30, pp. 25-35.

CONILL, J. (1993b): Ética económica. *Diálogo Filosófico*, no. 26, pp. 195-204.

CONRY, E. J.; NELSON, D. R. (1989): Business Law and Moral Growth. *American Business Law Journal*, vol. 27(1), pp. 1-39.

CONWAY, J.; HOULIHAN, J. (1982): The Real Estate Code of Ethics: Viable or Vaporous?. *Journal of Business Ethics,* vol. 1, pp. 201-210.

COOKE, R. A.; RYAN, L. V. (1989): The relevance of Ethics to Management Education. *Journal of Management Development*, vol. 7(2), pp. 28-38.

COOPER, R.; BURRELL, G. (1988): Modernism, Postmodernism and Organizational Analysis: An Introduction. *Organization Studies*, vol. 9(1), pp. 91-112.

CORBÍ, M. (1991): *La religió que ve. La gran transformació de la religió en la societat científico-tècnica*. Barcelona: Claret.

CORBÍ, M. (1992): *Proyectar la sociedad, reconvertir la religión. Los nuevos ciudadanos*. Barcelona: Herder.

CORBÍ, M. (1994): *El individuo libre y voluntario como eje de la organización inteligente*. Barcelona: ESADE.

CORNELLA, A. (1994): *Los recursos de la información. Ventaja competitiva de las empresas*. Madrid: McGraw Hill.

CORTINA, A. (1992): Ética filosófica. VIDAL, M.: *Conceptos fundamentales de ética filosófica*. Madrid: Trotta.

CORTINA, A. (1993): *Ética aplicada y democracia radical*. Madrid: Tecnos.

CORTINA, A. (1994): *Ética de la empresa*. Madrid: Trotta.

CRESSEY, D. R. & MOORE, C. A. (1983): Managerial Values and Corporate Codes of Ethics. *California Management Review*. vol. 25(4), pp. 53-77.

CROZIER, M. (1989): *L'entreprise a l'ecoute. Apprendre le management post-industriel*. París: InterEditions.

CHANDLER, A.D. (1977): *The Visible Hand. The Managerial Revolution in American Business*. Cambridge: Harvard University Press.

CHAMBRE DU COMMERCE DU QUÉBEC (1982): *Rapport du Comité sur la Responsabilité sociale de l'entreprise*. [Typescript].

CHATOV, R. (1980): What Corporate Ethics Statements Say. *California Management Review*, vol. 22(4), pp. 20-29.

CHEWNING, R. C. (1984): Can Free Enterprise Survive Ethical Schizophrenia? *Business Horizons*, vol. 27(2), pp. 5-11.

DANLEY, J. R. (1988): 'Ought' Implies 'Can', or, The Moral Relevance of a Theory of the Firm. *Journal of Business Ethics*, vol. 7(1-2), pp. 23-28.

DANLEY, J. R. (1991): Ethics and the Organizational Person: Revisiting De George. *Journal of Business Ethics*, vol. 10, pp. 935-950.

DAVIS, K. (1976): Social responsibility Is Inevitable. *California Management Review*, vol. 19(1), pp. 14-20.

DAVIS, M. (1991): L'Autorità morale di un codice professionale. *Etica degli Affari e delle Professioni*, vol. 4(4), 5-33.

DAVIS, M. The Special Role of Professionals in Business Ethics. *Business & Professional Ethics Journal*, vol. 7(2), pp. 51-62.

DAVIS, S.; BOTKIN, J. (1994): The Coming of Knowledge-Based Business. *Harvard Business Review*, Sept.-Oct., pp. 165-170.

De GEORGE, R.T. (1981): Can Corporations Have Moral Responsibility?. *University of Dayton Review*, Winter, no.5, pp. 3-15.

De GEORGE, R.T. (1982): What Is the American Business Value System? *Journal of Business Ethics*, vol. 1, pp. 267-275.

De GEORGE, R.T. (1983): The Social Business of Business. ROBISON, W. L.; PRITCHARD, M. S.; ELLIN, J. (ed.): *Profits and Professions. Essays in Business and Professional Ethics*. Clifton: Humana, 1983, pp. 157-174.

De GEORGE, R.T. (1986): Corporations and morality. CURTLER, H. (ed.): *Shame, responsibility and the corporation*. New York: Haven, 1986, pp. 57-75.

De GEORGE, R.T. (1987): The Status of Business Ethics: Past and Future. *Journal of Business Ethics*, vol. 6, pp. 201-211.

De GEORGE, R.T. (1989): There is Ethics in Business Ethics; But There's More As Well. *Journal of Business Ethics*, vol.8(5), pp. 337-339.

De GEORGE, R.T. (1990a): *Business Ethics*. New York: Macmillan.

De GEORGE, R.T. (1990b): Using the techniques of ethical analysis in corporate practice. ENDERLE, G.; ALMOND, B.; ARGANDOÑA, A. (eds.): *People in corporations*. London: Kluwer, pp. 25-33.

De GEORGE, R.T. (1991): Will Success Spoil Business Ethics?. FREEMAN, R.E. (ed.): *Business Ethics. The State of the Art*. Oxford: Oxford University Press, pp. 42-56.

De GEORGE, R.T. (1993): L'Etica degli Affari Di Fronte Al Futuro. *Etica degli affari e delle professioni*, no. 1, pp. 4-14.

DEAL, T.; KENNEDY, A. (1982): *Corporate Cultures*. Reading: Addison-Wesley Pub.

DEAN, P. J. (1992): Making Codes of Ethics 'Real'. *Journal of Business Ethics"*, vol. 11, pp. 285-290.

DEANER, C. M. D. (1994): A model of organization development ethics. *Public Administration Quarterly*, vol. 17(4), pp. 435-446.

DeMARCO, J.P.; FOX, R.M. (1986): The challenge of applied ethics. DeMARCO, J.P.; FOX, R.M. (eds.): *New directions in ethics. The challenge of applied ethics.* London: Routledge & Kegan Paul, pp. 1-18.

DENT, J. F. (1991):"Accounting and organizational cultures: a field study of the emergence of a new organizational reality. *Accounting Organizations and Society*, vol.16(8), pp. 705-732.

DERRY, R. (1991): Institutionalizing Ethical Motivation: Reflections on Goodpaster's Agenda. FREEMAN, R. E. (ed.): *Business Ethics. The State of the Art.* Oxford: Oxford University Press, pp. 121-135.

DOBSON, J. (1990): The Role of Ethics in Global Corporate Culture. *Journal of Business Ethics*, vol. 9(6), pp. 481-488.

DOMINGO, A.; BENNÀSSAR, B. (1992): Ética civil. VIDAL, M. (ed.): *Conceptos fundamentales de ética teológica.* Madrid: Trotta, pp. 269-291.

DONALDSON, J. (1989): *Key issues in Business Ethics*, London: Academic Press.

DONALDSON, J; SHELDRAKE, J. (1990): "The parameters of ethical decision-making in organisations". ENDERLE, G.; ALMOND, B.; ARGANDOÑA, A. (ed.): *People in corporations.* London: Kluwer, pp. 69-76.

DONALDSON, T. (1982): *Corporations and Morality.* Englewood Cliffs: Prentice Hall.

DONALDSON, T. (1986): "Personalizing corporate ontology: The French Way". CURTLER, H. (ed.): Shame, responsibility and the corporation. New York: Haven, 1986, pp. 99-111.

DONALDSON, T. (1989): *The Ethics of International Business.* Oxford: Oxford University Press.

DONALDSON, T. (1991): Rights in the Global Market. FREEMAN, R. E. (ed.): *Business Ethics. The State of the Art.* Oxford: Oxford University Press, pp. 139-162.

DONALDSON, T. (1992): The Language of International Corporate Ethics. *Business Ethics Quarterly*, vol. 2(3), pp. 271-281.

DONALDSON, T. (1994): When integration fails: the logic of prescription and description in Business Ethics. *Business Ethics Quarterly*, vol. 4(2), pp. 157-169.

DONALDSON, T.; DUNFEE, T. W. (1992): Integrative Social Contracts Theory: Ethics in Economic Life. EBEN'92 INTERNATIONAL CONFERENCE.

DONALDSON, T.; WERHANE, P. (eds.) (1988): *Ethical Issues in Business. A Philosophical Approach.* Englewood Cliffs: Prentice -Hall.

DORMIDO, S.; MELLADO, M. (1981): *La Revolución Informática.* Barcelona: Salvat.

DRAKE, B. H.; DRAKE, E. (1988): Ethical and Legal Aspects of Managing Corporate Cultures". *California Management Review*, vol. 30(2), pp. 107-123.

DRUCKER, P.F. (1989): Management and the world's work. *Harvard Business Review.*

DRUCKER, P.F. (1992): The New Society of Organizations. *Harvard Business Review*, Sept.-Oct., pp. 95-104.

DRUCKER, P.F. (1993): *Post-capitalist Society.* Oxford: Butterworth-Heinemann.

DURAN, P. (1994): L'home i l'empresa en la nova Europa. Barcelona. [Unpublished text].

DUSKA, R. F. (1993): Aristotle: a pre-modern post-modern?. Implications for Business Ethics. *Business Ethics Quarterly*, vol. 3(3), pp. 227-250.

EDEL, A. (1986): Ethical theory and moral practice: on the terms of their relation. DeMARCO, J. P.; FOX, R. M. (ed.): *New directions in ethics. The challenge of applied ethics.* London: Routledge & Kegan Paul, pp. 317-335.

ELM, D. R.; NICHOLS, M. L. (1993): An Investigation of the Moral Reasoning of Managers. *Journal of Business Ethics*, vol. 12, pp. 817-833.

EPSTEIN, E.M. (1973): Dimensions of Corporate Power (1). *California Management Review*, vol. 16(2), pp. 9-23.

EPSTEIN, E.M. (1974): Dimensions of Corporate Power (2). *California Management Review*, vol 16(4), pp. 32-47.

EPSTEIN, E.M. (1987a): The Corporate Social Policy Process and the process of corporate governance. *American Business Law Journal*, vol. 25(3), pp.361-383.

EPSTEIN, E.M. (1987b): The Corporate Social Policy Process: Beyond Business Ethics, Corporate Social Responsibility, and Corporate Social Responsiveness. *California Management Review*, vol. 29(3), pp. 99-114.

EPSTEIN, E.M. (1987c): Business Ethics, Corporate Good Citizenship, and the Corporate Social Policy Process. A view from the United States. *European Foundation for Management Development Conference on Business Ethics: Crucial Issues in Successful European Busines.*

ETHICS RESOURCE CENTER (1980): *Implementation and Enforcement od Codes of Ethics in Corporations and Associations.* [Typescript].

EVANS, J. (1982): El trabajador y el puesto de trabajo. FRIEDRICHS, G.; SCHAFF, A. (ed.): *Microelectrónica y sociedad para bien o para mal.* Madrid: Alhambra, pp. 130-155.

FALISE, M.; REGNIER, J. (1992): *Repères pour une éthique d'entreprise.* Lille: Centre d'Ethique Contemporaine.

FASCHING, D. J. (1981): A Case for Corporate and Management Ethics. *California Management Review*, vol. 23(4), pp. 62-76.

FERNÁNDEZ, J. L. (1992a): Prolegómenos a una docencia de la deontología profesional. *ICADE*, vol. 25, pp. 91-123.

FERNÁNDEZ, J. L. (1992b): ¿Ética "empresarial? *Razón y Fe*, no. 226, pp. 27-43.

FERNÁNDEZ, J. L. (1993): El papel de la ética en la estrategia empresarial. *Alta Dirección*, núm. 172, pp. 457-464.

FERNÁNDEZ, J.L. (1994a): *Ética para empresarios y directivos.* Madrid: ESIC.

FERNÁNDEZ, J. L. (1994b): La economía como oportunidad y reto de la ética profesional.

FERNÁNDEZ, J. L.; HORTAL, A. (eds.): *Ética de las profesiones.* Madrid: Comillas, pp. 83-107.

FERRATER, J. (1979): *De la materia a la razón.* Madrid: Alianza.

FERRATER, J.; COHN, P. (1981): *Ética aplicada. Del aborto a la violencia.* Madrid: Alianza.

FERRELL, O.C.; GRESHAM, L.G.; FRAEDRICH, J. (1989):"A Synthesis of Ethical Decision Models for Marketing. *Journal of Macromarketing,* Fall, pp. 55-64.

FILELLA, J. (1994): Persona y organización: de estructuras convencionales a formas funcionales. RECIO, E.M.; LOZANO, J.M.: *Persona y empresa. Libertad responsable o sujeción a las normas.* Barcelona: Hispano Europea, pp. 37-98.

FIOL, C.M.; LYLES, M.A. (1985): Organizational Learning. *Academy of Management Review*, vol. 10(4), pp. 803-813.

FORD, R.C.; RICHARDSON, W.D. (1994): Ethical Decision Making: A Review of the Empirical Literature. *Journal of Business Ethics*, vol. 13, pp. 205-221.

FRANKEL, M.S. (1990): Professional Codes: Why, How and with What Impact? *Journal of Business Ethics*, vol. 8(2-3), pp. 109-115.

FREDERICK, W.C. (1981): Free Market vs. Social Responsibility. Decision Time at the CED. *California Management Review*, vol. 23(3), pp. 20-28.

FREDERICK, W.C. (1986): Toward CSR3: Why Ethical Analysis is Indispensable and Unavoidable in Corporate Affairs. *California Management Review*, vol. 28(2), pp. 126-141.

FREDERICK, W.C. (1991): Commentary on Business Ethics as a Discipline: The Search for Legitimacy. FREEMAN, R.E. (ed.): *Business Ethics. The State of the Art.* Oxford: Oxford University Press, pp. 57-59.

FREDERICK, W.C.; DAVIS, K.; POST, J.E. (1988): *Business and Society. Corporate Strategy, Public Policy, Ethics.* New York: McGraw Hill.

FREEMAN, R.E. (1984): *Strategic Management: A Stakeholder Approach.* Boston: Pitman.

FREEMAN, R.E.; GILBERT, D.R. (1988): *Corporate Strategy and the Search for Ethics.* Englewood Cliffs: Prentice-Hall.

FREEMAN, R.E.; GILBERT, D.R. (1992): Business Ethics and Society: A Critical Agenda. *Business and Society*, vol. 31(1), pp. 9-17.

FREEMAN, R.E.; GILBERT, D.R. & HARTMAN, E. (1988): Values and the Foundations of Strategic Management. *Journal of Business Review*, vol. 7(11), pp. 821-834.

FREEMAN, R.E.; REED, D. (1983): Stockholders and Stakeholders: A New Perspective on Corporate Governance. *California Management Review*, vol. 25(3), pp. 88-106.

FRENCH, P. (1979): The Corporation as a Moral Person. *American Philosophical Quarterly*, vol. 16(3), pp. 207-215.

FRENCH, P. (1984): *Collective and Corporate Responsibility.* New York: Columbia University Press.

FRENCH, P.A. (1986): Principles of responsibility, shame and the corporation. CURTLER, H. (ed.): *Shame, responsibility and the corporation.* New York: Haven, 1986, pp. 17-56.

FRIEDMAN, M. (1962): *Capitalism and Freedom.* Chicago: University of Chicago Press. [*Capitalismo y libertad.* Madrid: Rialp, 1966].

FRIEDMAN, M. (1970): "The Social Responsibility of Business Is to Increase Its Profits". *New York Times Magazine*, Sept. 13. [BEAUCHAMP, T. L.; BOWIE, N.: *Ethical Theory and Business.* Englewood Cliffs: Prentice Hall, 1988, pp. 87-91].

FRIEDRICHS, G. and SCHAFF, A. (ed.) Microelectrónica y sociedad para bien o para mal, Alhambra, Madrid, pp. 130-155

FRITZSCHE, D. J. (1991): A Model of Decision-Making Incorporating Ethical Values. *Journal of Business Ethics*, vol. 10, pp. 841-852.

FRITZSCHE, D. J.; BECKER, H. (1983): Ethical Behavior of Marketing Managers. *Journal of Business Ethics*, vol. 2, pp. 291-299.

GAFFNEY, R. (1989): Systems Thinking in Business: Philosophy and Practice An Interview with Peter Senge. *Revision*, vol. 7, no. 2, pp. 30-37.

GAGLIARDI, P. (1986): The Creation and Change of Organizational Cultures: A Conceptual Framework. *Organization Studies*, vol.7(2), pp. 117-134.

GANDZ, J. and HAYES, N. (1988): Teaching Business Ethics. *Journal of Business Ethics*, vol. 7(9), pp. 657-669.

GARCÍA ECHEVARRÍA, S. (1982): *Responsabilidad social y balance social de la empresa*. Madrid: Fundación MAPFRE.

GARCÍA ECHEVARRÍA, S. (1992): La ética en el management europeo. Nuevas orientaciones en el contexto cultural europeo. *Instituto de Dirección y Organización de Empresas*, Special issue. 1ª quarter.

GARCÍA ECHEVARRÍA, S. (1993): Ética empresarial y comportamientos directivos. Cómo configurar corporaciones empresariales eficientes. *Alta Dirección*, no. 170, pp. 65-83.

GARCÍA, V. D. (1994): Características básicas de una asesoría ético-empresarial. ÉTICA, ECONOMÍA Y DIRECCIÓN: *La ética en la empresa: la puesta en práctica*. Barcelona, pp. 17-19.

GARCÍA MARZÁ, V. D. (1995): Las relaciones banca-industria. ARGANDOÑA, A, (ed.): *La dimensión ética de las instituciones y mercados financieros*. Madrid: Fundación BBV, pp. 117-142.

GARCÍA-RAMOS, L. A. (1990): Hacia nuevas formas organizativas basadas en la información: las redes. *Datamation*, pp. 38-45.

GARRATT, B. (1990): *Creating a Learning Organisation. A Guide to Leadership, Learning & Development*. Cambridge: Director Books.

GARRIGA, R. (1991): Dossier Tecnología y organización. *Quaderns de Tecnologia. Institut Català de Tecnologia*, vol. 4, October, p. 118.

GELLERMAN, S.W. (1986): Why 'good' managers make bad ethical choices. *Harvard Business Review*, July.-August, pp. 85-90.

GELLERMAN, S.W. (1989): Managing Ethics from the Top Down. *Sloan Management Review*, Winter, pp. 73-79.

GEORGE, R. J. (1987): Teaching Business Ethics: Is There a Gap Between Rhetoric and Reality?. *Journal of Business Ethics*, vol. 6, pp. 513-518.

GEWIRTH, A. (1986): Professional Ethics: The Separatist Thesis. *Ethics. The University of Chicago*, vol. 96, pp. 282-300.

GIBBONS, M.; METCALFE, J. S. (1991): La tecnología procedente de la Universidad como apoyo para la industria. *Quaderns de Tecnología. Institut Català de Tecnologia*. vol.4, October, pp. 107-110.

GILBERT, D.R. (1986): Corporate Strategy and Ethics. *Journal of Business Ethics*, vol. 5, pp. 137-150.

GILBERT, D.R. (1991): Respect for Persons, Management Theory, and Business Ethics. FREEMAN, R.E. (ed.): *Business Ethics. The State of the Art.* Oxford: Oxford University Press, pp. 111- 120.

GONZÁLEZ, J. (1994): Las profesiones en la sociedad corporativa". FERNÁNDEZ, J. L.; HORTAL, A. (eds.): *Ética de las profesiones*, Madrid: Comillas, pp. 21-34.

GOODPASTER, K.E. (1982): Kohlbergian Theory: A Philosophical Counterinvitation. *Ethics*, April, pp. 491-498.

GOODPASTER, K.E. (1983): The Concept of Corporate Responsibility. *Journal of Business Ethics*, vol. 2, pp. 1-22.

GOODPASTER, K.E. (1984a): *Ethics in Management.* Boston: Harvard Business School.

GOODPASTER, K.E. (1984b): *Ethics in Management. Teacher's Manual.* Boston: Harvard Business School.

GOODPASTER, K.E. (1985): Business Ethics, Ideology, and the Naturalistic Fallacy. *Journal of Business Ethics*, vol. 4, pp. 227-232.

GOODPASTER, K.E. (1987): The Principle of Moral Projection: A Reply to Professor Ranken. *Journal of Business Ethics*, vol. 6, pp. 329-332.

GOODPASTER, K.E. (1991a): Business Ethics and Stakeholder Analysis. *Business Ethics Quarterly*, vol. 1(1), pp. 53-72.

GOODPASTER, K.E. (1991b): Ethical Imperatives and Corporate Leadership. FREEMAN, R.E. (ed.): *Business Ethics. The State of the Art.* Oxford: Oxford University Press, pp. 89-110.

GOODPASTER, K.E.; MATTHEWS, J.B. (1982): Can a corporation have a conscience? *Harvard Business Review.*

GRACIA, D. (1991): *Procedimientos de decisión en ética clínica.* Madrid: Eudema.

GRACIA, D. (1992): Planteamiento general de la bioética. VIDAL, M.: *Conceptos fundamentales de ética filosófica.* Madrid: Trotta, pp. 421-438.

GRANGER, C.H. (1978): The Hierarchy of Objectives. *Harvard-Deusto Business Review* (2a sèrie), pág. 3-16.

GRANT, C. (1991): Friedman Fallacies. *Journal of Business Ethics*, vol. 10, pp. 907-914.

GRUSON, P. (1989): Préoccupations éthiques aux Etats-Unis. A propos de la *Business Ethics. Etudes*, Oct., pp. 327- 337.

GUERRETTE, R.H. (1994): Management by ethics. A new paradigm and model for corporate ethics. LEWIS, A.; WÄRNERYD, K.E.: *Ethics and economic affairs.* London: Routledge, pp. 51-114.

GUEST, R. H. (1986): Management Imperatives for the Year 2000. *California Management Review*, vol. 28(4), pp. 62-70.

GUPTARA, P. (1993): Building intelligent organisations: truisms and truths from 15 years of work in organisational renewal. *The 1993 global management development forum.*

GUTIÉRREZ, M. (1994):¿Recursos o personas?. *EL PAÍS,* March 27th

GUY, M. E. (1990): *Ethical Decision Making in Everyday Work Situations.* New York: Quorum Books.

HABERMAS, J. (1986a): Gerechtigkeit und Solidarität. *Zur Bestimmung der Moral. Philosophische und sozialwissenschaftlichte.* Frankfurt: Suhrkamp

HABERMAS, J. (1986b): Moralität und Sittlichkeit. Trefen Hegels Einwände gegen Kant auch auf die Diskursethik zu? *Moralität und sittilichkeit*. Frankfurt: Suhrkamp.

HABERMAS, J. (1991): Vom pragmatischen, ethischen und moralischen Gebrauch der praktischen Vernunft. *Erläuterungen zur Diskursethik*.

HAFFENDEN, M. (1993): Learning at all Organisational Levels-Agenda. *The 1993 global management development forum*.

HEDBERG, B. (1981): How organizations learn and unlearn. NYSTROM, P. C.; STARBUCK, W. H.: *Handbook of Organizational Design*. London: Oxford University Press, pp. 3-27.

HOFFMAN, W. M. (1986): What is Necessary for Corporate Moral Excellence?. *Journal of Business Ethics*, vol. 5, pp. 233-242.

HOFFMAN, W. M.; MOORE, J. M. (1982a): Results of a Business Ethics Curriculum Survey Conducted by the Center for Business Ethics. *Journal of Business Ethics*, vol. 1, pp. 81-83.

HOFFMAN, W. M.; MOORE, J. M. (1982b): What is Business Ethics? A Reply to Peter Drucker. *Journal of Business Ethics*, vol. 1, pp. 293-300.

HORTAL, A. (1979): "El sujeto ético en la era tecnológica". DOU, A. (ed.): *Aspectos éticos del desarrollo tecnológico*. Bilbao: Mensajero, 1979, pp. 185-212.

HORTAL, A. (1994a): "Planteamiento de una ética professional". FERNÁNDEZ, J.L.; HORTAL, A. (eds.) *Ética de las profesiones*, Madrid: Comillas, pp. 55-73.

HORTAL, A. (1994b): "Ética y tecnificación de las profesiones". FERNÁNDEZ, J. L.; HORTAL, A. (eds.): *Ética de las profesiones*, Madrid: Comillas, pp. 75-82.

HOSMER, L. (1985): The Other 338: Why a Majority of Our Schools of Business Administration Do Not Offer a Course in Business Ethics. *Journal of Business Ethics*, vol. 4, pp. 17-22.

HOSMER, L. (1988): Adding Ethics to the Business Curriculum. *Business Horizons*, vol. 31(4), pp. 9-15.

HUBER, G. P. (1991). Organizational learning: the contributing processes and the literatures. *Organization Science*, vol. 2(1), pp. 88-115.

HUNT, S. D.; CHONKO, L. B. (1984): Marketing and Machiavellianism; *Journal of Marketing*, vol. 48, pp. 30-42.

INFORME FAST (1986): *Europa 1995. Nuevas Tecnologías y Cambio Social*. Madrid: Fundesco.

JAYARAMAN, L. L.; MIN, B. K. (1993): "Business Ethics - A Developmental Perspective: The Evolutions of the Free and Mature Corporation. *Journal of Business Ethics*, vol. 12, pp. 665-675.

JENNINGS, B. (1991): The Regulation of Virtue: Cross-Currents in Professional Ethics. *Journal of Business Ethics*, vol. 10, pp. 561-568.

JONES, T.M. (1980): Corporate Social Responsibility Revisited, Redefined. *California Management Review*, vol. 22, pp. 59-67.

JONES, T.M. (1991): Ethical decision making by individuals in organizations: an issue-contingent model. *Academy of Management Review*, vol. 16(2), pp. 366-395.

JUNGERMANN, H. (1986): The two camps on rationality. ARKES, H. R.; HAMMOND, K. R. (ed.): *Judgement and Decision Making*. Cambridge: Cambridge University Press, 1986, pp. 627-641.

KAHN, W.A. (1990): Toward an Agenda for Business Ethics Research. *Academy of Management Review*, vol. 15(2), pp. 311-328.

KELLY, C. M. (1987): The Interrelationship of ethics and power in today's organizations". *Organizational Dynamics*, vol. 16(1), pp. 5-18.

KERHUEL, A. (1989): L'entreprise saisie par l'éthique. *Projet*, no. 220, pp. 102-107.

KERHUEL, A. (1990): De part et d'autre de l'Atlantique. *Projet*, no. 224, pp. 15-21.

KIDD, P. T. (1991): El diseño interdisciplinario de sistemas de producción. *Quaderns de Tecnologia. Institut Català de Tecnologia*, vol. 4, October, pp. 119-122.

KIM, D.H. (1993): The Link between Individual and Organizational Learning. *Sloan Management Review*, pp. 37-51.

KING, A. (1982a):¿Nueva revolución industrial o simplemente otra tecnología?. FRIEDRICHS, G.; SCHAFF, A. (ed.): *Microelectrónica y sociedad para bien o para mal*. Madrid: Alhambra, pp. 1-27.

KING, A. (1982b): Microelectrónica e interdependencia mundial. FRIEDRICHS, G.; SCHAFF, A. (ed.): *Microelectrónica y sociedad para bien o para mal*. Madrid: Alhambra, pp. 255-274.

KING, A.; SCHNEIDER, B. (1991): *The first global revolution*.

KLEIN, S. (1988a): Is a Moral Organization Possible?. *Business & Professional Ethics Journal*, vol. 7(1), pp.51-73.

KLEIN, S. (1988b): Plato's *Statesman* and the Nature of Business Leadership: An Analysis from an Ethical Point of View. *Journal of Business Ethics*, vol.7(4), pp. 283-294.

KLEIN, S. (1989): Platonic Virtue Theory and Business Ethics. *Business & Professional Ethics Journal*, vol. 8 (4), pp. 59-82.

KLEINIG, J. & ZHANG, Y. (ed.) (1993): *Professional Law Enforcement Codes. A Documentary Collection*. Westport: Greenwood Press.

KOHLBERG, L. (1985): The Just Community Approach to Moral Education in Theory and Practice. BERKOWITZ, M.; OSER, F.: *Moral education: theory and application*. London: Lawrence Erlbaum, pp. 27-87.

KOHLBERG, L.; CANDEE, D. (1984): The Relationship of Moral Judgement to Moral Action. KURTINES, W. M.; GEWIRTZ, J. L.: *Morality, Moral Behavior and Moral Development*. NewYork: John Winley & Sons, 1984, pp. 52-73.

KOHLBERG, L.; HIGGINS, A.; POWER, C. (1984): The Relationship of Moral Atmosphere to Judgements of Responsibility. KURTINES, W. M.; GEWIRTZ, J.L.: *Morality, Moral Behavior and Moral Development*. New York: John Winley & Sons, 1984, pp. 74-106.

KOHLBERG, L.; LEVINE, C.; HOWER, A. (1983): *Moral Stages: A Current Formulation and a Response to Critics*. New York: Karger.

KOSLOWSKI, P. (1987): *Moralidad y eficiencia: líneas fundamentales de la ética económica*. Pamplona: Empresa y Humanismo.

KUHN, T. S. (1962): *The Structure of Scientific Revolution*. Chicago: University of Chicago Press.

KULTGEN, J. (1983): Evaluating Codes of Professional Ethics. ROBISON, W. L.; PRITCHARD, M. S.; ELLIN, J. (ed.): *Profits and Professions. Essays in Business and Professional Ethics*. Clifton: Humana, 1983, pp. 225-264.

L'ETANG, J. (1992): A Kantian Approach to Codes of Ethics. *Journal of Business Ethics*, vol. 11, pp. 737-744.

LACZNIAK, G. R.; MURPHY, P. E. (1993): *Ethical Marketing Decisions. The Higher Road*. Needham Heights: Allyn & Bacon.

LADD, J. (1970): Morality and the Ideal of Rationality in Formal Organizations. DONALDSON, T.; WERHANE, P.H. (ed.): *"Ethical issues in Business. A Philosophical Approach*. Englewood Cliffs: Prentice Hall, 1988, pp. 110-122.

LADD, J. (1980): The Quest for a Code of Professional Ethics: An Intellectual and Moral Confusion. JOHNSON, D.G.: *Ethical Issues in Engineering*. Englewood Cliffs: Prentice Hall, 1991, pp. 130-136.

LADD, J. (1986): Person and responsibility: Ethical concepts and impertinent analogies. CURTLER, H. (ed.): *Shame, responsibility and the corporation*. New York: Haven, 1986, pp. 77-97.

LE MOUËL, J. (1991): *Critique de l'efficacité*. Paris: du Seuil.

LESOURNE, J. (1988): *Education & Societé. Les défis de l'an 2000*. Paris: La Découverte.

LEVITT, B.; MARCH, J.G. (1988): Organizational learning. *Annual Review of Sociology*, no. 14, pp. 319-340.

LEVITT, T. (1958): "The Dangers of Social Responsibility". *Harvard Business Review*, Sept.-Oct., pp. 41-50.

LIPOVETSKY, G. (1992): *Le crépuscle du devoir. L'éthique indolore des nouveaux temps démocratiques*. Paris: Gallimard.

LUTHANS, F. HODGETTS, R.M. & THOMPSON. K.R. (1987): *Social Issues in Business. Strategic and Public Policy Perspectives*. New York: Macmillan Publishing Company.

LLANO, A. (1993): Ética empresarial. *AEDIPE*, Sept., pp. 3-9.

MACCOBY, M. (1976): The corporate climber. *Fortune*, December, pp. 98-101.

MAHONEY, J. (1990): *Teaching Business Ethics in the UK, Europe and the USA. A Comparative Study*. London: The Athlone Press.

MAITLAND, I. (1985): The Limits of Self-Regulation". *California Management Review*, vol. 27(3). ["I Limiti dell'Autoregulazione del Mondo degli Affari". *Etica degli affari e delle professioni*, 1992, vol. 2, pp. 46-54].

MANLEY, W.W. (1991): *Executive's Handbook of Model Business Conduct Codes*. Englewood Cliffs: Prentice-Hall.

MARSICK, V.J. (1988): Learning in the workplace: the case for reflectivity and critical reflectivity. *Adult Education Quarterly*, vol. 38(4), pp. 187-198.

MARTIN, F.; LEAL, A. G. (1989): ¿Cómo cambiar la cultura de la organización? *Alta Dirección*, vol. 25(147), pp. 363-373.

MARTÍNEZ, J. (1979): Tecnología, burocracia y ética. DOU, A. (ed.): *Aspectos éticos del desarrollo tecnológico*. Bilbao: Mensajero, 1979, pp. 105-144.

MARZAL, A. (1983): *Análisis político de la empresa. Razón dominante y modelos de empresa*. Barcelona: Ariel.

MASIFERN, E. (1993): Estrategia, hoy. *Alta Dirección*, no. 172, pp. 401-408.

MASUDA, Y. (1980): *The Information Society as Post-Industrial Society*. [*La sociedad informatizada como sociedad post-industrial*. Madrid: Tecnos].

MASUDA, Y. (1990): *Managing in the Information Society*. Cambridge: Basil Blackwell.

MAYO, A. (1993): Learning at all organisational levels. *The 1993 global management development forum*.

McCOY, C. S. (1988): *Management of Values. The Ethical Difference in Corporate Policy and Performance*. Boston: Pitman.

McKERSIE, R. B.; WALTON, R. E. (1991): Organizational Change. SCOTT, M. S. (ed.): *The Corporation of the 1990s. Information Technology and Organizational Transformation*. Oxford: Oxford Universitiy Press, pp. 244-277.

McMURRY, R. N. (1973): Power and the ambitious executive. *Harvard Business Review*, vol. 51, pp. 140-145.

McHUGH, F.P. (1988): *Keyguide to information sources in Business Ethics*. New York: Nichols Publishing.

MELE, D. (1991): Etica y empresa. *Información Comercial Española*, no. 691, pp. 122-134.

MELENDO, T. (1990): *Las claves de la eficacia empresarial*. Madrid: Rialp.

MEYER, J.W.; ROWAN, B. (1977): Institucionalized Organizations: Formal Structure as Myth and Ceremony. *American Journal of Sociology*, vol. 83(2), pp. 340-363.

MINTZBERG, H. (1975): The Manager's Job: Folklore and Fact". *Harvard Business Review*, July-August.

MINTZBERG, H. (1979a): *The Structuring of Organizations. (A Synthesis of the Research)*. Englewood Cliffs: Prentice-Hall.

MINTZBERG, H. (1987): Making Management Decisions: The Role of Intuition and Emotion". *Academy of Management Review*.

MINTZBERG, H. (1989): The Case for Corporate Social Responsibility. *The Journal of Business Strategy*, vol. 4(2), pp. 3-15. [IANNONE, A.P. (ed.): *Contemporary Issues in Business*. Oxford: Oxford University Press, 1989, pp. 165-177].

MINTZBERG, H.; WATERS, J. (1990): Does Decision Get in the Way? *Organization Studies*, pp. 1-6.

MITROFF, I.I. (1983): *Stakeholders of the Organizational Mind*. San Francisco: Jossey-Bass.

MORÁN, J. M. (1991): La nueva competitividad: tecnología, liderazgo y educación. *Quaderns de Tecnologia. Institut Català de Tecnologia*, vol. 4, Oct., pp. 132-135.

MORGAN, G. (1980): Paradigms, Metaphors, and Puzzle Solving in Organization Theory. *Administrative Science Quarterly*, vol. 25(4), pp. 605-622.

MORGAN, G. (1986): *Images of Organisation*. London: Sage.

MORILLAS, L. M. (1994): *La sociedad del conocimiento*. Barcelona: Cristianisme i Justícia.

MOSER, M.R. (1986): A Framework for Analyzing Corporate Social Responsability. *Journal of Business Ethics*, vol. 5, pp. 69-72.

MULLIGAN, T.M. (1987): The Two Cultures in Business Education. *Academy of Management Review*, vol. 12(4), pp. 593-599.

MURPHY, P.E. (1988): Implementing Business Ethics. *Journal of Business Ethics*, vol. 7(12), pp. 907-915.

MURPHY, P.E. (1989): Creating Ethical Corporate Structures. *Sloan Management Review*, Winter, pp. 81-87.

MURRAY, E.A. (1986): Ethics and Corporate Strategy. DICKIE, R.B.; ROUNER, L.S.: *Corporations and the Common Good*. Notre Dame: University of Notre Dame Press, pp. 91-117.

NAISBITT, J. (1983): *Megatrends: Ten new directions transforming our lives*. Warner Books.

NAISBITT, J.; ABURDENE, P. (1985): *Reinventing the Corporation*. Megatrends.

NAISBITT, J.; ABURDENE, P. (1990): *Megatrends 2000*. Megatrends.

NASH, L.L. (1983): Ethics without the sermon. *Harvard Business Review*.

NEWTON, L. (1983): Professionalization. The Intractable Plurality of Values. ROBISON, W.L.; PRITCHARD, M.S.; ELLIN, J. (ed.): *Profits and Professions. Essays in Business and Professional Ethics*. Clifton: Humana, 1983, pp. 23-36.

NEWTON, L. (1990): I professionistici e l'etica professionale negli Stati Uniti. *Etica deggli affari*, vol. 3(1), pp. 63-76.

NICHOLSON, N. (1994): Ethics in Organizations: A Framework for Theory and Research. *Journal of Business Ethics*, vol. 13, pp. 581-596.

NIELSEN, R.P. (1988): Limitations of Ethical Reasoning as an Action (Praxis) Strategy. *Journal of Business Ethics*, vol. 7:10, pp. 725-733.

NIELSEN, R.P. (1989): Negotiating As An Ethics Action (Praxis) Strategy. *Journal of Business Ethics*, vol. 8(5), pp. 383-390.

NIELSEN, R.P. (1993): Varieties of postmodernism as moments in ethics action-learning. *Business Ethics Quarterly*, vol. 3(3), pp. 251-269.

NORA, S.; MINC, A. (1978): *L'informatisation de la societé*. Paris: du Seuil.

NORCIA, V. di. (1988): An Enterprise/Organization Ethic. *Business & Professional Ethics Journal*, vol. 7(3-4), pp. 61-79.

NORTON, D. L. (1988): Character Ethics and Organizational Life. WRIGHT, N. D.: *Papers in the Ethics of Administration*. Provo: BrighamYoung University, pp. 47-66.

NUENO, P. (1991): La *learning organization. Expansión-Orbis*, pp. 305-324.

OBESO, C. (1989): La organización reglamentada: los orígenes del taylorismo-fordismo. *Papers ESADE*, no. 22.

OUCHI, W.G.; WILKINS, A.L. (1985): Organizational Culture. *Annual Review f Sociology*, vol. 11, pp. 457-483.

PADIOLEAU, J.G. (1988): Les entreprises americaines et la morale des affaires. *Chroniques d'actualité de la S.É.D.É.I.S.*, vol. 37(9), pp. 362-367.

PADIOLEAU, J.G. (1989): L'éthique est-elle un outil de gestion? *Revue Française de Gestion*, June, pp. 82-91.

PAINE, L. S. (1991). Ethics as Character Development: Reflections on the Objective of Ethics Education. FREEMAN, R. E. (ed.): *Business Ethics. The State of the Art*. Oxford: Oxford University Press, pp. 67-85.

PASCALE, R. (1985): The Paradox of "Corporate Culture: Reconciling Ourselves to Socialization". *California Management Review*, vol. 27(2), pp. 26-41.

PERROW, C. (1986): *Complex Organizations*. London: McGraw Hill.

PERROW, C. (1987): A society of organizations. Macro Organizational Behavior Society.

PETERS, T.J.; WATERMAN, R.H. (1982): *In Search of Excellence*. New York: Harper & Row.

PETTIGREW, A. (1979): On Studying Organizational Cultures. *Administrative Science Quarterly*, vol. 24, pp. 570-581.

PETTIGREW, A. (1990): Studying Strategic Choice and Strategic Change. A Comment on Mintzberg and Waters: 'Does Decision Get in the Way?'. *Organization Studies*, pp. 7-11.

PFEIFFER, R. S. (1990): The Central Distinction in the Theory of Corporate Moral Personhood. *Journal of Business Ethics*, vol. 9(6), pp. 473-480.

PHILLIPS, N. (1991): The Sociology of Knowledge: Toward an Existential View of Business Ethics. *Journal of Business Ethics*, vol. 10, pp. 787-795.

PRANDSTRALLER, G.P. (1991): "I codici deontologici delle professioni come risposta ai bisogni delle società avanzate". *Etica degli Affari e delle Professioni*, vol. 4(4), pp. 63-67.

PRESTON, L. E.; POST, J. (1975): *Private management and Public Policy*. Englewood Cliffs: Prentice-Hall.

PRESTON, L. E. (1975): Corporation and Society: The Search for a Paradigm. *Journal of Economic Literature*, vol. 13(2), pp. 434-453.

PRICE WATERHOUSE - CRANFIELD (1992): *Informe de conclusiones*. Barcelona: ESADE.

PRUZAN, P.; THYSSEN, O. (1990): Conflict and Consensus: Ethics as a Shared Value Horizon for Strategic Planning. *Human Systems Management*, vol. 9, pp. 135-151.

PUGÈS, L. M. (1970): *Economía, beneficio y ética*. Barcelona: Hispano Europea.

QUINN, J. B. (1992): *Intelligent enterprise*. New York: The Free Press.

RAIBORN, C.A. & PAYNE, D. (1990): Corporate Codes of Conduct: A Collective Conscience and Continuum. *Journal of Business Ethics*, vol. 9(11), pp. 879-889.

RAMÍREZ, R. (1983): Action Learning: A Strategic Approach for Organizations Facing Turbulent Conditions. *Human Relations*, vol. 36(8), pp. 725-742.

RAWLS, J. (1971): *A Theory of Justice*.

REECK, D. (1982): *Ethics for the Professions. A Christian Perspective*. Minneapolis: Augsburg Publishing House.

RIESMAN, D. (1950): *The Lonely Crowd. A Study of the Changing American Character*. New Haven: Yale University Press.

RISPA, R. (1982): *La Revolución de la Información*. Barcelona: Salvat.

RITCHIE, J. B. (1988): Organizational Ethics: Paradox and Paradigm. WRIGHT, N. D.: *Papers in the Ethics of Administration*. Provo: Brigham Young University, pp. 159-184.

ROBERTSON, D. C. (1991): Corporate ethics programs: the impact of firm size. HARVEY, B.; VAN LUIJIK, H.; CORBETTA, G. (ed.) (1991): *Market Morality and Company Size*. Dordrecht: Kluwer, pp. 119-136.

ROBIN, D.P.; REIDENBACH, R.E. (1988): Integrating Social Responsibility and Ethics into the Strategic Planning Process. *Business & Professional Ethics Journal*, vol. 7(3-4), pp. 29-46.

ROBIN, D.P.; REIDENBACH, R.E. (1991): A Conceptual Model of Corporate Moral Development. *Journal of Business Ethics*, vol. 10, pp. 273-284.

ROCKART, J. F.; SHORT, J. S. (1991): The Networked Organization and the Management of Interdependence. SCOTT, M. S. (ed.): *The Corporation of the 1990s. Information Technology and Organizational Transformation.* Oxford: Oxford Universitiy Press, pp. 189-219.

RUBIO, J. (1987): *El hombre y la ética.* Barcelona: Anthropos.

RUBIO, J. (1989): La psicología moral (de Piaget a Kohlberg). CAMPS, V. (ed.): *Historia de la ética (III).* Barcelona: Crítica, 1989, pág. 481-532.

RUBIO, J. (1992): Educación moral. VIDAL, M.: *Conceptos fundamentales de ética filosófica.* Madrid: Trotta, pp. 293-313.

RUDDICK, W. (1980): Philosophy and Public Affairs. *Social Research*, vol. 47, pp. 734-748.

SACCONI, L. (1990): Etica degli affari: origine, collocazione e definizione 'comprensiva'. *Notizie di POLITEIA*, no. 17, pp. 16-26.

SACCONI, L. (1991a): *Etica degli affari.* Milan: Il Saggiatore.

SACCONI, L. (1991b): Etica manageriale (II): responsabilità, democrazia ed etica della virtù a confronto. *Etica degli Affari e delle Professioni*, vol. 4(1), pp. 5-26.

SCHAFF, A. (1985): *Wohin fürth der weg? Die gesellsschaftlichen folgen der zweiten industriellen revolution.* Vienna: Europa Verlag.

SCHEIN, E.H. (1984): Coming to a New Awareness of Organizational Culture. *Sloan Management Review*, Winter, pp. 3-16.

SCHEIN, E.H. (1985): *Organizational Culture and Leadership.* London: Jossey-Bass.

SENGE, P.M. (1990): *The Fifth Discipline.* Bantam Doubleday Dell

SETHI, S. P. (1975): Dimensions of Corporate Social Perfomance: An Analytical Framework. *California Management Review*, vol. 17(3), pp. 58-64.

SHAW, W. BARRY, V. (1989): *Moral Issues in Business.* Belmont: Wadsworth.

SHERWIN, D. (1983): The ethical roots of the business system. *Harvard Business review*, pp. 183-192.

SHERWOOD, J. (1988): Creating Work Cultures With Competitive Advantage. *Organizational Dynamics*, vol. 16(3), pp. 5-27.

SIMON, J. G.; POWERS, C. W.; GUNNEMANN, J. P. (1972): The Responsabilities of Corporations and Their Owners. BEAUCHAMP, T. L.; BOWIE, N. E. (ed.): *Ethical Theory and Business.* Englewood-Cliffs: Prentice-Hall, 1988, pp. 92-96.

SIMON, H.A. (1979): Rational Decision Making in Business Organizations. *The American Economic Review*, Sept., pp. 493-513.

SIMON, H.A. (1983): Alternative visions of rationality. *Reason in human afairs.* Stanford: Standford University Press, pp.. 7-35. ARKES, H.R.; HAMMOND, K.R. (ed.): *Judgement and Decision Making.* Cambridge, Cambridge University Press, 1986, pp. 97-113.

SIMS, R.R. (1991): The Institutionalization of Organizational Ethics. *Journal of Business Ethics*, vol. 10, pp. 493-506.

SINCLAIR, A. (1991): After excellence: models of organisational culture for the public sector. *Australian Journal of Public Administration*, vol. 50(3), pp. 321-332.

SINCLAIR, A. (1993): Approaches to Organisational Culture and Ethics. *Journal of Business Ethics*, vol.12, pp. 63-73.

SKIDD, D.R.A. (1988): Corporate Responsibility: Morality Without Consciousness. *Business & Professional Ethics Journal*, vol. 7(1), ppg.75-89.

SMIRCICH, L. (1983): Concepts of Culture and Organizational Analysis. *Administrative Science Quarterly*, vol. 28, pp. 339-358.

SOETERS, J. L. (1986): Excellent Companies as Social Movements. *Journal of Management Studies*, May, pp. 299-312.

SOHN, H. F. (1982): Prevailing Rationales in the Corporate Social Responsibility Debate. *Journal of Business Ethics*, vol. 1, pp. 139-133.

SOLÉ PARELLADA, F.; BRAMANTI, A. (1991): "El porqué de las redes de cooperación tecnológica". *Quaderns de Tecnología. Institut Català de Tecnologia*, vol. 4, October, pp. 114-117.

SOLER, C. (1994): El conflicto como bien social y factor de desarrollo: las personas en un contexto de cambio organitzativo que respete a las personas. RECIO, E. M.; LOZANO, J. M.: *Persona y empresa. Libertad responsable o sujeción a las normas*. Barcelona: Hispano Europea, pp. 141-178.

SOLOMON, R.C. (1991): Business Ethics, Literacy, and the Education of the Emotions. FREEMAN, R.E. (ed.): *Business Ethics. The State of the Art*. Oxford: Oxford University Press, pp. 188-211.

SOLOMON, R.C. (1992): Corporate roles, personal virtues: an Aristotelian approach to Business Ethics. *Business Ethics Quarterly*. vol. 2(3), pág. 317-339.

SOLOMON, R.C. (1993): *Ethics and Excellence. Cooperation and Integrity in Business*. Oxford: Oxford University Press.

SRICA, V. (1993): Learning and creativity in the knowledge based economy. *The 1993 global management development forum*.

SRIVASTVA, S.; BARRETT, F.J. (1988): Foundations for Executive Integrity: Dialogue, Diversity, Development". SRIVASTVA, S. and Associates. (ed.): *Executive Integrity. The Search for High Human Values in Organizational Life*. San Francisco: Jossey-Bass, 1988, pp. 290-319.

STATA, R. (1989): Organizational Learning-The Key to Management Innovation. *Sloan Management Review*, Spring, pp. 63-74.

STEAD, W. E.; WORRELL, D. L.; STEAD, J. G. (1990): An Integrative Model for Understanding and Managing Ethical Behavior in Business Organizations. *Journal of Business Ethics*, vol. 9(3), pp. 233-242.

STEINER, G. A.; STEINER J. F. (1977): *Issues in Business and Society*. New York: Random House.

STEINER, G. A.; STEINER, J. F. (1988): *Business, Government, and Society. A Managerial Perspective*. New York: Random House.

STEVENS, B. (1994): An Analysis of Corporate Ethical Code Studies: Where Do We Go From Here? *Journal of Business Ethics*. vol. 13, pp. 63-69.

STEVENSON, J. T. (1989): Reasonableness in Morals. *Journal of Business Ethics*, vol. 8(2-3), pp. 95-107.

STONE, C.D. (1975): *Where de the Law Ends. The Social Control of Corporate Behavior.* Prospect Heights: Waveland Press.

STRONG, K. C.; MEYER, G. D. (1992): An Integrative Descriptive Model of Ethical Decision Making. *Journal of Business Ethics*, vol. 11, pp. 89-94.

TAYLOR, L.P. (1987): Management: Agent of Human Cultural Evolution. *Futures*, vol. 19(5), pp. 513-527.

TEULINGS, Ch. (1978): Standards and Values in the Business Enterprise. DAM, C. van; STALLAERT, L. (ed.): *Trends in Business Ethics"*. Boston: Martinus Nijhoff Social Sciences Division, 1978, pp. 10-22.

THE BUSINESS ROUNDTABLE (1988): *Corporate Ethics: A Prime Business Asset, Report on policy and Practice in Companies' Conduct.*

THE CONFERENCE BOARD (1988): *Corporate Ethics*. New York: The Conference Board.

THIEBAUT, C. (1992a): *Los límites de la comunidad*. Madrid: Centro de Estudios Constitucionales.

THIEBAUT, C. (1992b): Neoaristotelismos contemporáneos. CAMPS, V.; GUARIGLIA, O.; SALMERÓN, F. (ed.): *Concepciones de la ética*. Madrid: Trotta, pp. 29-52.

THOMPSON, P. B. (1986): Why do we need a theory of corporate responsibility?.CURTLER, H. (ed.): *Shame, responsibility and the corporation*. New York: Haven, 1986, pág. 113-135.

THUROW, L. (1991): Foreword. SCOTT, M. S. (ed.): *The Corporation of the 1990s. Information Technology and Organizational Transformation*. Oxford: Oxford Universitiy Press, pág. v-vii.

THUROW, L. (1992a): *Head to Head*. William Morrow.

THUROW, L. (1992b): Communitarian vs. Individualistic Capitalism. *The Responsive Community*, vol. 2(4), pp. 24-30.

TOFFLER, A. (1990): *Power Shift*. New York: Bantam.

TOURAINE, A. (1969): *La société post-industrielle*. Paris: Gonthier.

TREVINO, L.K. (1986): Ethical Decision Making in Organizations: A Person-Situation Interactionist Model. *Academy of Management Review*, vol. 11(3), pp. 601-617.

TREVINO, L.K. (1990): A cultural perspective on changing and developing organizational ethics. *Research in Organizational Change and Development*, vol. 4, pp. 195-230.

TREVINO, L.K. (1992): Moral Reasoning and Business Ethics: Implications for Research, Education, and Management. *Journal of Business Ethics*, vol. 11, pp. 445-459.

TREVINO, L.K.; WEAVER, G.R. (1994): Business ETHICS/BUSINESS Ethics: one field or two?. *Business Ethics Quarterly*, vol. 4(2), pp. 113-128.

TULEJA, T. (1985): *Beyond the bottom line*. New York: Facts On File Pub.

UNNIA, M. (1990): Lo specifico italiano dell'etica delle professioni. *Etica deggli affari*, vol. 3(1), pp. 91-102.

VALADIER, P. (1987): Notre precarieté, une chance pour la vie morale. *Christus*, vol. 34, pp. 234-244.

VALADIER, P. (1988): La morale dans une société pluraliste. *Études*, no. 368, pp. 189-200.

VELASQUEZ, M.G. (1983): Why Corporations Are Not Morally Responsible for Anything They Do. *Bussiness & Professional Ethics Journal*, no. 2, pp. 1-17. BEAUCHAMP, T.L.; BOWIE, N.E. (eds.): *Ethical Theory and Business*. Englewood Cliffs: Prentice Hall, 1988, pp. 69-76.

VELASQUEZ, M.G. (1988): *Business Ethics. Concepts and cases*. Englewood Cliffs: Prentice Hall.

VICTOR, B.; CULLEN, J. B. (1988): The Organizational Bases of Ethical Work Climates. *Administrative Science Quarterly*, vol. 33, pp. 101-125.

VIDAL, M. (1984): *Ética civil y sociedad democrática*. Bilbao: Desclée.

VIDAL, M. (1990a): Paradigma de ética razonable para la empresa. Exigencias básicas del discurso ético sobre la actividad empresarial. *ICADE*, vol. 19, pp. 13-38.

VIDAL, M. (1990b): La moral pública en el contexto de la ética civil. *SAL TERRAE*, vol. 78(7-8), pp. 501-512.

WALTERS, K. D. (1977): Corporate Social Responsibility and Political Ideology. *California Management Review*, vol. 19(3), pp. 40-51.

WALZER, M. (1983): *Spheres of Justice*. Oxford: Basil Blackwell.

WANG, J.; DEWHIRST, H. D. (1992): Board of Directors and Stakeholder Orientation. *Journal of Business Ethics*, vol. 11, pp. 115-123.

WARREN, R. C. (1993): Codes of Ethics: Bricks without Straw. *Business Ethics. A European Review*, vol. 2(4), pp. 187-191.

WATERS, J.A.; BIRD, F.(1987): The Moral Dimension of Organizational Culture. *Journal of Business Ethics*, vol. 6, pp. 15-22.

WATKINS, K.E.; MARSICK, V.J. (1993a): *Sculpting the learning organisation*. San Francisco: Jossey-Bass.

WATKINS, K.E.; MARSICK, V.J. (1993b): Sculpting the Learning Organization: Consulting Using Action Tecnologies". *New Directions for Adult and Continuing Education*, no. 58, pp. 81-90.

WEAVER, G.R. (1993): Corporate codes of ethics: purpose, process and content issues. *Business & Society*, vol. 32(1), pp. 44-58.

WEBER, J. (1990): Managers' Moral Reasoning: Assessing Their Responses to Three Moral Dilemmas. *Human Relations*, vol. 43(7), pp. 687-702.

WEBER, J. (1993): Institutionalizing ethics into business organizations: a model and research agenda. *Business Ethics Quarterly*, vol. 3(4), pp. 419-436.

WEBER, J.; GREEN, S. (1991): Principled Moral Reasoning: Is it a Viable Approach to Promote Ethical Integrity? *Journal of Business Ethics*, vol. 10, pp. 325-333.

WEISS, W. L. (1986): Minerva's Owl: Building A Corporate Value System. *Journal of Business Ethics*, vol. 5, pp. 243-247.

WELLER, S. (1988): The Effectiveness of Corporate Codes of Ethics. *Journal of Business Ethics*, vol. 7(5), pp. 389-395.

WERHANE, P. (1994): The normative/descriptive distinction in methodologies of Business Ethics. *Business Ethics Quarterly*, vol. 4(2), pp. 175-180.

WERHANE, P. (1985): *Persons, Rights & Corporations*. Englewood Cliffs: Prentice-Hall.

WHITE, B. J.; MONTGOMERY, B. R. (1980): Corporate Codes of Conduct. *California Management Review*, vol.23(2), pp. 80-87.

WILBUR, J. B. (1982): The Foundations of Corporate Responsibility. *Journal of Business Ethics*, vol. 1, pp. 145-155.

WOBBE, W. (1991): Tecnología y antropocentrismo: Modificación del "Leitbild" de los ingenieros para llegar a ser competitivo. *Quaderns de Tecnologia. Institut Català de Tecnologia*, vol. 4, october, pp. 123-125.

WOOD, D. J. (1991): Corporate Social Perfomance Revisited. *Academy of Managament Review*, vol. 16(4), pp. 691-718.

WOOD, J. A.; LONGENECKER, J. G.; McKINNEY, J. A.; MOORE, C. W. (1988): Ethical Attitudes of Students and Business Professionals: A Study of Moral Reasoning. *Journal of Business Ethics*, vol. 7, pp. 249-257.

WOOT, P. de. (1992): Towards a European management model". *EFMD Annual Conference*.

YATES, J.; BENJAMIN, R. I. (1991): The Past and the Present as a Window on the Future. SCOTT, M. S. (ed.): *The Corporation of the 1990s. Information Technology and Organizational Transformation*. Oxford: Oxford Universitiy Press, pp. 61-97.

ZELENY, M. (1990): Amoeba: The New Generation of Self-Managing Human Systems. *IOS Press. Human Systems Management*, vol. 9, ppg. 57-59.

ZENISECK, T.J. (1979): Corporate Social Responsibility: A Conceptualization Based On Organizational Literature. *Academy of Management Review*, vol. 4(3), pp. 359-368.

INDEX

applied ethics 6, 7, 9, 119, 144

business ethics
    as a toolbox 36, 37, 38, 39
    as academic discipline 17, 22, 30, 31, 32, 33, 49, 65
    as applied ethics 7, 8, 30, 31, 32, 36
    as process 10, 12, 61, 101, 116, 125, 126, 128, 129, 133, 134, 135, 137, 141, 158, 164, 165, 167
    framework 38, 40, 45, 65, 100, 124, 138, 139, 164, 165
    history of development, 18, 19, 20, 21, 22
    in social context 1, 2, 6, 17, 35, 39, 60, 88, 91, 105, 113, 119, 128, 129, 130, 154
    integration of approaches 31, 32, 35, 37, 38, 43, 45, 74, 79, 85, 100, 101, 116, 120, 126, 128, 129, 131, 167
    "macro" perspective 23, 25, 26, 68
    "meso" approach 23, 68, 123, 129, 131, 133, 135
    "micro" level 24, 25, 27, 68, 72, 112, 126, 128, 133, 135
    paradigm for 17, 30, 31, 126, 165
    three levels 24, 26, 28, 46, 68, 167
bioethics 8, 20
business schools 22

casuistry 8
character 106, 115, 116
civic ethics 39, 40, 41, 99, 100
communitarism 11, 117, 119
consequentialism 13, 15, 120, 126, 127, 138, 167, 168
constructivism 38, 144, 168
conventional morality, 15, 26, 33, 34, 37, 91, 95, 100, 120, 123, 125, 126, 138, 167, 168
conventionalism 16, 137, 138

corporate code 1, 87, 91, 93, 94, 95, 96, 97, 98, 99, 100, 119, 120, 137, 138, 150, 168
crisis of ideologies 6
culture: related to ethical climate 34, 38, 108
culture: related to moral reasoning 34
culture: related to organizational ethics 33, 102, 106, 107, 108, 109, 119, 120, 125, 130, 134, 137, 138

decisions 73, 80, 81, 82, 86, 115, 126, 127, 128, 129, 135, 139, 141, 151
deontological ethics 12, 101, 115
deontology 8, 14, 90, 101
dialogical ethics 37, 84, 100, 120, 124

economic ethics 26, 28, 52, 53
environment 56, 73, 114
ethical space 14, 119, 132
ethics of humanity 14, 15, 16, 100, 120, 123, 124
ethics of organizations 27, 28, 79, 82, 85, 92, 102, 132
excellence 108, 109, 110, 111, 113, 117, 125, 137

good 12, 86, 92, 93, 101, 116, 123, 131

hermeneutics of responsibility 12, 14, 86, 120, 125, 141, 167, 168
heteronomy of results 12
hierarchy 72, 76, 152

individual values 6, 109, 111, 113, 114, 118
information society 142
institutionalization of ethics 132, 133, 134, 135, 136, 137, 138, 139
integrationism 11
interdisciplinary approach 11, 29